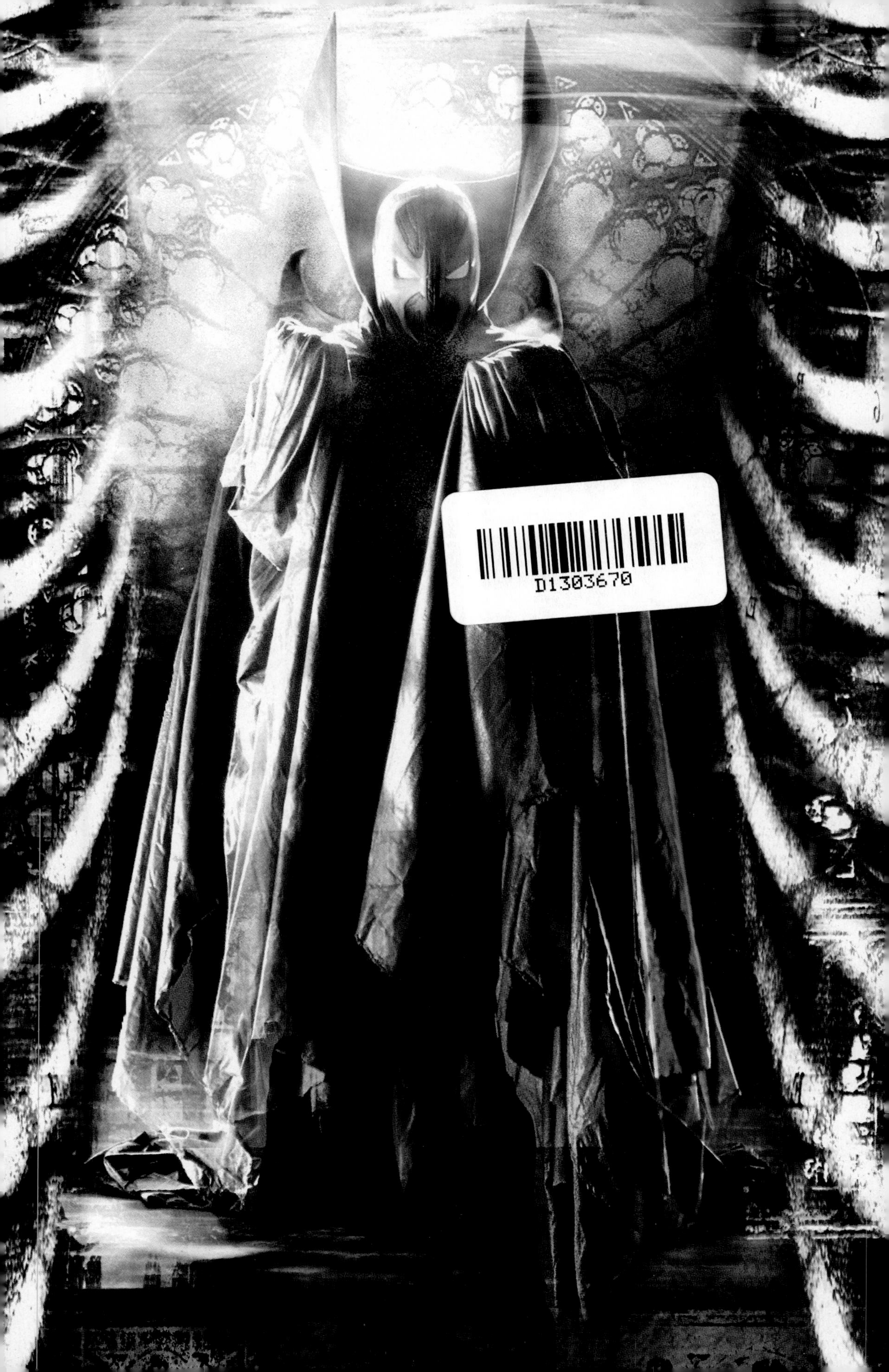

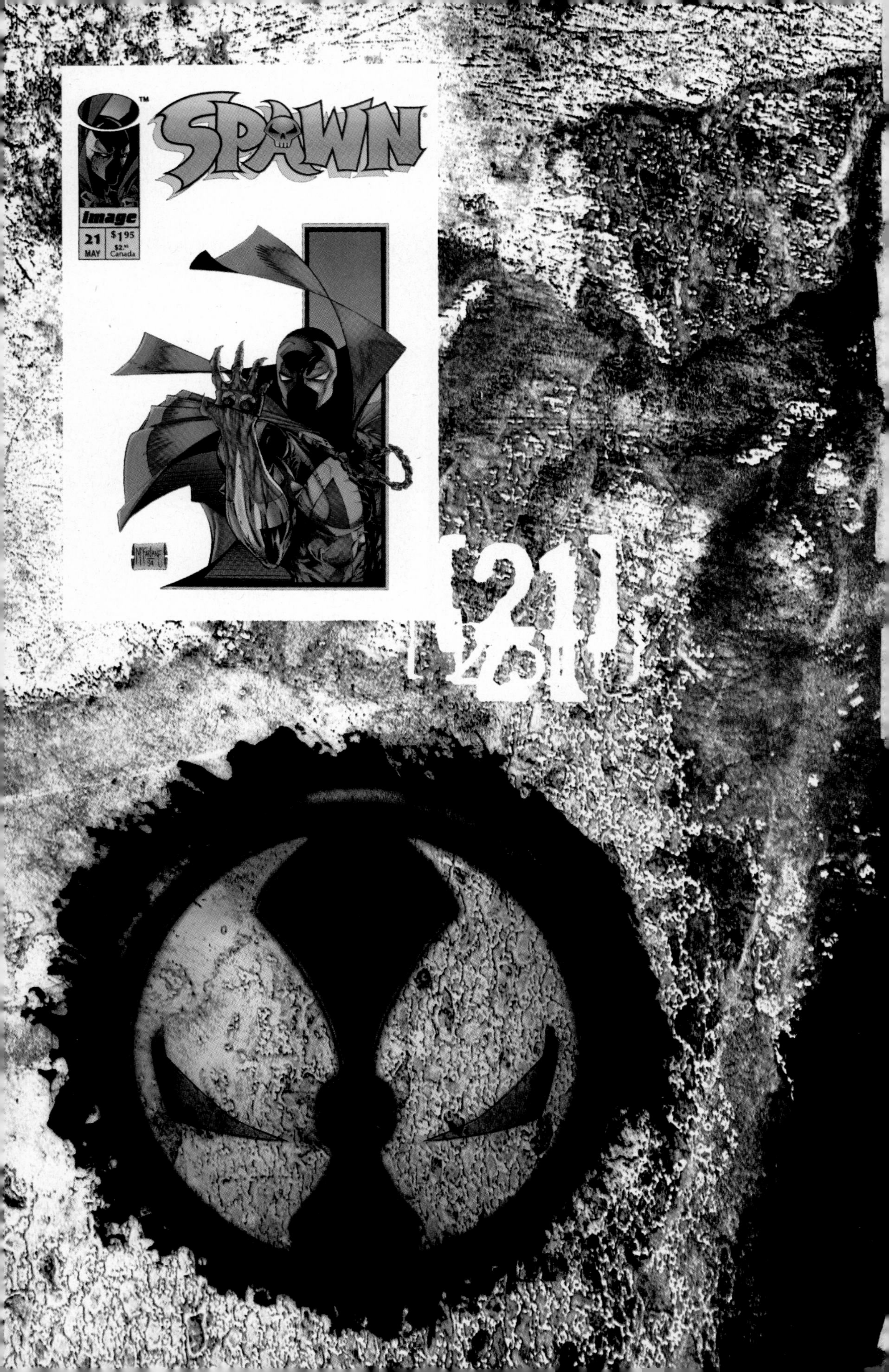
SPAWN
image
21
MAY
$1.95
Canada
[21]

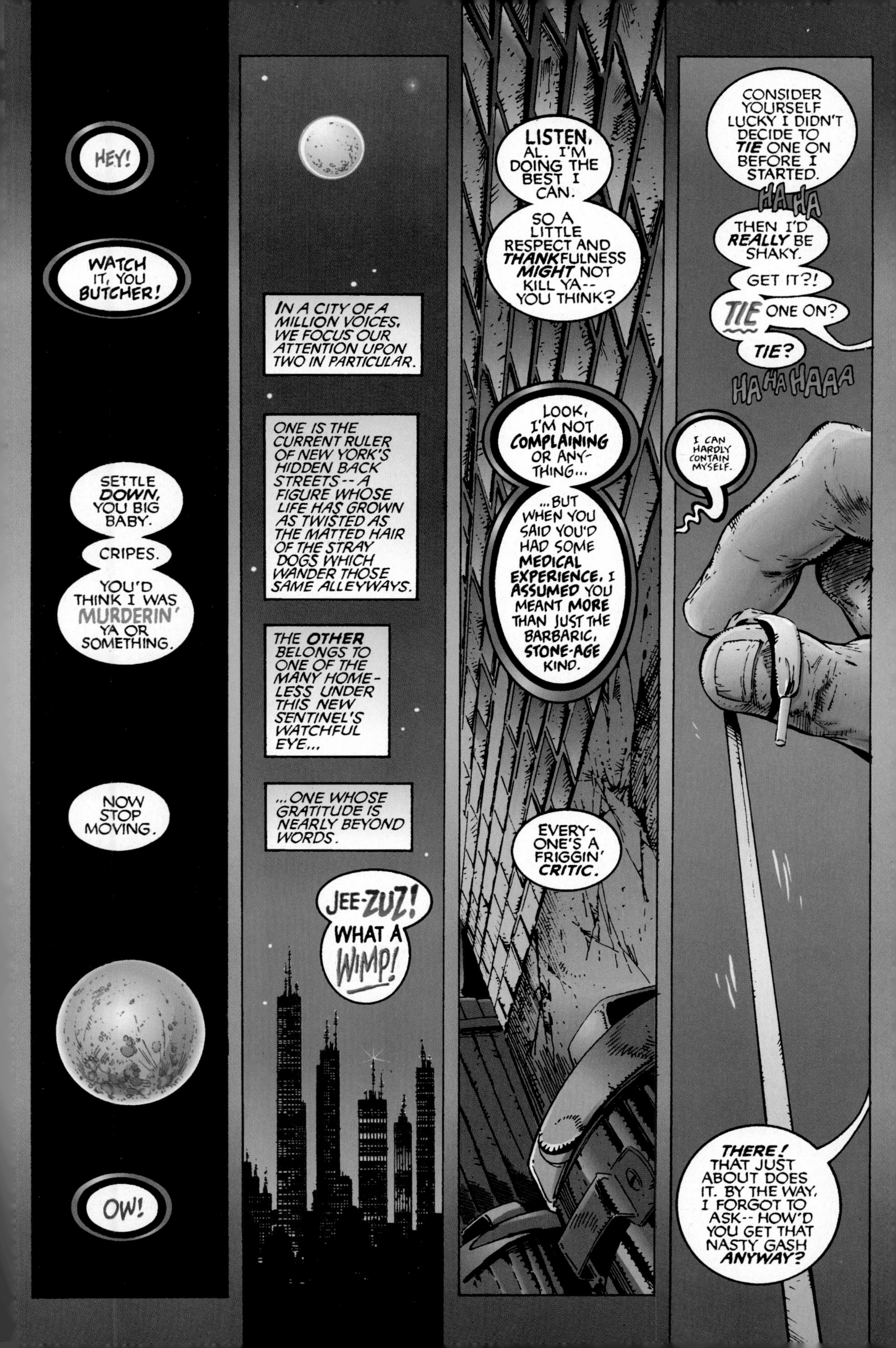
HEY!
WATCH IT, YOU BUTCHER!
SETTLE DOWN, YOU BIG BABY.
CRIPES.
YOU'D THINK I WAS MURDERIN' YA OR SOMETHING.
NOW STOP MOVING.
OW!
IN A CITY OF A MILLION VOICES, WE FOCUS OUR ATTENTION UPON TWO IN PARTICULAR.
ONE IS THE CURRENT RULER OF NEW YORK'S HIDDEN BACK STREETS-- A FIGURE WHOSE LIFE HAS GROWN AS TWISTED AS THE MATTED HAIR OF THE STRAY DOGS WHICH WANDER THOSE SAME ALLEYWAYS.
THE OTHER BELONGS TO ONE OF THE MANY HOME-LESS UNDER THIS NEW SENTINEL'S WATCHFUL EYE...
...ONE WHOSE GRATITUDE IS NEARLY BEYOND WORDS.
JEE-ZUZ! WHAT A WIMP!
LISTEN, AL. I'M DOING THE BEST I CAN.
SO A LITTLE RESPECT AND THANKFULNESS MIGHT NOT KILL YA-- YOU THINK?
LOOK, I'M NOT COMPLAINING OR ANY-THING...
...BUT WHEN YOU SAID YOU'D HAD SOME MEDICAL EXPERIENCE, I ASSUMED YOU MEANT MORE THAN JUST THE BARBARIC, STONE-AGE KIND.
EVERY-ONE'S A FRIGGIN' CRITIC.
CONSIDER YOURSELF LUCKY I DIDN'T DECIDE TO TIE ONE ON BEFORE I STARTED.
HA HA
THEN I'D REALLY BE SHAKY.
GET IT?!
TIE ONE ON?
TIE?
HA HA HAAA
I CAN HARDLY CONTAIN MYSELF.
THERE! THAT JUST ABOUT DOES IT. BY THE WAY, I FORGOT TO ASK-- HOW'D YOU GET THAT NASTY GASH ANYWAY?

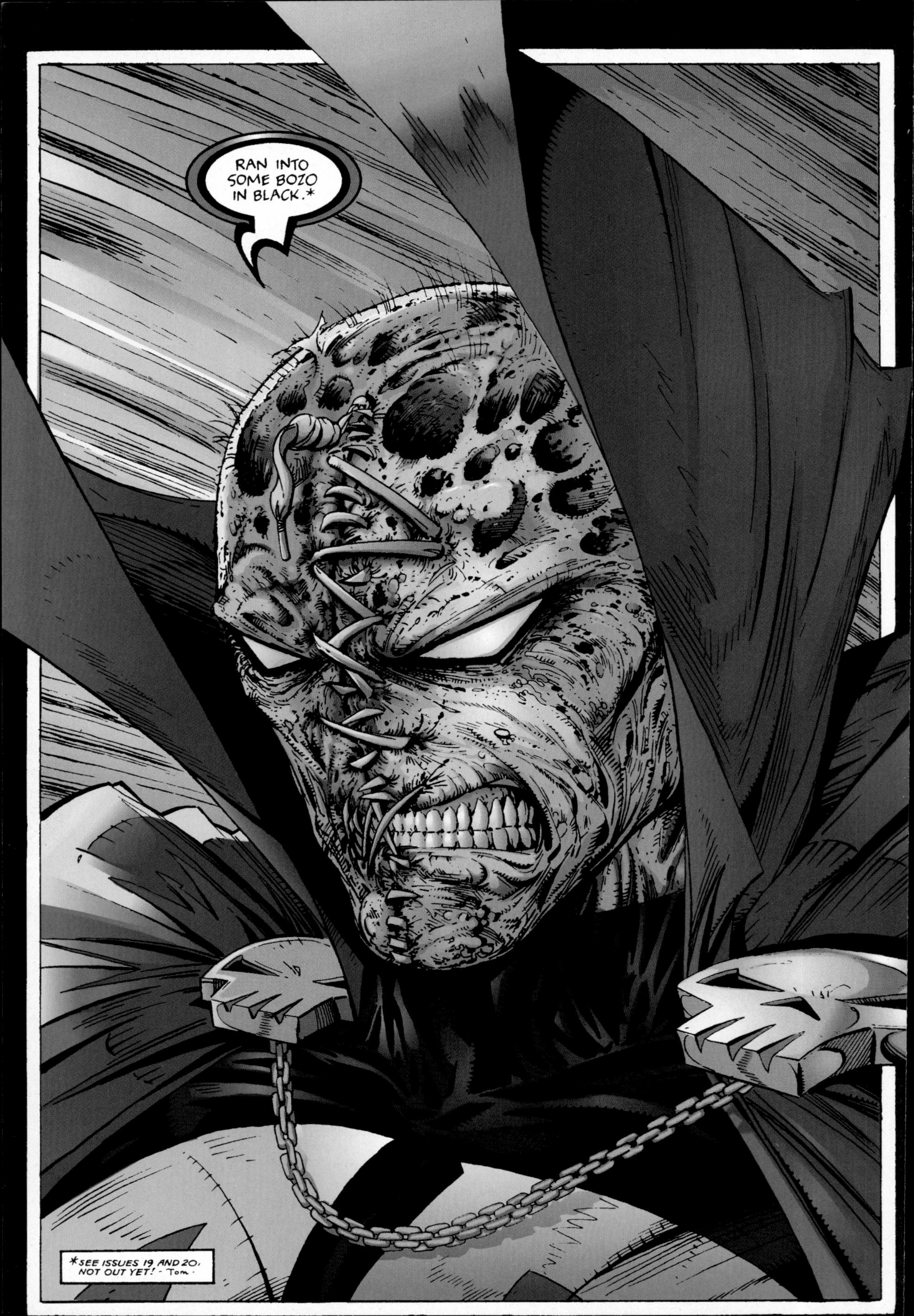
RAN INTO SOME BOZO IN BLACK.*
*SEE ISSUES 19 AND 20. NOT OUT YET! - Tom -

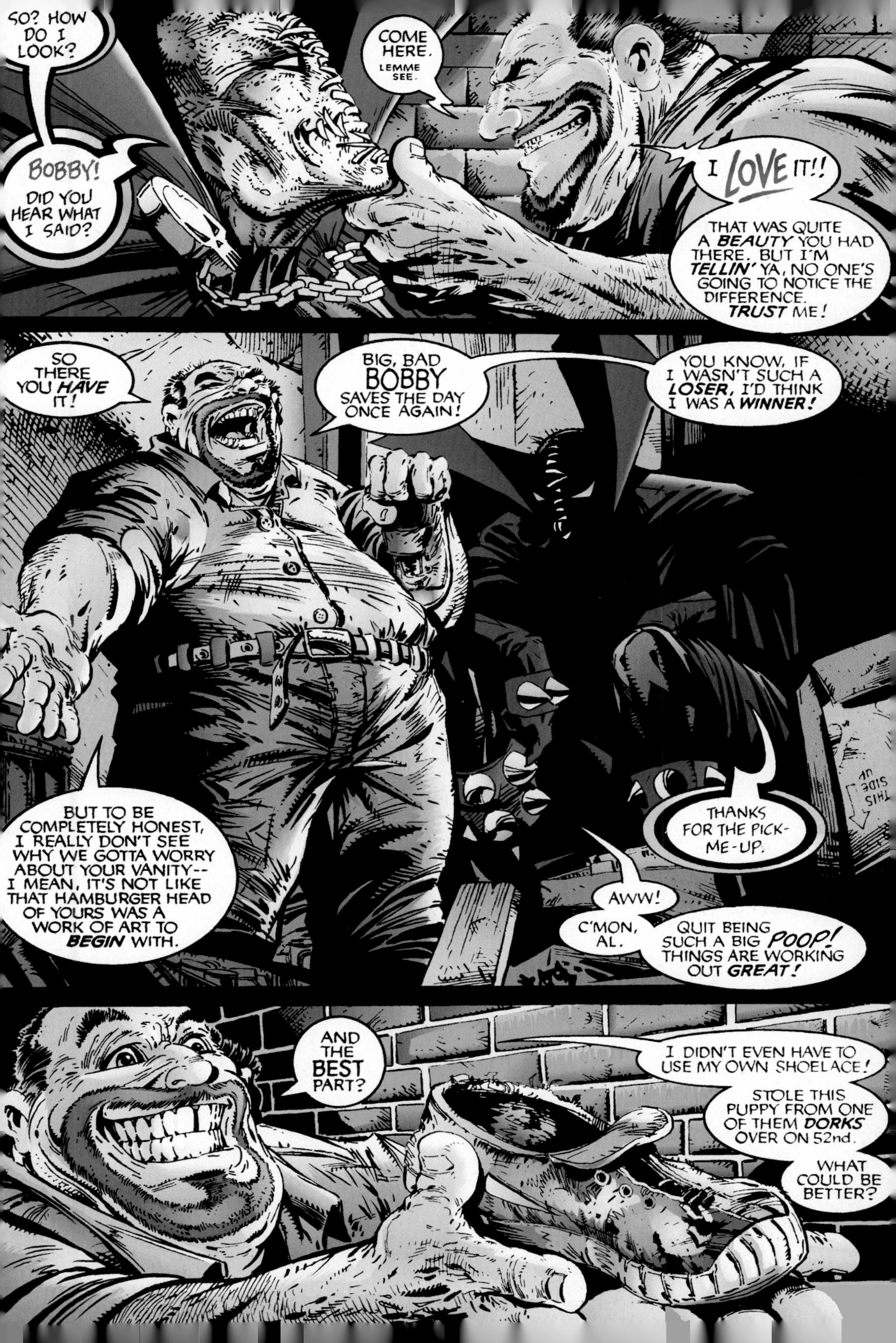
SO? HOW DO I LOOK?
COME HERE. LEMME SEE.
BOBBY! DID YOU HEAR WHAT I SAID?
I LOVE IT!!
THAT WAS QUITE A BEAUTY YOU HAD THERE. BUT I'M TELLIN' YA, NO ONE'S GOING TO NOTICE THE DIFFERENCE. TRUST ME!
SO THERE YOU HAVE IT!
BIG, BAD BOBBY SAVES THE DAY ONCE AGAIN!
YOU KNOW, IF I WASN'T SUCH A LOSER, I'D THINK I WAS A WINNER!
BUT TO BE COMPLETELY HONEST, I REALLY DON'T SEE WHY WE GOTTA WORRY ABOUT YOUR VANITY-- I MEAN, IT'S NOT LIKE THAT HAMBURGER HEAD OF YOURS WAS A WORK OF ART TO BEGIN WITH.
THANKS FOR THE PICK-ME-UP.
AWW!
C'MON, AL.
QUIT BEING SUCH A BIG POOP! THINGS ARE WORKING OUT GREAT!
AND THE BEST PART?
I DIDN'T EVEN HAVE TO USE MY OWN SHOELACE!
STOLE THIS PUPPY FROM ONE OF THEM DORKS OVER ON 52nd.
WHAT COULD BE BETTER?

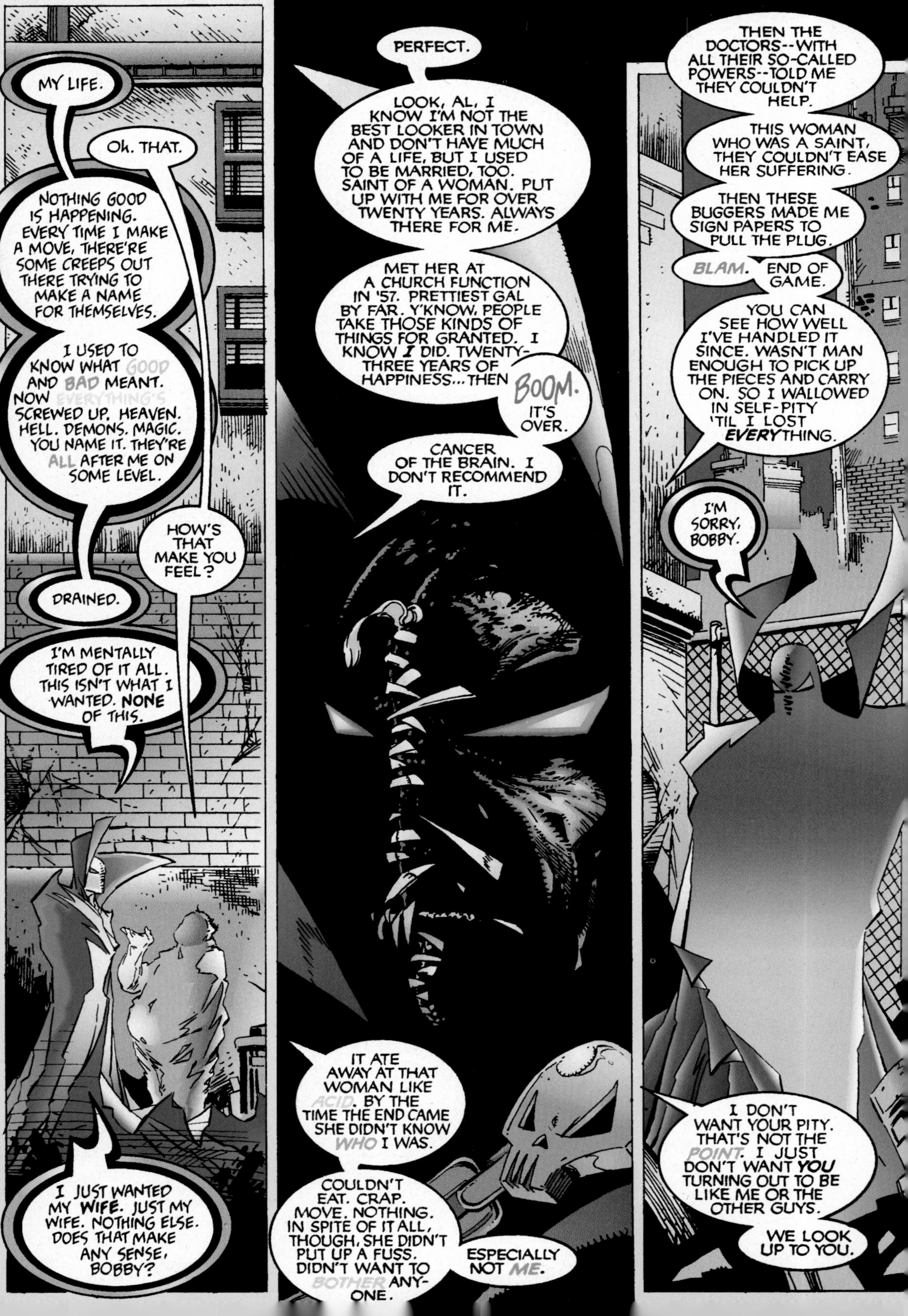
MY LIFE.
Oh. THAT.
NOTHING GOOD IS HAPPENING. EVERY TIME I MAKE A MOVE, THERE'RE SOME CREEPS OUT THERE TRYING TO MAKE A NAME FOR THEMSELVES.
I USED TO KNOW WHAT GOOD AND BAD MEANT. NOW EVERYTHING'S SCREWED UP. HEAVEN. HELL. DEMONS. MAGIC. YOU NAME IT. THEY'RE ALL AFTER ME ON SOME LEVEL.
HOW'S THAT MAKE YOU FEEL?
DRAINED.
I'M MENTALLY TIRED OF IT ALL. THIS ISN'T WHAT I WANTED. NONE OF THIS.
I JUST WANTED MY WIFE. JUST MY WIFE. NOTHING ELSE. DOES THAT MAKE ANY SENSE, BOBBY?
PERFECT.
LOOK, AL, I KNOW I'M NOT THE BEST LOOKER IN TOWN AND DON'T HAVE MUCH OF A LIFE, BUT I USED TO BE MARRIED, TOO. SAINT OF A WOMAN. PUT UP WITH ME FOR OVER TWENTY YEARS. ALWAYS THERE FOR ME.
MET HER AT A CHURCH FUNCTION IN '57. PRETTIEST GAL BY FAR. Y'KNOW, PEOPLE TAKE THOSE KINDS OF THINGS FOR GRANTED. I KNOW I DID. TWENTY-THREE YEARS OF HAPPINESS... THEN
BOOM.
IT'S OVER.
CANCER OF THE BRAIN. I DON'T RECOMMEND IT.
IT ATE AWAY AT THAT WOMAN LIKE ACID. BY THE TIME THE END CAME SHE DIDN'T KNOW WHO I WAS.
COULDN'T EAT. CRAP. MOVE. NOTHING. IN SPITE OF IT ALL, THOUGH, SHE DIDN'T PUT UP A FUSS. DIDN'T WANT TO BOTHER ANY-ONE.
ESPECIALLY NOT ME.
THEN THE DOCTORS--WITH ALL THEIR SO-CALLED POWERS--TOLD ME THEY COULDN'T HELP.
THIS WOMAN WHO WAS A SAINT, THEY COULDN'T EASE HER SUFFERING.
THEN THESE BUGGERS MADE ME SIGN PAPERS TO PULL THE PLUG.
BLAM.
END OF GAME.
YOU CAN SEE HOW WELL I'VE HANDLED IT SINCE. WASN'T MAN ENOUGH TO PICK UP THE PIECES AND CARRY ON. SO I WALLOWED IN SELF-PITY 'TIL I LOST EVERYTHING.
I'M SORRY, BOBBY.
I DON'T WANT YOUR PITY. THAT'S NOT THE POINT. I JUST DON'T WANT YOU TURNING OUT TO BE LIKE ME OR THE OTHER GUYS.
WE LOOK UP TO YOU.

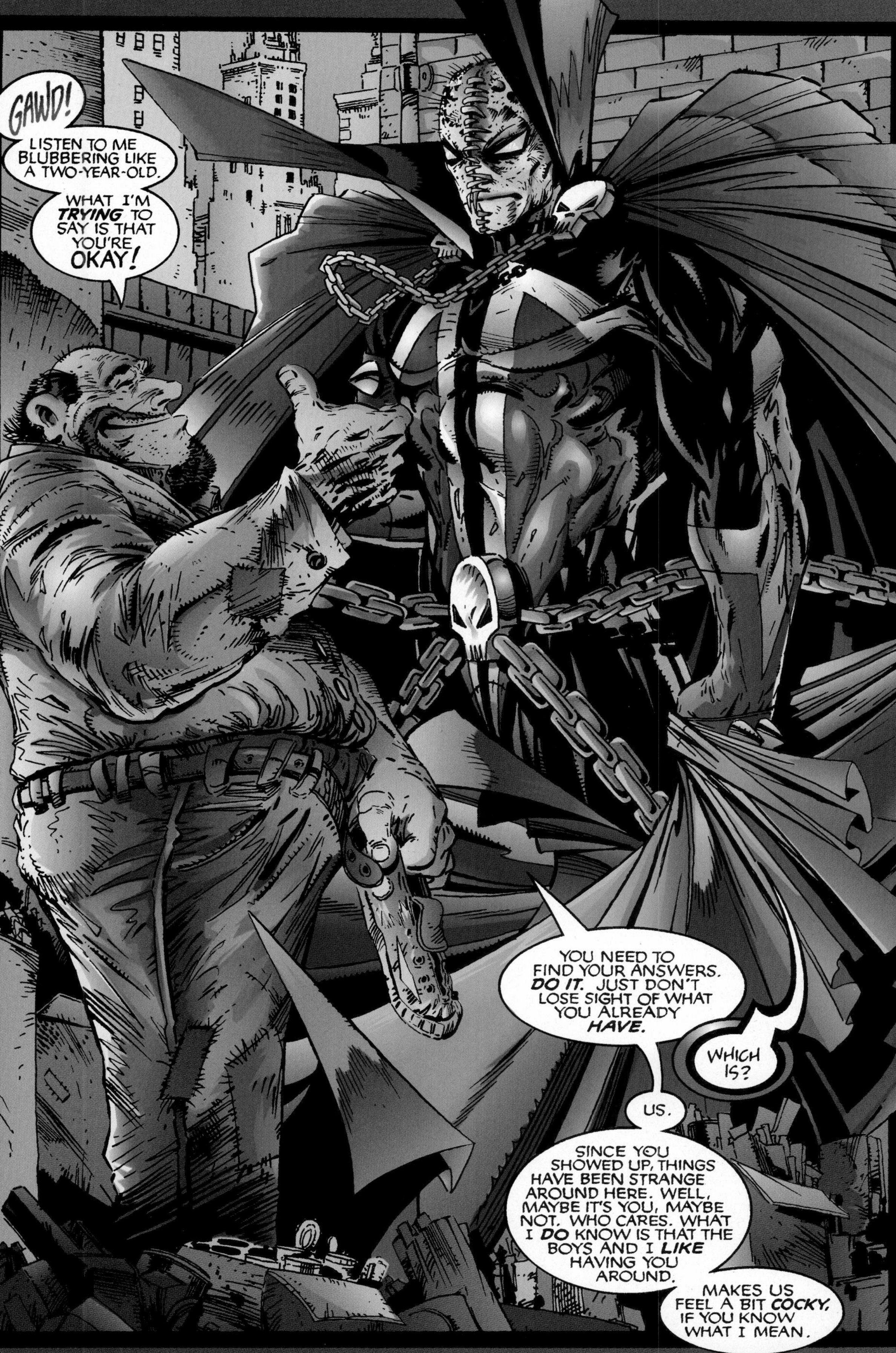
GAWD!
LISTEN TO ME BLUBBERING LIKE A TWO-YEAR-OLD.
WHAT I'M TRYING TO SAY IS THAT YOU'RE OKAY!
YOU NEED TO FIND YOUR ANSWERS. DO IT. JUST DON'T LOSE SIGHT OF WHAT YOU ALREADY HAVE.
WHICH IS?
US.
SINCE YOU SHOWED UP, THINGS HAVE BEEN STRANGE AROUND HERE. WELL, MAYBE IT'S YOU, MAYBE NOT. WHO CARES. WHAT I DO KNOW IS THAT THE BOYS AND I LIKE HAVING YOU AROUND.
MAKES US FEEL A BIT COCKY, IF YOU KNOW WHAT I MEAN.

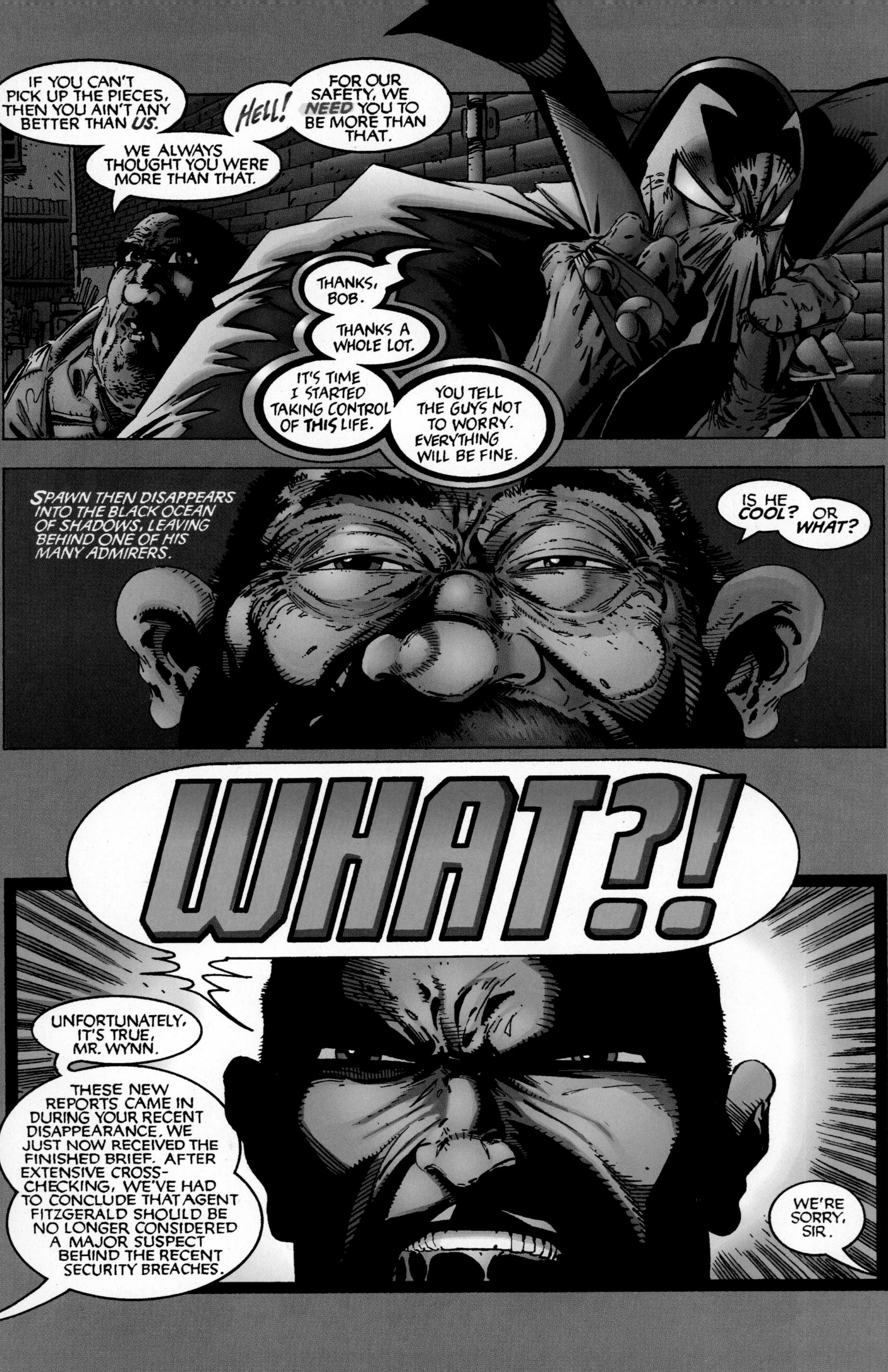
IF YOU CAN'T PICK UP THE PIECES, THEN YOU AIN'T ANY BETTER THAN US.
WE ALWAYS THOUGHT YOU WERE MORE THAN THAT.
HELL!
FOR OUR SAFETY, WE NEED YOU TO BE MORE THAN THAT.
THANKS, BOB.
THANKS A WHOLE LOT.
IT'S TIME I STARTED TAKING CONTROL OF THIS LIFE.
YOU TELL THE GUYS NOT TO WORRY. EVERYTHING WILL BE FINE.
SPAWN THEN DISAPPEARS INTO THE BLACK OCEAN OF SHADOWS, LEAVING BEHIND ONE OF HIS MANY ADMIRERS.
IS HE COOL? OR WHAT?
WHAT?!
UNFORTUNATELY, IT'S TRUE, MR. WYNN.
THESE NEW REPORTS CAME IN DURING YOUR RECENT DISAPPEARANCE. WE JUST NOW RECEIVED THE FINISHED BRIEF. AFTER EXTENSIVE CROSS-CHECKING, WE'VE HAD TO CONCLUDE THAT AGENT FITZGERALD SHOULD BE NO LONGER CONSIDERED A MAJOR SUSPECT BEHIND THE RECENT SECURITY BREACHES.
WE'RE SORRY, SIR.

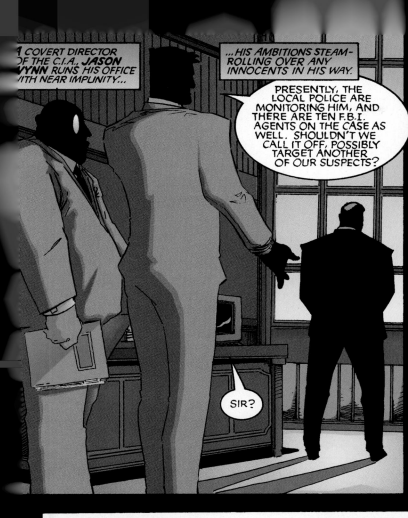

A COVERT DIRECTOR OF THE C.I.A., **JASON WYNN** RUNS HIS OFFICE WITH NEAR IMPUNITY...

...HIS AMBITIONS STEAM-ROLLING OVER ANY INNOCENTS IN HIS WAY.

PRESENTLY, THE LOCAL POLICE ARE MONITORING HIM, AND THERE ARE TEN F.B.I. AGENTS ON THE CASE AS WELL. SHOULDN'T WE CALL IT OFF, POSSIBLY TARGET ANOTHER OF OUR SUSPECTS?

SIR?

TRAPPED. IT'S NOT... JASON WYNN HAS... HIMSELF IN VERY O... TWO-DAY DISAPPE... HAS FURTHER COM... THE SITUATION. THE... WASN'T SATISFIED W... EXPLANATION. TO... FROM AN OPERATIO... BE A CLEAR ADMIS... ERROR...

...AND WEAKN...

CONTINUE SURVEILLANCE AS USUAL.

FITZGERALD REMAINS OUR PRIME TARGET.

*ISSUES 16 TO 18 -- Tom

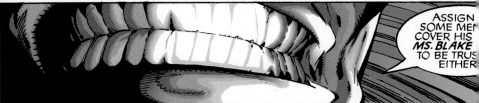

ASSIGN... SOME MEN... COVER HIS... **MS. BLAKE**... TO BE TRUS... EITHER...

...HEN WAIT ...OR FURTHER ...STRUCTIONS.

BUT, SIR-- THE REPORT! ARE YOU SURE THAT...

BY THE WAY, AGENT ROENICK...

...HAVE IT ...ESTROYED.

NOW.

THUS, WYNN PROTECTS HIMSELF FROM ANY PERCEIVED WRONGDOING AND REINFORCES HIS AUTHORITY.

QU... ORD... I'LL... H...

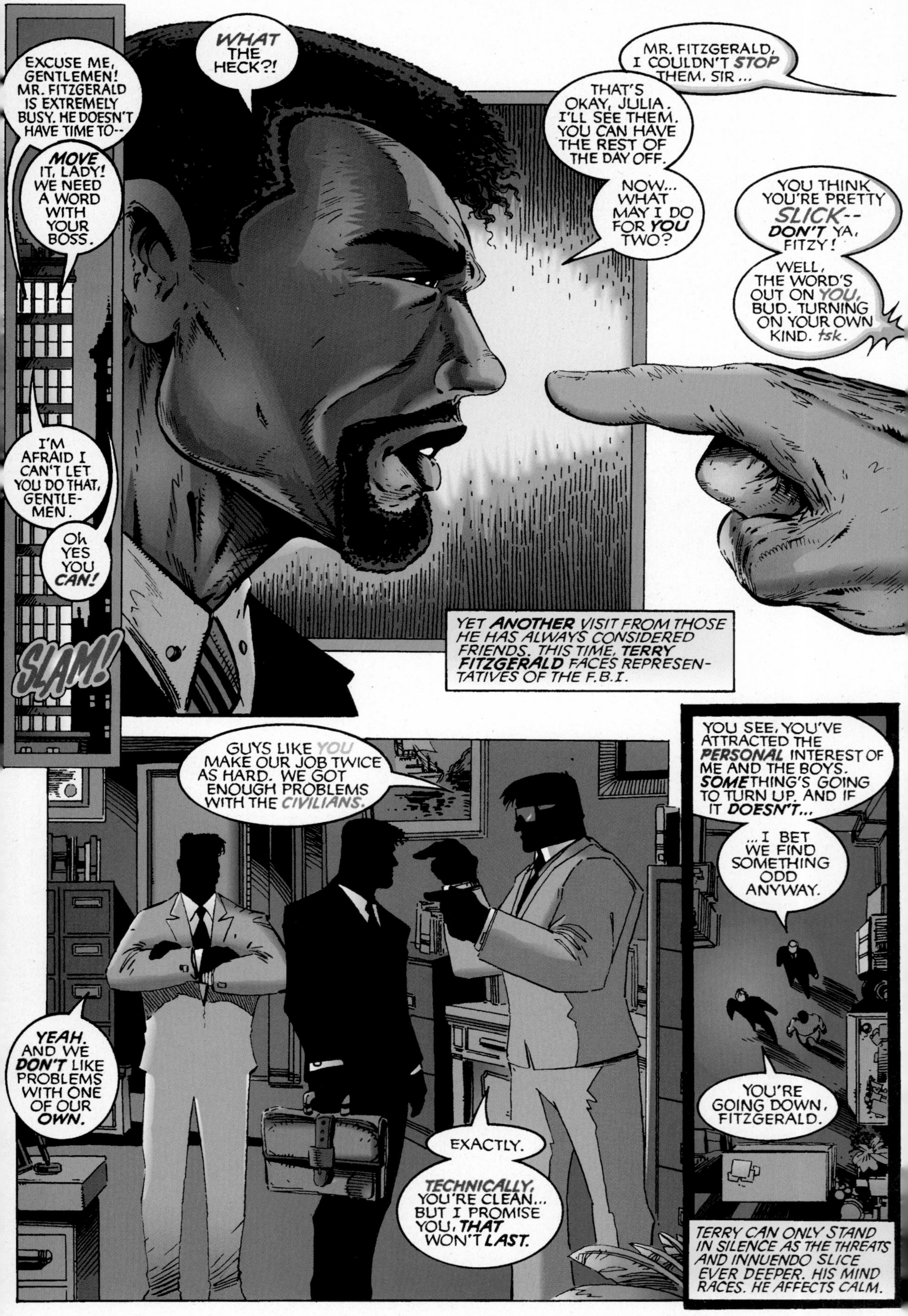
EXCUSE ME, GENTLEMEN! MR. FITZGERALD IS EXTREMELY BUSY. HE DOESN'T HAVE TIME TO--
MOVE IT, LADY! WE NEED A WORD WITH YOUR BOSS.
I'M AFRAID I CAN'T LET YOU DO THAT, GENTLE-MEN.
Oh YES YOU CAN!
SLAM!
WHAT THE HECK?!
MR. FITZGERALD, I COULDN'T STOP THEM, SIR...
THAT'S OKAY, JULIA. I'LL SEE THEM. YOU CAN HAVE THE REST OF THE DAY OFF.
NOW... WHAT MAY I DO FOR YOU TWO?
YOU THINK YOU'RE PRETTY SLICK-- DON'T YA, FITZY!
WELL, THE WORD'S OUT ON YOU, BUD. TURNING ON YOUR OWN KIND. tsk.
YET ANOTHER VISIT FROM THOSE HE HAS ALWAYS CONSIDERED FRIENDS. THIS TIME, TERRY FITZGERALD FACES REPRESEN-TATIVES OF THE F.B.I.
GUYS LIKE YOU MAKE OUR JOB TWICE AS HARD. WE GOT ENOUGH PROBLEMS WITH THE CIVILIANS.
YEAH. AND WE DON'T LIKE PROBLEMS WITH ONE OF OUR OWN.
EXACTLY.
TECHNICALLY, YOU'RE CLEAN... BUT I PROMISE YOU, THAT WON'T LAST.
YOU SEE, YOU'VE ATTRACTED THE PERSONAL INTEREST OF ME AND THE BOYS. SOMETHING'S GOING TO TURN UP. AND IF IT DOESN'T...
...I BET WE FIND SOMETHING ODD ANYWAY.
YOU'RE GOING DOWN, FITZGERALD.
TERRY CAN ONLY STAND IN SILENCE AS THE THREATS AND INNUENDO SLICE EVER DEEPER. HIS MIND RACES. HE AFFECTS CALM.

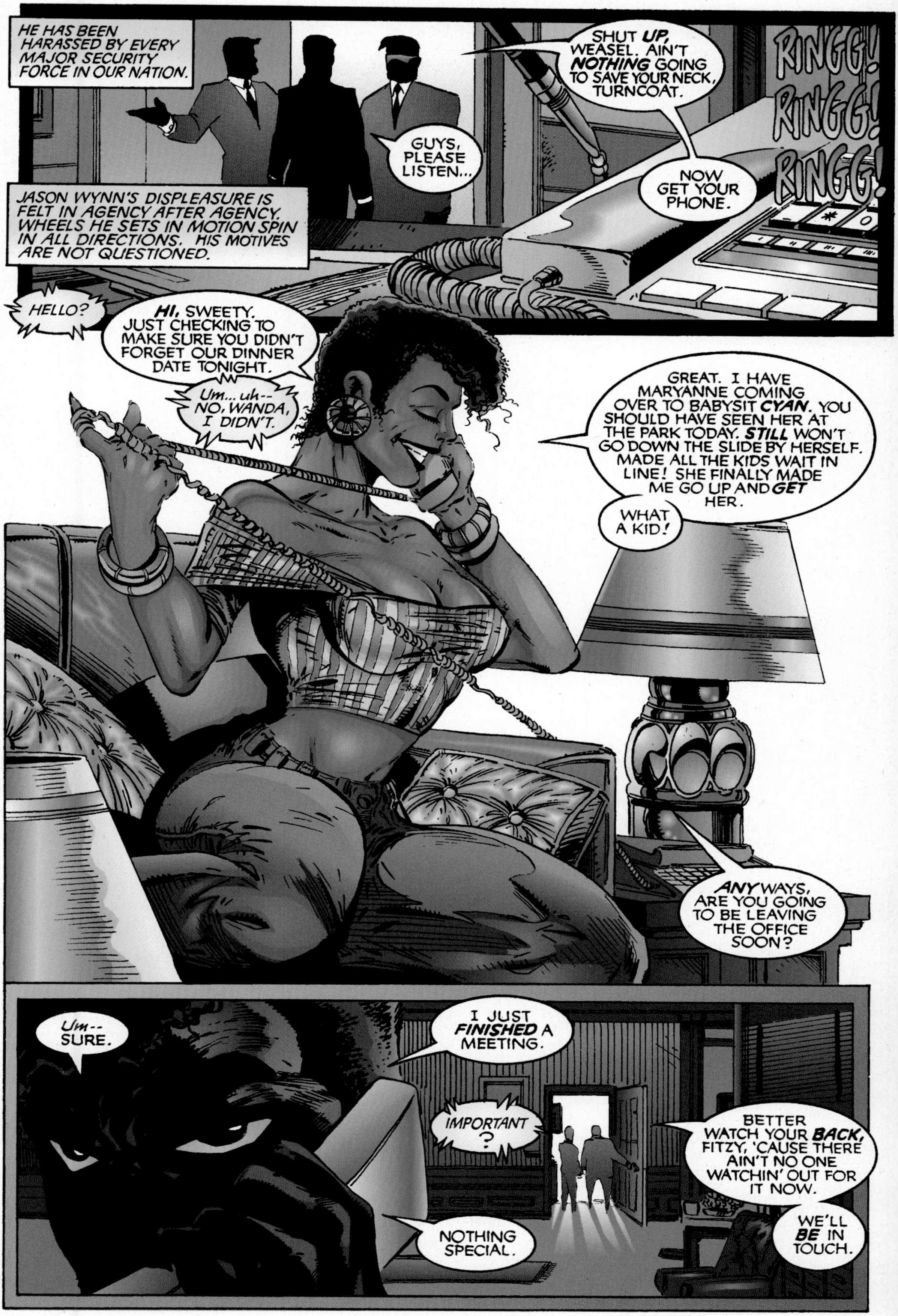
HE HAS BEEN HARASSED BY EVERY MAJOR SECURITY FORCE IN OUR NATION.
SHUT UP, WEASEL. AIN'T NOTHING GOING TO SAVE YOUR NECK, TURNCOAT.
RINGG! RINGG! RINGG!
GUYS, PLEASE LISTEN...
NOW GET YOUR PHONE.
JASON WYNN'S DISPLEASURE IS FELT IN AGENCY AFTER AGENCY. WHEELS HE SETS IN MOTION SPIN IN ALL DIRECTIONS. HIS MOTIVES ARE NOT QUESTIONED.
HELLO?
HI, SWEETY. JUST CHECKING TO MAKE SURE YOU DIDN'T FORGET OUR DINNER DATE TONIGHT.
Um... uh-- NO, WANDA, I DIDN'T.
GREAT. I HAVE MARYANNE COMING OVER TO BABYSIT CYAN. YOU SHOULD HAVE SEEN HER AT THE PARK TODAY. STILL WON'T GO DOWN THE SLIDE BY HERSELF. MADE ALL THE KIDS WAIT IN LINE! SHE FINALLY MADE ME GO UP AND GET HER.
WHAT A KID!
ANYWAYS, ARE YOU GOING TO BE LEAVING THE OFFICE SOON?
Um-- SURE.
I JUST FINISHED A MEETING.
IMPORTANT ?
BETTER WATCH YOUR BACK, FITZY, 'CAUSE THERE AIN'T NO ONE WATCHIN' OUT FOR IT NOW.
NOTHING SPECIAL.
WE'LL BE IN TOUCH.

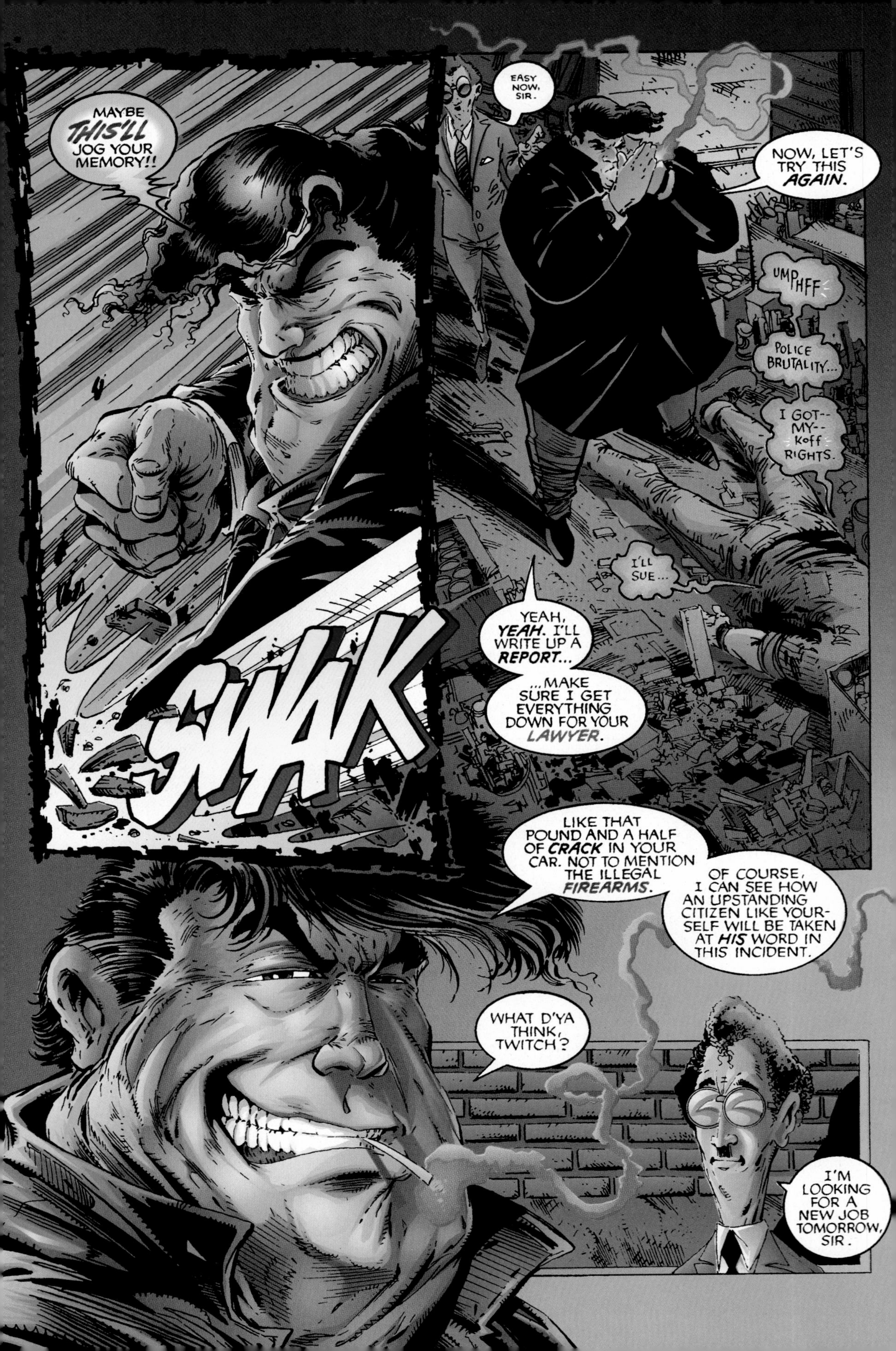
MAYBE THIS'LL JOG YOUR MEMORY!!
SWAK
EASY NOW, SIR.
NOW, LET'S TRY THIS AGAIN.
UMPHFF
POLICE BRUTALITY...
I GOT-- MY-- KOFF RIGHTS.
I'LL SUE...
YEAH, YEAH. I'LL WRITE UP A REPORT...
...MAKE SURE I GET EVERYTHING DOWN FOR YOUR LAWYER.
LIKE THAT POUND AND A HALF OF CRACK IN YOUR CAR. NOT TO MENTION THE ILLEGAL FIREARMS.
OF COURSE, I CAN SEE HOW AN UPSTANDING CITIZEN LIKE YOURSELF WILL BE TAKEN AT HIS WORD IN THIS INCIDENT.
WHAT D'YA THINK, TWITCH?
I'M LOOKING FOR A NEW JOB TOMORROW, SIR.

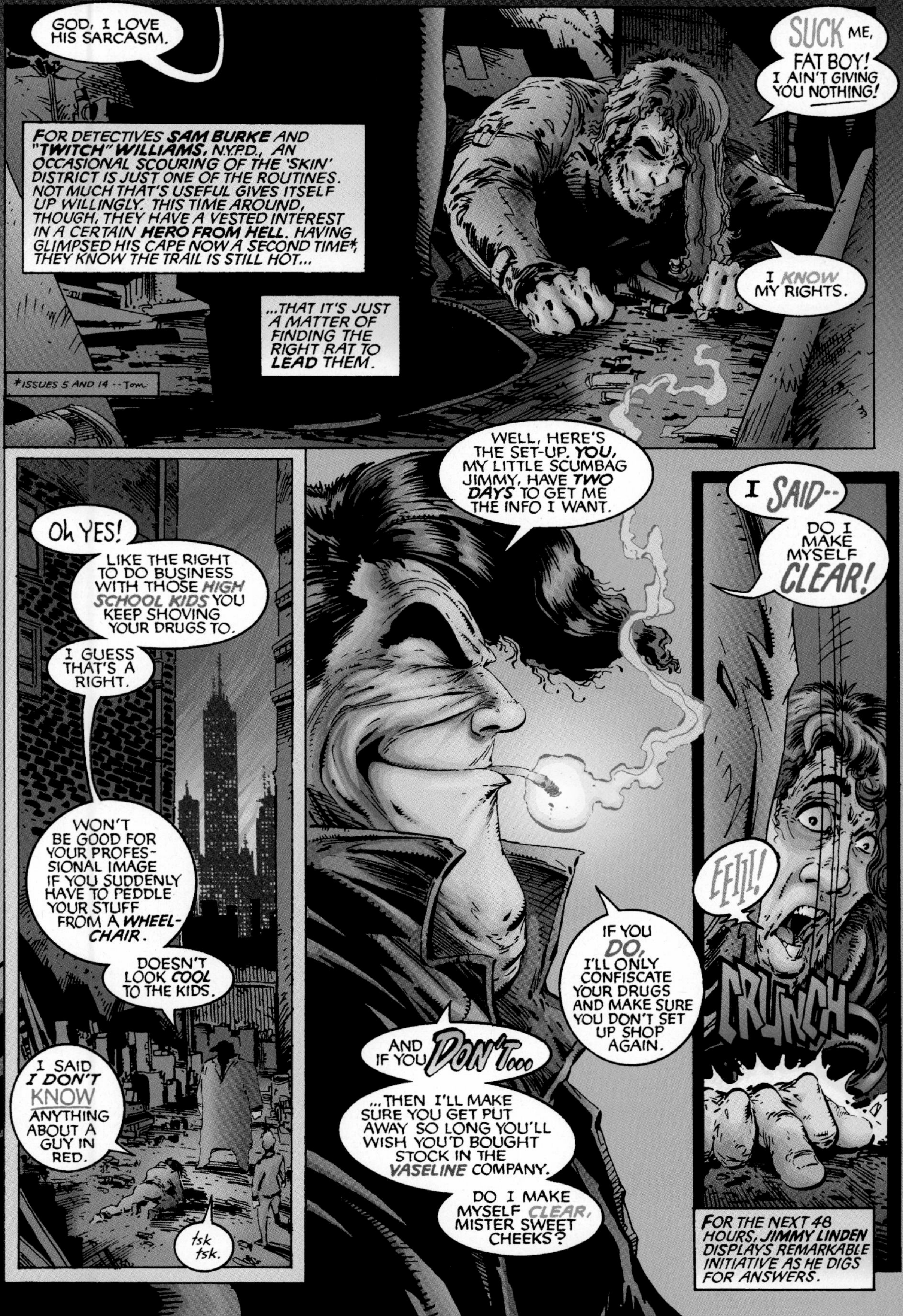
GOD, I LOVE HIS SARCASM.
SUCK ME, FAT BOY! I AIN'T GIVING YOU NOTHING!
FOR DETECTIVES SAM BURKE AND "TWITCH" WILLIAMS, N.Y.P.D., AN OCCASIONAL SCOURING OF THE 'SKIN' DISTRICT IS JUST ONE OF THE ROUTINES. NOT MUCH THAT'S USEFUL GIVES ITSELF UP WILLINGLY. THIS TIME AROUND, THOUGH, THEY HAVE A VESTED INTEREST IN A CERTAIN HERO FROM HELL. HAVING GLIMPSED HIS CAPE NOW A SECOND TIME*, THEY KNOW THE TRAIL IS STILL HOT...
...THAT IT'S JUST A MATTER OF FINDING THE RIGHT RAT TO LEAD THEM.
*ISSUES 5 AND 14 --Tom
I KNOW MY RIGHTS.
Oh YES!
LIKE THE RIGHT TO DO BUSINESS WITH THOSE HIGH SCHOOL KIDS YOU KEEP SHOVING YOUR DRUGS TO.
I GUESS THAT'S A RIGHT.
WON'T BE GOOD FOR YOUR PROFES-SIONAL IMAGE IF YOU SUDDENLY HAVE TO PEDDLE YOUR STUFF FROM A WHEEL-CHAIR.
DOESN'T LOOK COOL TO THE KIDS.
I SAID I DON'T KNOW ANYTHING ABOUT A GUY IN RED.
tsk tsk.
WELL, HERE'S THE SET-UP. YOU, MY LITTLE SCUMBAG JIMMY, HAVE TWO DAYS TO GET ME THE INFO I WANT.
IF YOU DO, I'LL ONLY CONFISCATE YOUR DRUGS AND MAKE SURE YOU DON'T SET UP SHOP AGAIN.
AND IF YOU DON'Tooo
...THEN I'LL MAKE SURE YOU GET PUT AWAY SO LONG YOU'LL WISH YOU'D BOUGHT STOCK IN THE VASELINE COMPANY.
DO I MAKE MYSELF CLEAR, MISTER SWEET CHEEKS?
I SAID--
DO I MAKE MYSELF CLEAR!
EEIII!
CRUNCH
FOR THE NEXT 48 HOURS, JIMMY LINDEN DISPLAYS REMARKABLE INITIATIVE AS HE DIGS FOR ANSWERS.

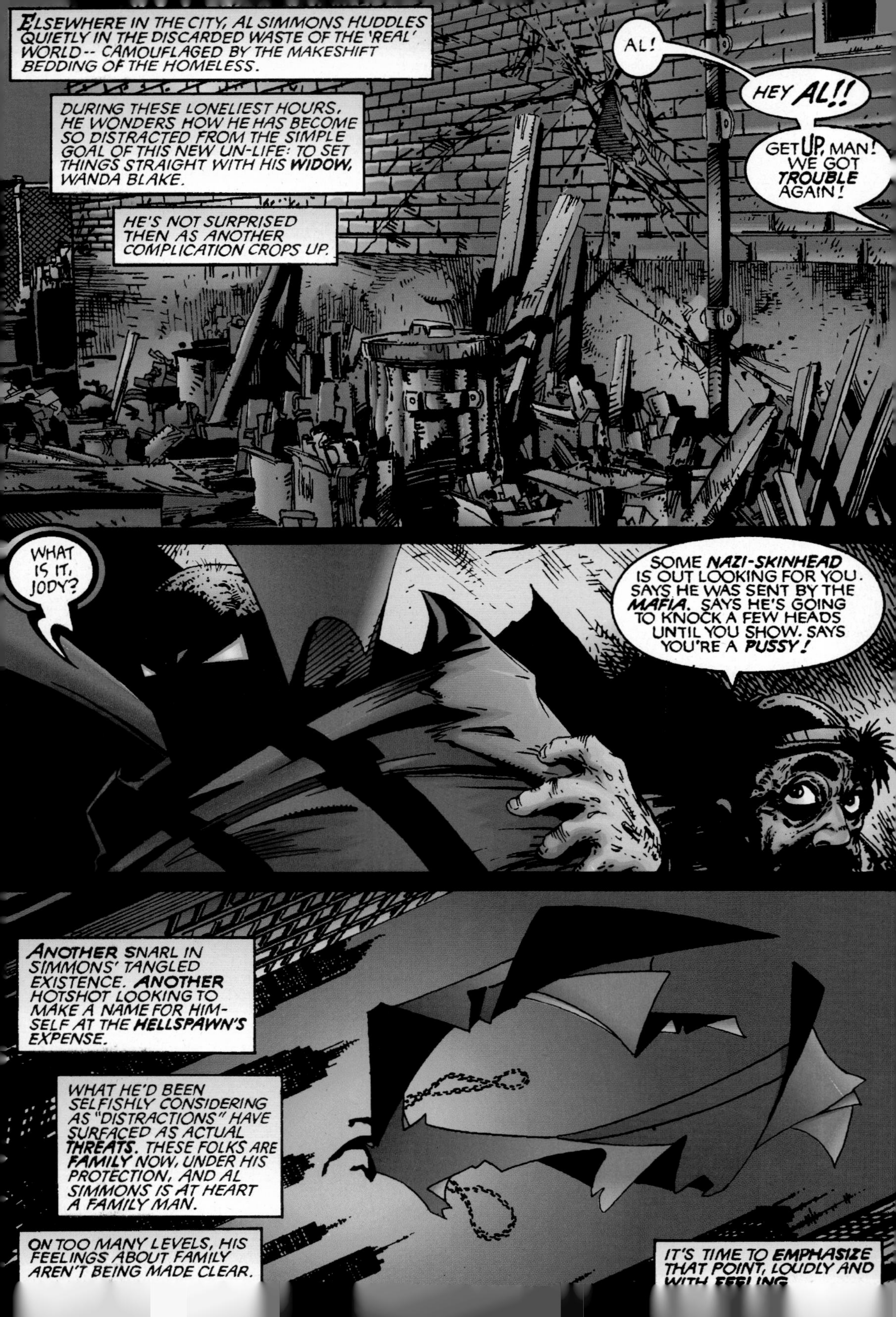
ELSEWHERE IN THE CITY, AL SIMMONS HUDDLES QUIETLY IN THE DISCARDED WASTE OF THE 'REAL' WORLD-- CAMOUFLAGED BY THE MAKESHIFT BEDDING OF THE HOMELESS.
DURING THESE LONELIEST HOURS, HE WONDERS HOW HE HAS BECOME SO DISTRACTED FROM THE SIMPLE GOAL OF THIS NEW UN-LIFE: TO SET THINGS STRAIGHT WITH HIS WIDOW, WANDA BLAKE.
HE'S NOT SURPRISED THEN AS ANOTHER COMPLICATION CROPS UP.
AL!
HEY AL!!
GET UP, MAN! WE GOT TROUBLE AGAIN!
WHAT IS IT, JODY?
SOME NAZI-SKINHEAD IS OUT LOOKING FOR YOU. SAYS HE WAS SENT BY THE MAFIA. SAYS HE'S GOING TO KNOCK A FEW HEADS UNTIL YOU SHOW. SAYS YOU'RE A PUSSY!
ANOTHER SNARL IN SIMMONS' TANGLED EXISTENCE. ANOTHER HOTSHOT LOOKING TO MAKE A NAME FOR HIMSELF AT THE HELLSPAWN'S EXPENSE.
WHAT HE'D BEEN SELFISHLY CONSIDERING AS "DISTRACTIONS" HAVE SURFACED AS ACTUAL THREATS. THESE FOLKS ARE FAMILY NOW, UNDER HIS PROTECTION, AND AL SIMMONS IS AT HEART A FAMILY MAN.
ON TOO MANY LEVELS, HIS FEELINGS ABOUT FAMILY AREN'T BEING MADE CLEAR.
IT'S TIME TO EMPHASIZE THAT POINT, LOUDLY AND WITH FEELING.

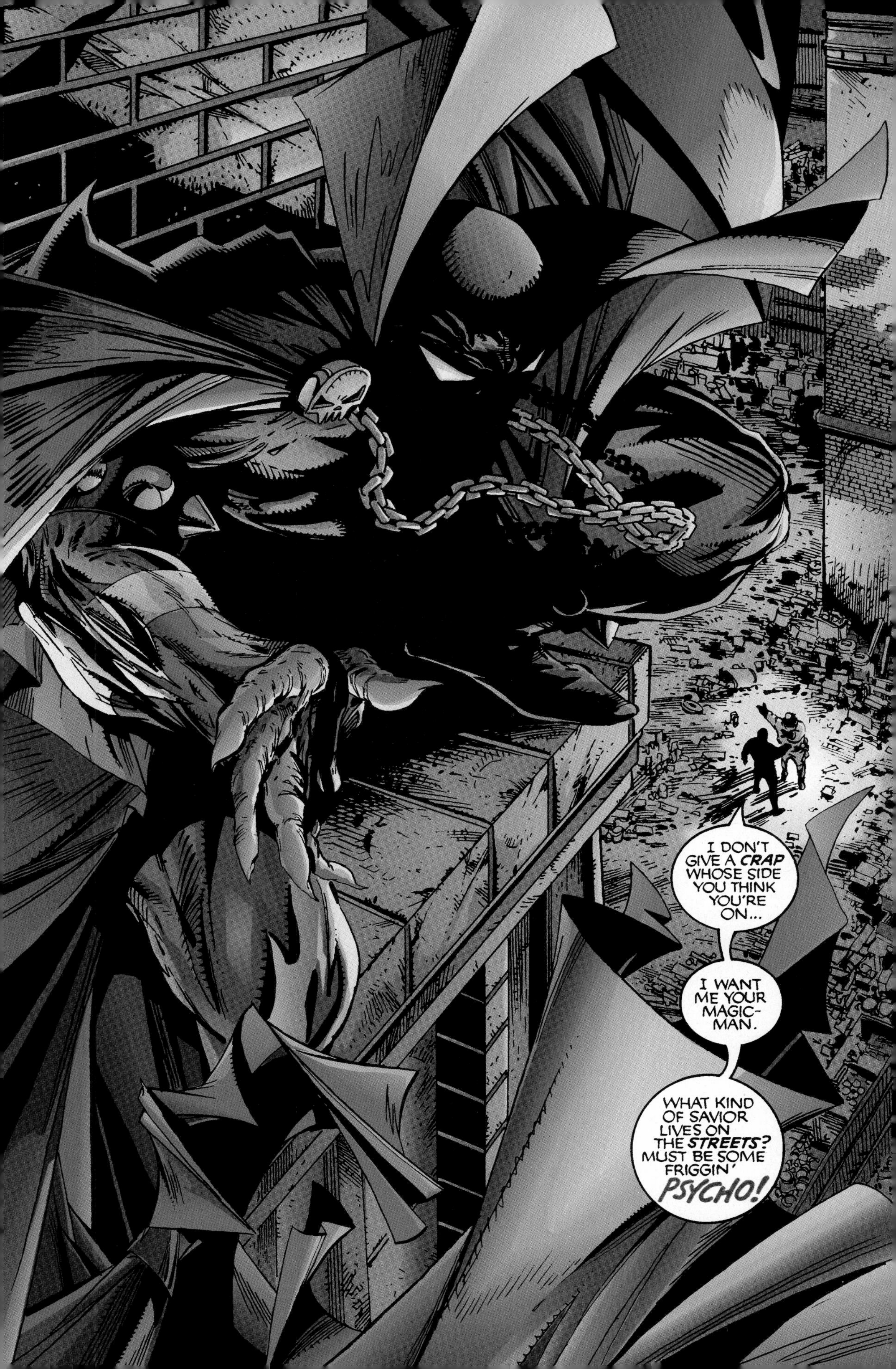
I DON'T GIVE A CRAP WHOSE SIDE YOU THINK YOU'RE ON...
I WANT ME YOUR MAGIC-MAN.
WHAT KIND OF SAVIOR LIVES ON THE STREETS? MUST BE SOME FRIGGIN' PSYCHO!

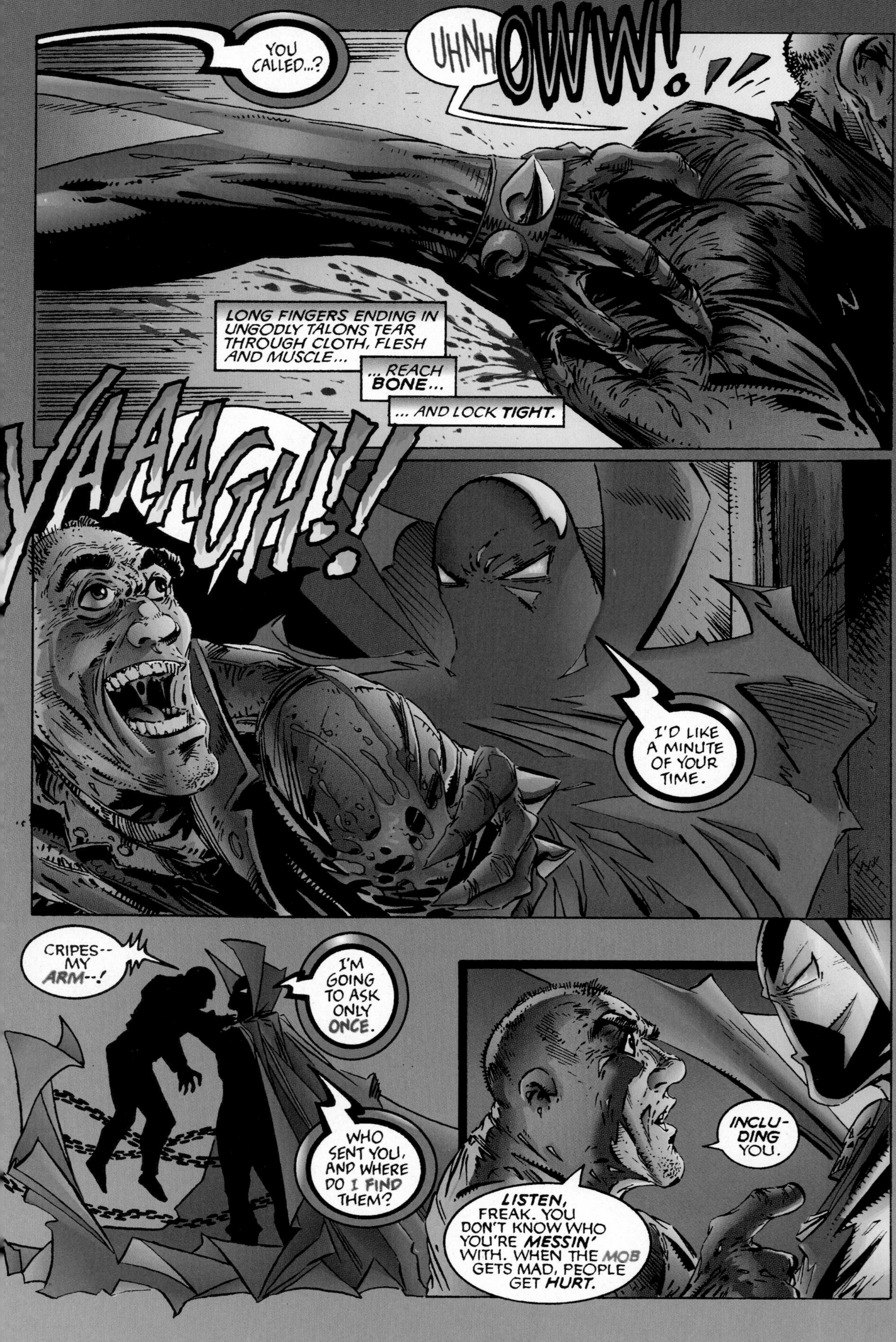
YOU CALLED...?
UHNH OWW!
LONG FINGERS ENDING IN UNGODLY TALONS TEAR THROUGH CLOTH, FLESH AND MUSCLE...
...REACH BONE...
... AND LOCK TIGHT.
YAAAGH!!
I'D LIKE A MINUTE OF YOUR TIME.
CRIPES-- MY ARM--!
I'M GOING TO ASK ONLY ONCE.
WHO SENT YOU, AND WHERE DO I FIND THEM?
LISTEN, FREAK. YOU DON'T KNOW WHO YOU'RE MESSIN' WITH. WHEN THE MOB GETS MAD, PEOPLE GET HURT.
INCLU- DING YOU.

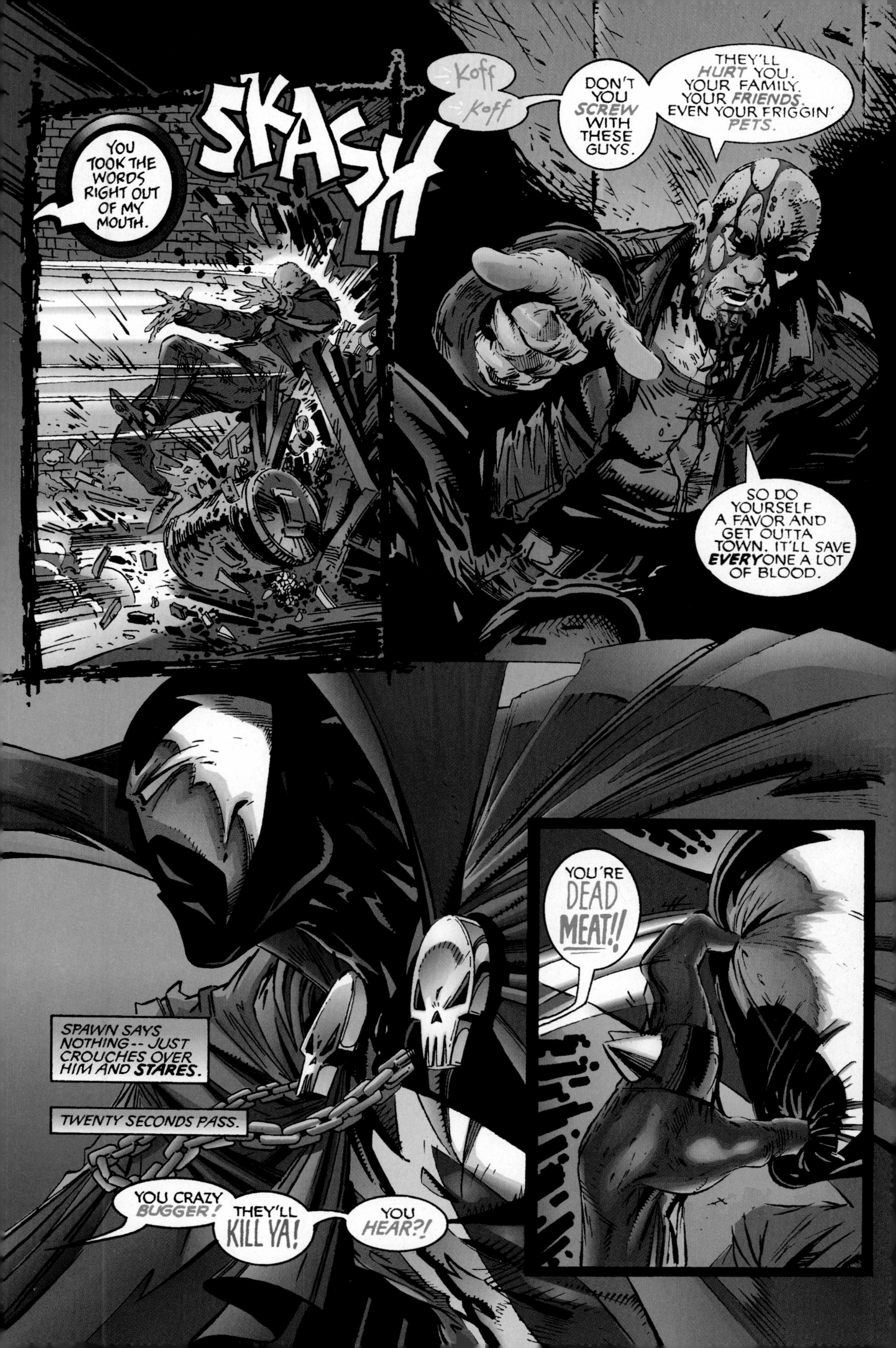
SKASH
YOU TOOK THE WORDS RIGHT OUT OF MY MOUTH.
Koff
Koff
DON'T YOU SCREW WITH THESE GUYS.
THEY'LL HURT YOU. YOUR FAMILY. YOUR FRIENDS. EVEN YOUR FRIGGIN' PETS.
SO DO YOURSELF A FAVOR AND GET OUTTA TOWN. IT'LL SAVE EVERYONE A LOT OF BLOOD.
SPAWN SAYS NOTHING-- JUST CROUCHES OVER HIM AND STARES.
TWENTY SECONDS PASS.
YOU CRAZY BUGGER!
THEY'LL KILL YA!
YOU HEAR?!
YOU'RE DEAD MEAT!!

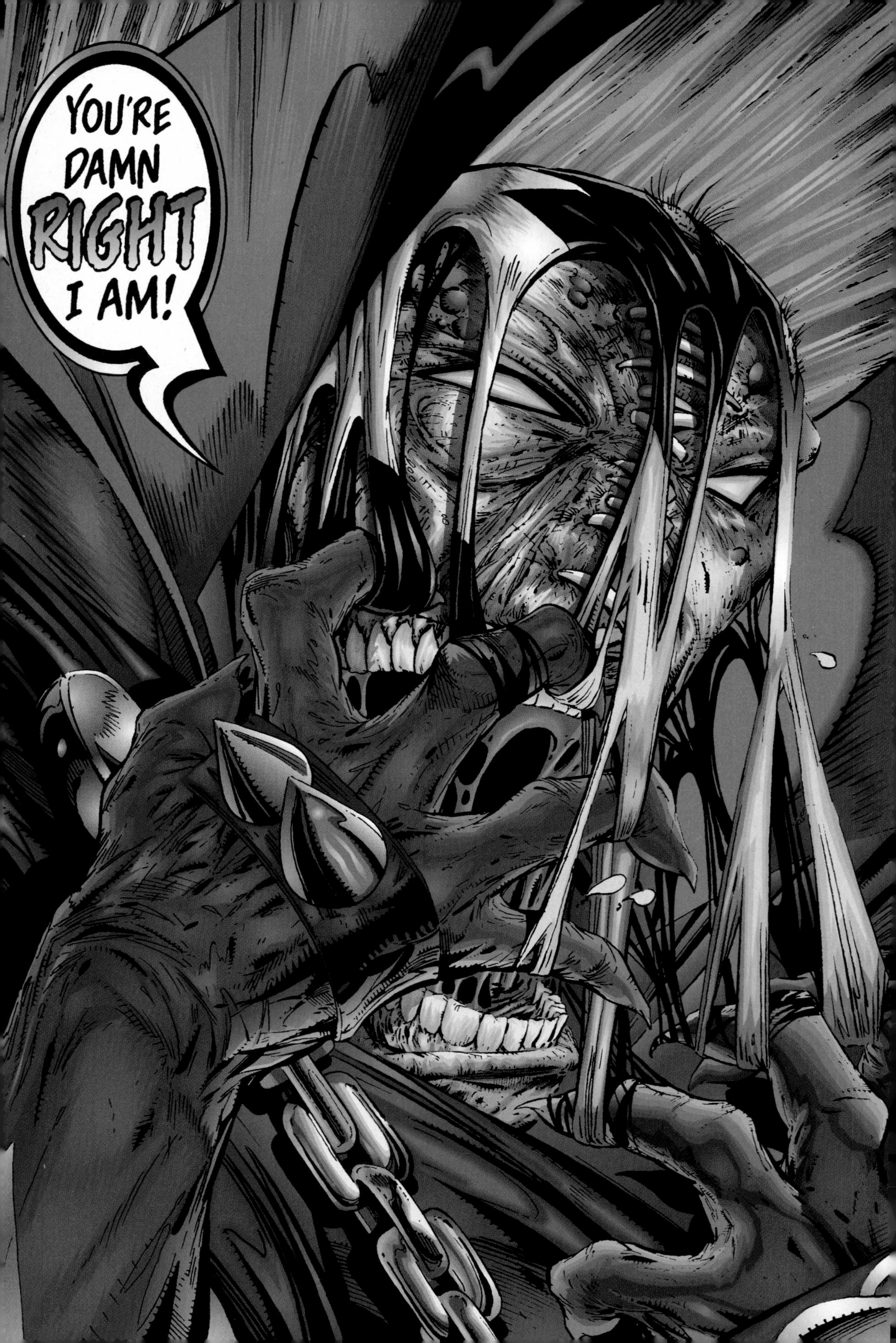
YOU'RE DAMN RIGHT I AM!

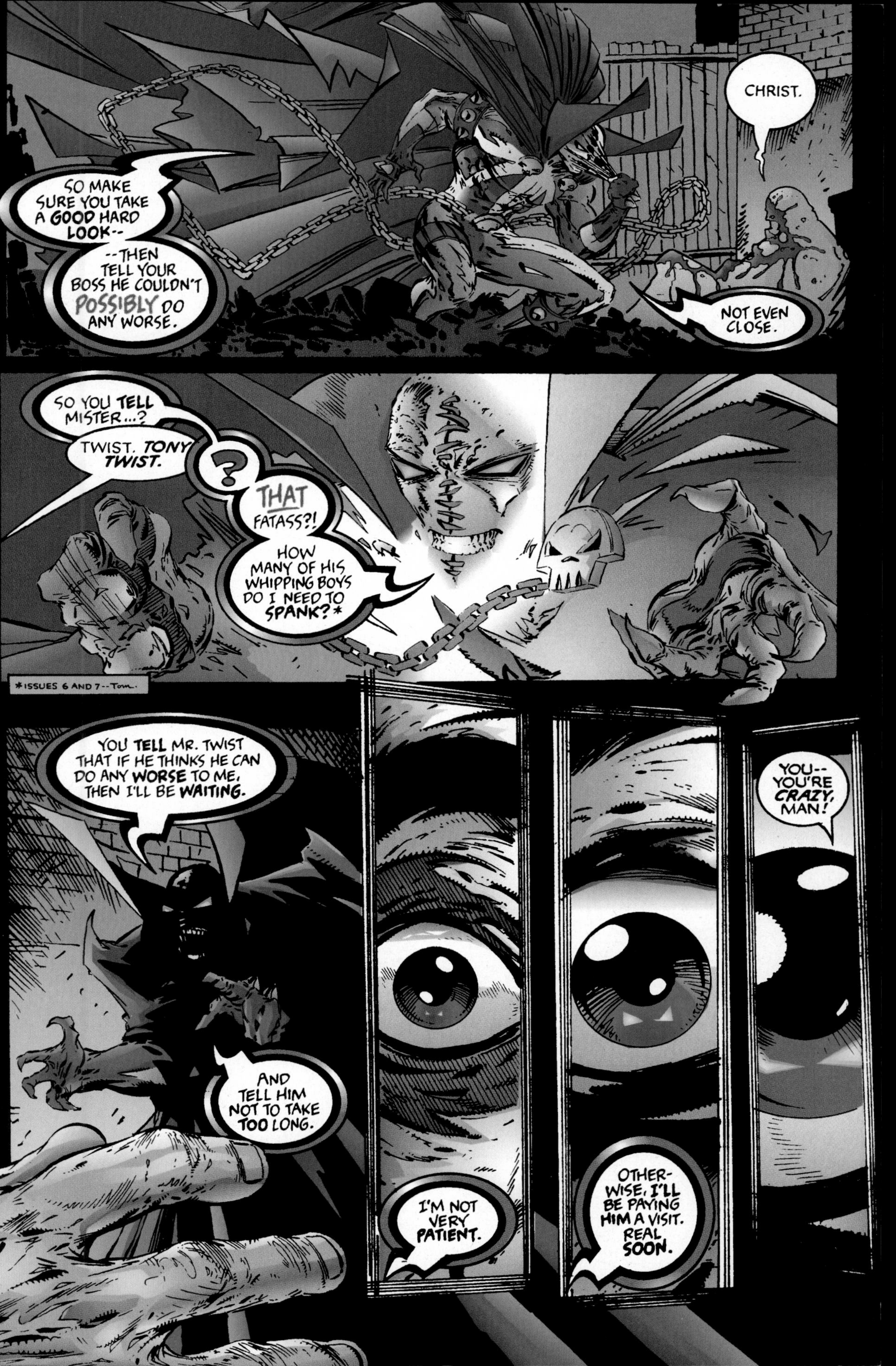
CHRIST.
SO MAKE SURE YOU TAKE A GOOD HARD LOOK--
--THEN TELL YOUR BOSS HE COULDN'T POSSIBLY DO ANY WORSE.
NOT EVEN CLOSE.
SO YOU TELL MISTER...?
TWIST. TONY TWIST.
?
THAT FATASS?!
HOW MANY OF HIS WHIPPING BOYS DO I NEED TO SPANK?*
*ISSUES 6 AND 7--Tom.
YOU TELL MR. TWIST THAT IF HE THINKS HE CAN DO ANY WORSE TO ME, THEN I'LL BE WAITING.
AND TELL HIM NOT TO TAKE TOO LONG.
I'M NOT VERY PATIENT.
OTHER-WISE, I'LL BE PAYING HIM A VISIT. REAL SOON.
YOU-- YOU'RE CRAZY, MAN!

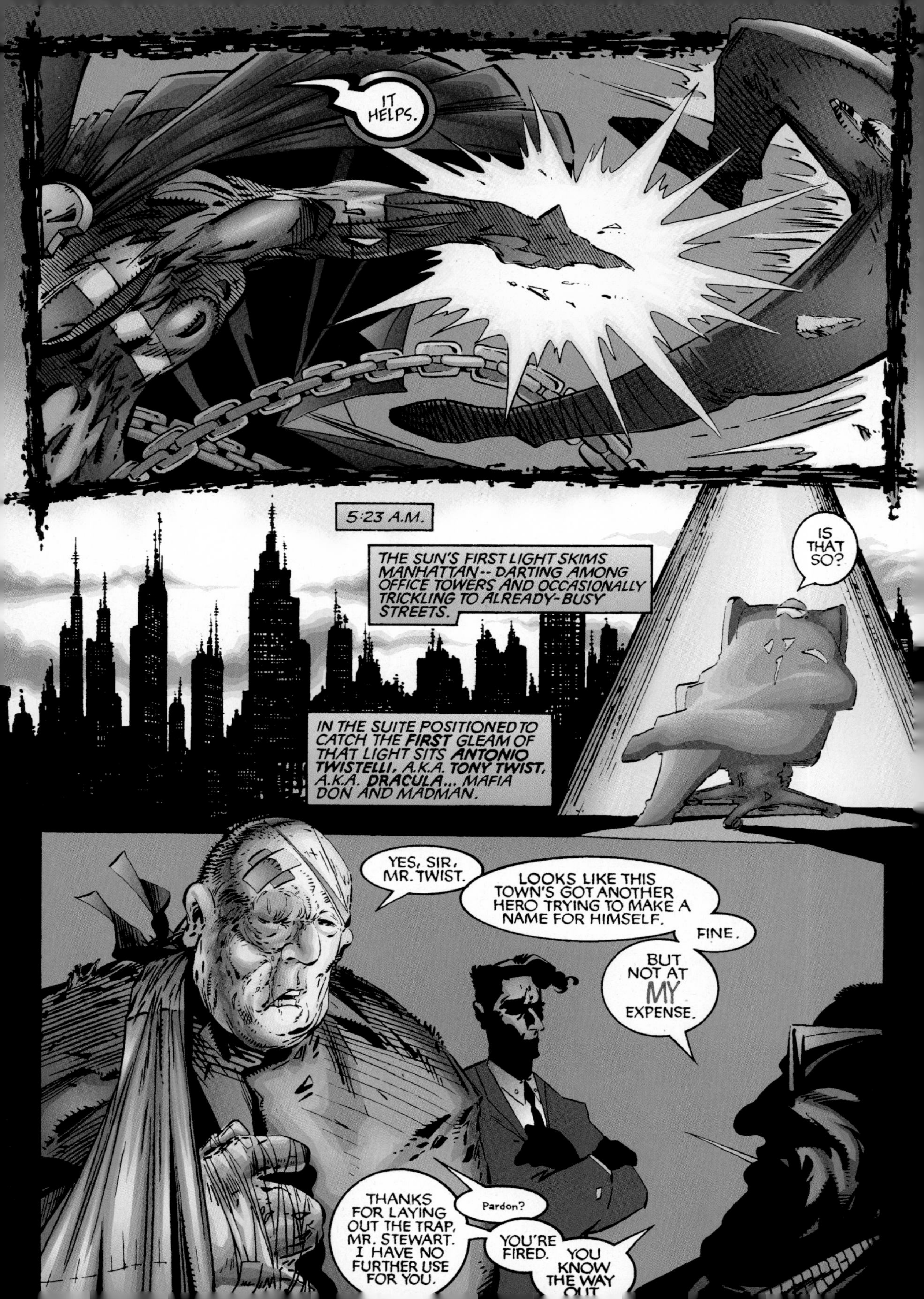
IT HELPS.
5:23 A.M.
THE SUN'S FIRST LIGHT SKIMS MANHATTAN-- DARTING AMONG OFFICE TOWERS AND OCCASIONALLY TRICKLING TO ALREADY-BUSY STREETS.
IN THE SUITE POSITIONED TO CATCH THE FIRST GLEAM OF THAT LIGHT SITS ANTONIO TWISTELLI, A.K.A. TONY TWIST, A.K.A. DRACULA... MAFIA DON AND MADMAN.
IS THAT SO?
YES, SIR, MR. TWIST.
LOOKS LIKE THIS TOWN'S GOT ANOTHER HERO TRYING TO MAKE A NAME FOR HIMSELF.
FINE.
BUT NOT AT MY EXPENSE.
THANKS FOR LAYING OUT THE TRAP, MR. STEWART. I HAVE NO FURTHER USE FOR YOU.
Pardon?
YOU'RE FIRED.
YOU KNOW THE WAY OUT

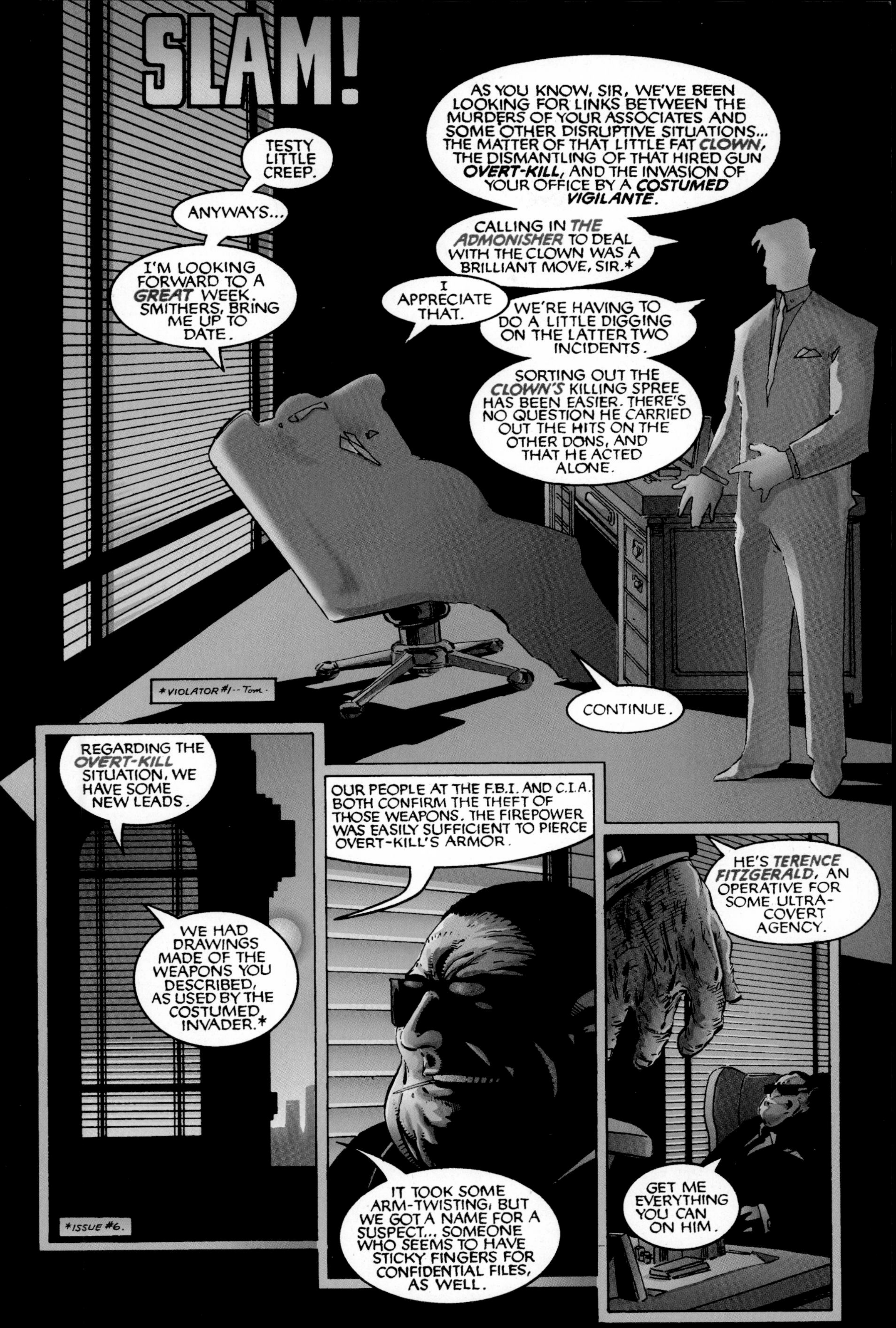
SLAM!
TESTY LITTLE CREEP.
ANYWAYS...
I'M LOOKING FORWARD TO A GREAT WEEK. SMITHERS, BRING ME UP TO DATE.
AS YOU KNOW, SIR, WE'VE BEEN LOOKING FOR LINKS BETWEEN THE MURDERS OF YOUR ASSOCIATES AND SOME OTHER DISRUPTIVE SITUATIONS... THE MATTER OF THAT LITTLE FAT CLOWN, THE DISMANTLING OF THAT HIRED GUN OVERT-KILL, AND THE INVASION OF YOUR OFFICE BY A COSTUMED VIGILANTE.
CALLING IN THE ADMONISHER TO DEAL WITH THE CLOWN WAS A BRILLIANT MOVE, SIR.*
I APPRECIATE THAT.
WE'RE HAVING TO DO A LITTLE DIGGING ON THE LATTER TWO INCIDENTS.
SORTING OUT THE CLOWN'S KILLING SPREE HAS BEEN EASIER. THERE'S NO QUESTION HE CARRIED OUT THE HITS ON THE OTHER DONS, AND THAT HE ACTED ALONE.
*VIOLATOR #1 -- Tom.
CONTINUE.
REGARDING THE OVERT-KILL SITUATION, WE HAVE SOME NEW LEADS.
WE HAD DRAWINGS MADE OF THE WEAPONS YOU DESCRIBED, AS USED BY THE COSTUMED INVADER.*
*ISSUE #6.
OUR PEOPLE AT THE F.B.I. AND C.I.A. BOTH CONFIRM THE THEFT OF THOSE WEAPONS. THE FIREPOWER WAS EASILY SUFFICIENT TO PIERCE OVERT-KILL'S ARMOR.
IT TOOK SOME ARM-TWISTING, BUT WE GOT A NAME FOR A SUSPECT... SOMEONE WHO SEEMS TO HAVE STICKY FINGERS FOR CONFIDENTIAL FILES, AS WELL.
HE'S TERENCE FITZGERALD, AN OPERATIVE FOR SOME ULTRA-COVERT AGENCY.
GET ME EVERYTHING YOU CAN ON HIM.

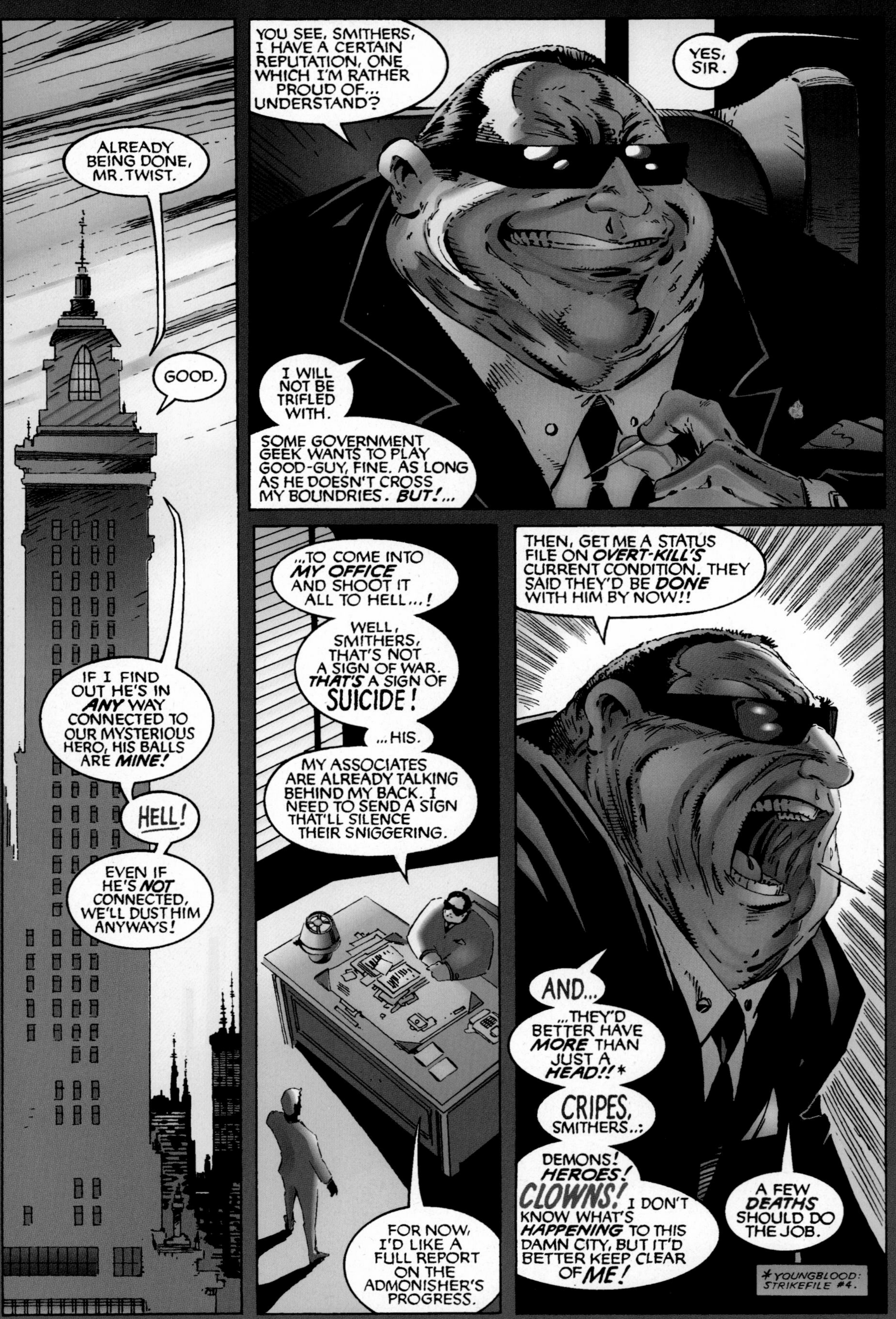
YOU SEE, SMITHERS, I HAVE A CERTAIN REPUTATION, ONE WHICH I'M RATHER PROUD OF... UNDERSTAND?
YES, SIR.
ALREADY BEING DONE, MR. TWIST.
GOOD.
I WILL NOT BE TRIFLED WITH.
SOME GOVERNMENT GEEK WANTS TO PLAY GOOD-GUY, FINE. AS LONG AS HE DOESN'T CROSS MY BOUNDRIES. BUT!...
IF I FIND OUT HE'S IN ANY WAY CONNECTED TO OUR MYSTERIOUS HERO, HIS BALLS ARE MINE!
HELL!
EVEN IF HE'S NOT CONNECTED, WE'LL DUST HIM ANYWAYS!
...TO COME INTO MY OFFICE AND SHOOT IT ALL TO HELL...!
WELL, SMITHERS, THAT'S NOT A SIGN OF WAR. THAT'S A SIGN OF SUICIDE!
...HIS.
MY ASSOCIATES ARE ALREADY TALKING BEHIND MY BACK. I NEED TO SEND A SIGN THAT'LL SILENCE THEIR SNIGGERING.
FOR NOW, I'D LIKE A FULL REPORT ON THE ADMONISHER'S PROGRESS.
THEN, GET ME A STATUS FILE ON OVERT-KILL'S CURRENT CONDITION. THEY SAID THEY'D BE DONE WITH HIM BY NOW!!
AND...
...THEY'D BETTER HAVE MORE THAN JUST A HEAD!!*
CRIPES, SMITHERS..:
DEMONS! HEROES! CLOWNS! I DON'T KNOW WHAT'S HAPPENING TO THIS DAMN CITY, BUT IT'D BETTER KEEP CLEAR OF ME!
A FEW DEATHS SHOULD DO THE JOB.
*YOUNGBLOOD: STRIKEFILE #4.

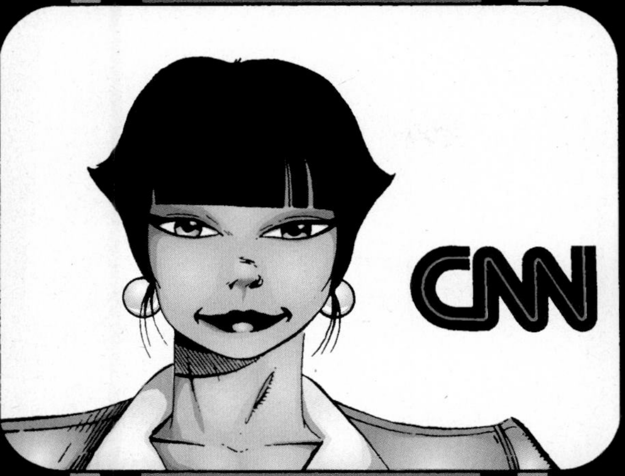
CNN

...AN UNEXPECTED NAME IN THE NEWS TODAY IS ***JASON WYNN***, A PREVIOUSLY LITTLE-KNOWN DEPARTMENT HEAD AT THE C.I.A. WYNN RECEIVED A CLEAN BILL OF HEALTH FROM HIS DOCTORS, ACCORDING TO REPORTS RELEASED TODAY, AND HAS ALREADY BEEN BACK AT WORK SINCE MONDAY.

HE UNDERWENT SOME SIXTY PHYSICAL AND PSYCHOLOGICAL TESTS AFTER BEING DISCOVERED CRUMPLED ON HIS OFFICE FLOOR THE PREVIOUS FRIDAY. THERE ARE STILL FEW DETAILS REGARDING HIS ABSENCE WEDNESDAY AND THURSDAY OF LAST WEEK, THOUGH ABDUCTION BY A HOSTILE AGENCY HAS NOT BEEN RULED OUT.

WYNN CLAIMS NO RECOLLECTION OF ANYTHING THAT OCCURED DURING HIS ABSENCE. ACCORDING TO A **WITNESS**, THE DIRECTOR WAS SPIRITED MYSTERIOUSLY OUT OF A C.I.A. GYMNASIUM. THE DISAPPEARANCE LED TO AN EXHAUSTIVE SEARCH WHICH ENDED WHEN A NIGHT CUSTODIAN FOUND HIM. APPARENTLY, WYNN HAD SOMEHOW RETURNED UNDETECTED TO HIS OWN PRIVATE OFFICE ON THE TENTH FLOOR, WHICH WAS LOCKED FROM THE OUTSIDE.

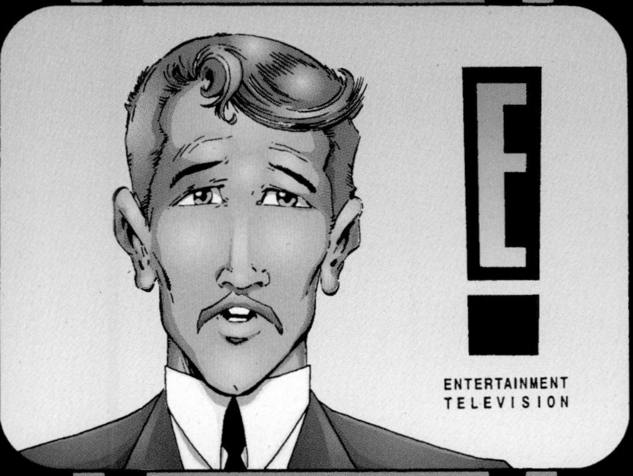
E!
ENTERTAINMENT TELEVISION

WHAT HAS DOCTORS CONCERNED IS WYNN'S UNEXPLAINABLE PARA-AMNESIA. REPEATED PROBES AND C.A.T. SCANS OF THE DIRECTOR'S BRAIN AND CENTRAL NERVOUS SYSTEM HAS REVEALED NO INDICATIONS OF PHYSICAL TRAUMA OR INVASIVE MANIPULATION OF ANY SORT.

A HOSPITAL SPOKESPERSON, SPEAKING ON CONDITION OF ANONYMITY, EMPHASIZED THAT THERE IS NO SIGN OF INJURY WHATSOEVER AND THAT WYNN IS IN TOP PHYSICAL HEALTH. HOWEVER, HE WILL CONTINUE TO BE TESTED OVER THE NEXT SEVERAL WEEKS IN CASE SIMILAR SYMPTOMS ARISE.

WYNN WAS UNAVAILABLE FOR COMMENT, BUT HIS PERSONAL AIDE HAS RELATED THAT MR. WYNN IS BACK TO WORK *"IN FULL FORCE"* AND PROCEEDING AS IF THE ENTIRE EVENT NEVER OCCURED. THE C.I.A., N.S.A. AND N.S.C. ALL HAD NO COMMENT BUT THAT MR. WYNN IS BEING WATCHED CLOSELY FOR ANY SIGNS OF FUTURE ABNORMALITY.

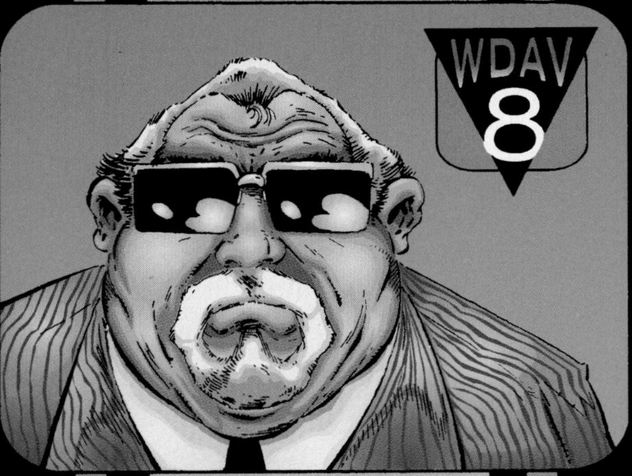
WDAV
8

GREAT DAY IN THE MORNING! LET'S GO OVER THE FACTS, IF THE C.I.A. DOESN'T MIND. A MEMBER OF THEIR ***DIRECTORATE*** DISAPPEARS, ala *"STAR TREK,"* APPARENTLY OFF THE FACE OF THE ***EARTH***, AND THEN JUST SHOWS UP TWO DAYS LATER, THUMB IN HIS MOUTH, HUDDLED IN A FETAL BALL IN HIS OFFICE. HE REMEMBERS ***SQUAT***, BUT THAT'S OKAY, 'CAUSE HE'S ONE OF THE GOOD OL' BOYS. SO, THEY GET HIM TO PEE IN A CUP, A DOZEN TOP-SECURITY DOCTORS WRITE UP A DOZEN UNREADABLE REPORTS, AND THEY SEND HIM BACK TO WORK WITH AN APPLE IN HIS LUNCHBOX. AT THE SAME TIME, THEY DECLARE IT ***MIGHT*** HAVE BEEN AN ENEMY ACTION AND YET DON'T BLINK AN EYE AT THE POSSIBILITY OUR TOP-SECRET BOY SCOUT IS ***COMPROMISED!***

WAS HE KIDNAPPED OR ***WASN'T*** HE? PERHAPS HE WAS OFF IN ARUBA WITH MISS MONEYPENNY--OUR TAX PENNIES AT WORK! I BET IF YOU OR I TRIED THIS CRAP WE'D BE WALKING THE STREETS IN TEN SECONDS FLAT. I KNOW ***I'LL*** SLEEP BETTER KNOWING THAT BOYS LIKE THIS ARE IN CHARGE OF OUR ***NATIONAL SECURITY!***

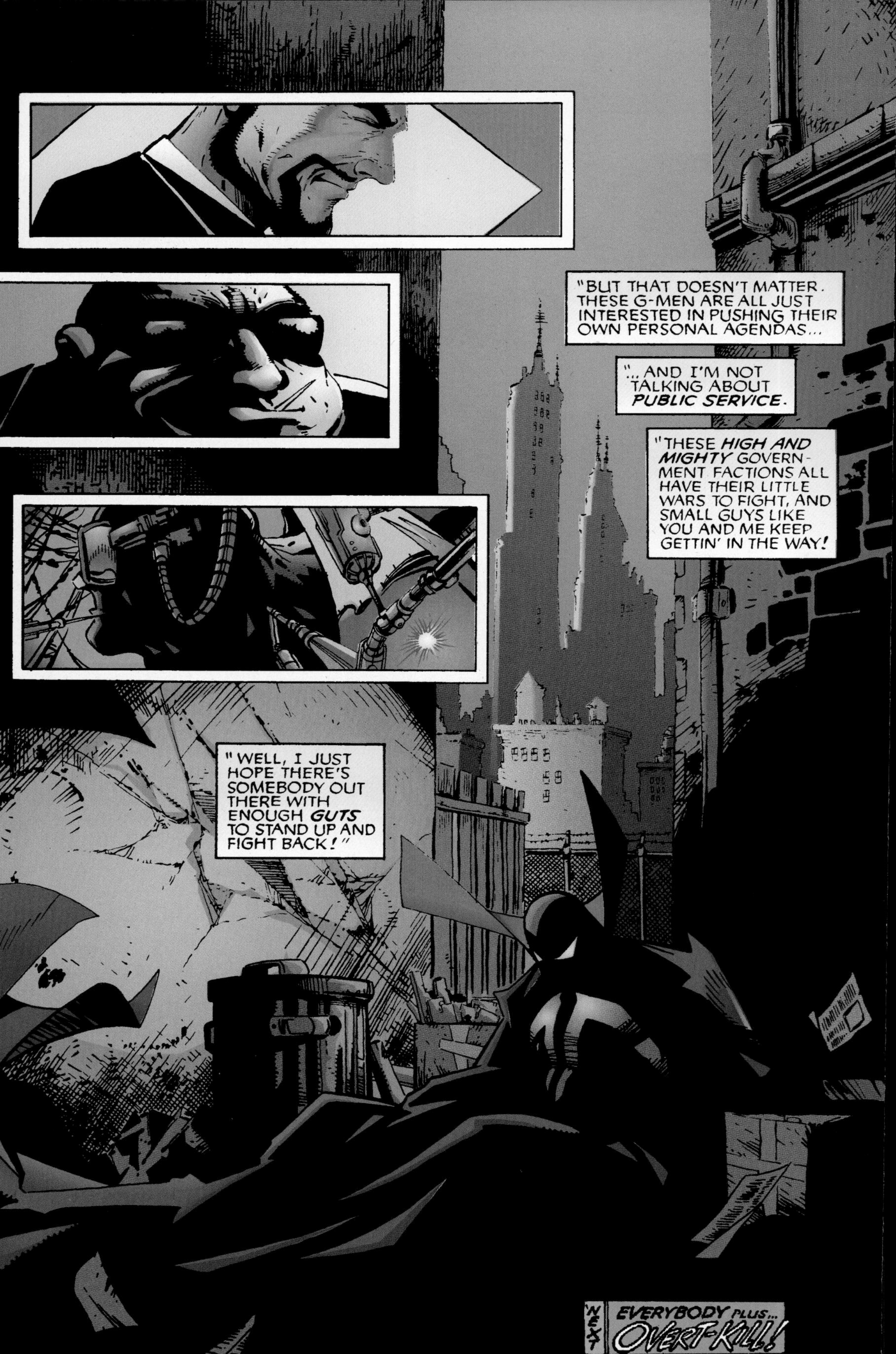
"BUT THAT DOESN'T MATTER. THESE G-MEN ARE ALL JUST INTERESTED IN PUSHING THEIR OWN PERSONAL AGENDAS...
"...AND I'M NOT TALKING ABOUT PUBLIC SERVICE.
"THESE HIGH AND MIGHTY GOVERNMENT FACTIONS ALL HAVE THEIR LITTLE WARS TO FIGHT, AND SMALL GUYS LIKE YOU AND ME KEEP GETTIN' IN THE WAY!
"WELL, I JUST HOPE THERE'S SOMEBODY OUT THERE WITH ENOUGH GUTS TO STAND UP AND FIGHT BACK!"
NEXT
EVERYBODY PLUS... OVERT-KILL!

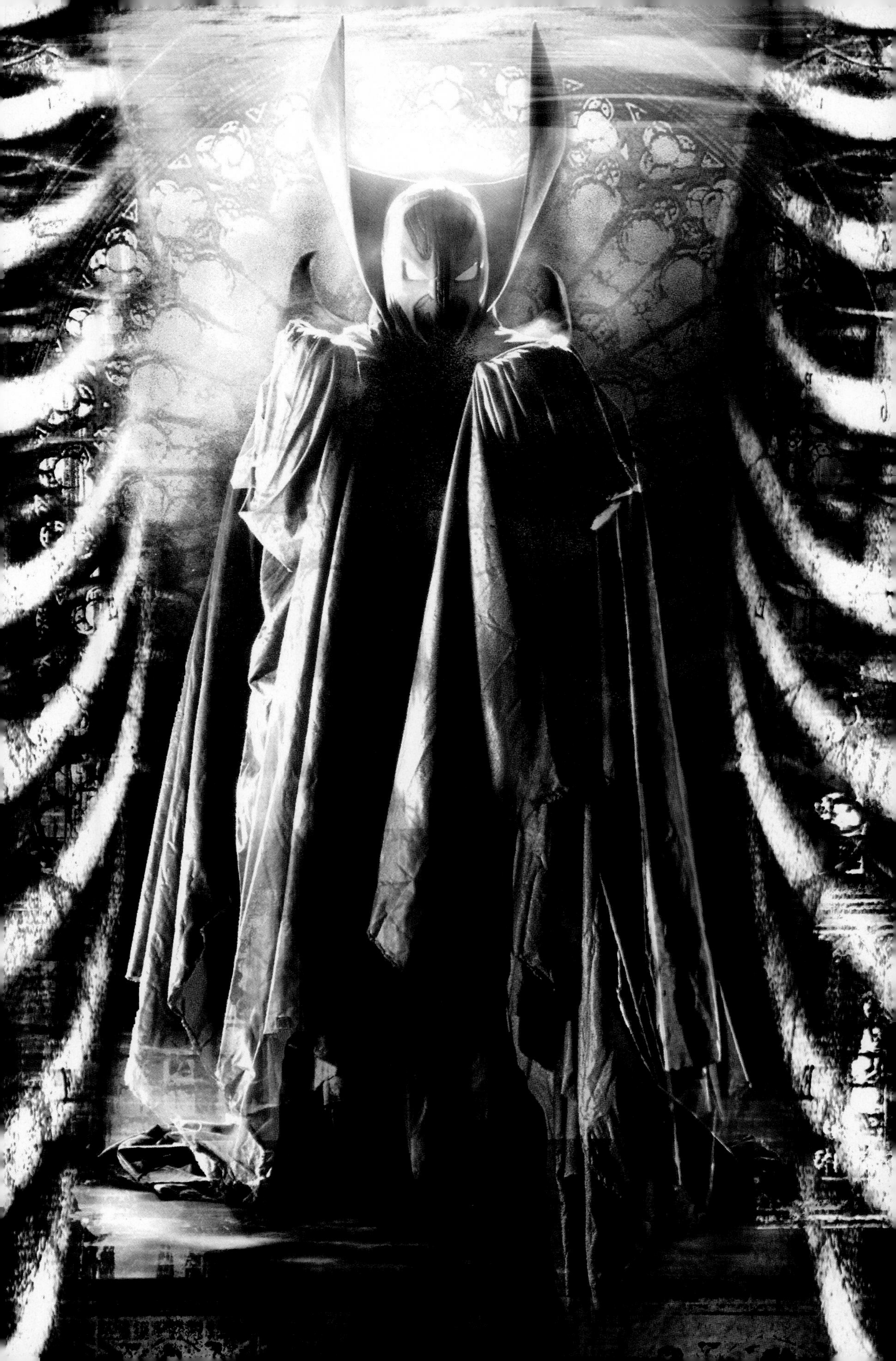

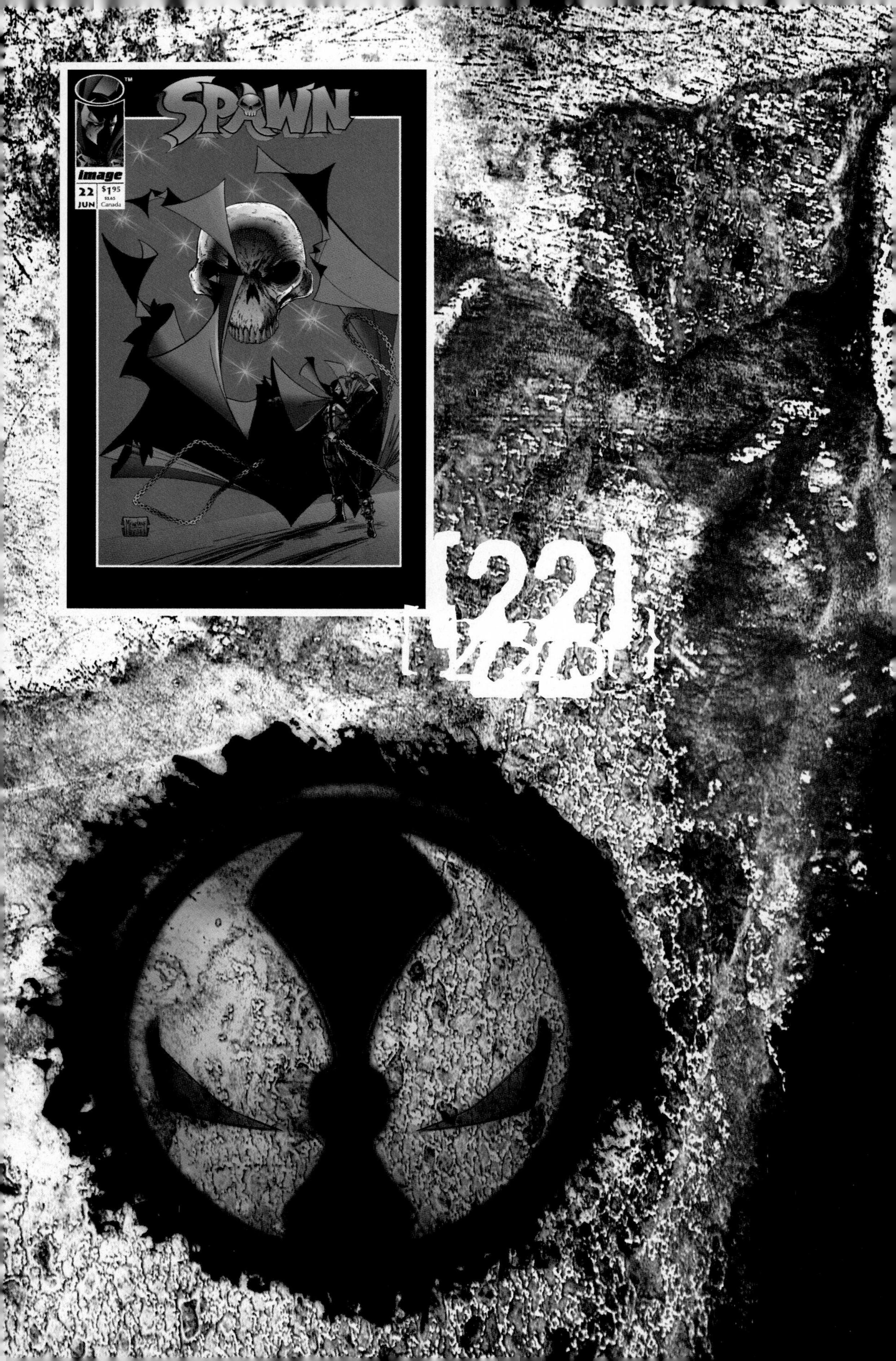
SPAWN
image
22
JUN
$1.95
$2.65 Canada

[22]

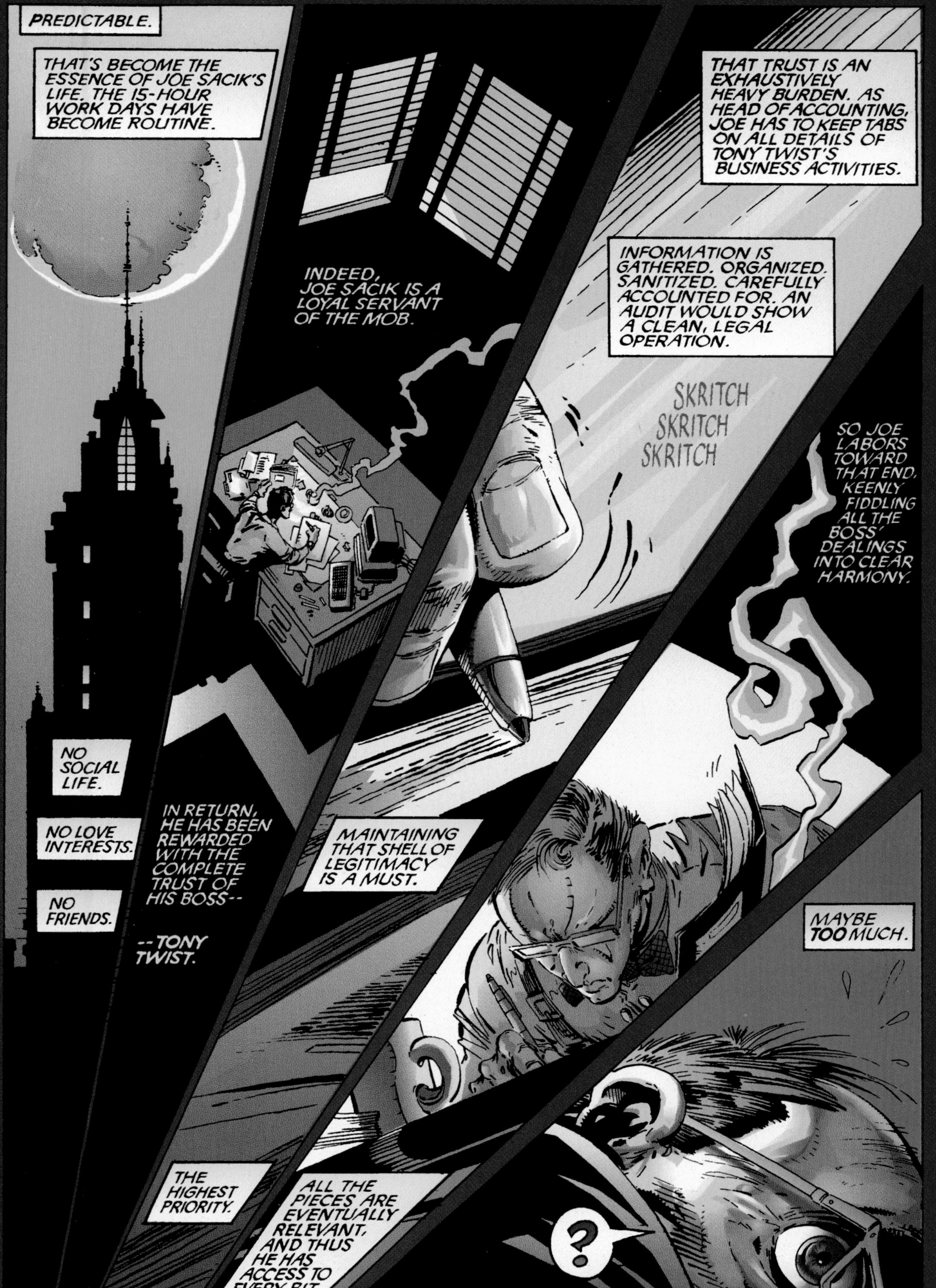
PREDICTABLE.
THAT'S BECOME THE ESSENCE OF JOE SACIK'S LIFE. THE 15-HOUR WORK DAYS HAVE BECOME ROUTINE.
NO SOCIAL LIFE.
NO LOVE INTERESTS.
NO FRIENDS.
INDEED, JOE SACIK IS A LOYAL SERVANT OF THE MOB.
IN RETURN, HE HAS BEEN REWARDED WITH THE COMPLETE TRUST OF HIS BOSS--
--TONY TWIST.
THAT TRUST IS AN EXHAUSTIVELY HEAVY BURDEN. AS HEAD OF ACCOUNTING, JOE HAS TO KEEP TABS ON ALL DETAILS OF TONY TWIST'S BUSINESS ACTIVITIES.
THE HIGHEST PRIORITY.
INFORMATION IS GATHERED. ORGANIZED. SANITIZED. CAREFULLY ACCOUNTED FOR. AN AUDIT WOULD SHOW A CLEAN, LEGAL OPERATION.
SKRITCH
SKRITCH
SKRITCH
MAINTAINING THAT SHELL OF LEGITIMACY IS A MUST.
ALL THE PIECES ARE EVENTUALLY RELEVANT, AND THUS HE HAS ACCESS TO EVERY BIT OF DATA.
SO JOE LABORS TOWARD THAT END, KEENLY FIDDLING ALL THE BOSS' DEALINGS INTO CLEAR HARMONY.
MAYBE TOO MUCH.
?

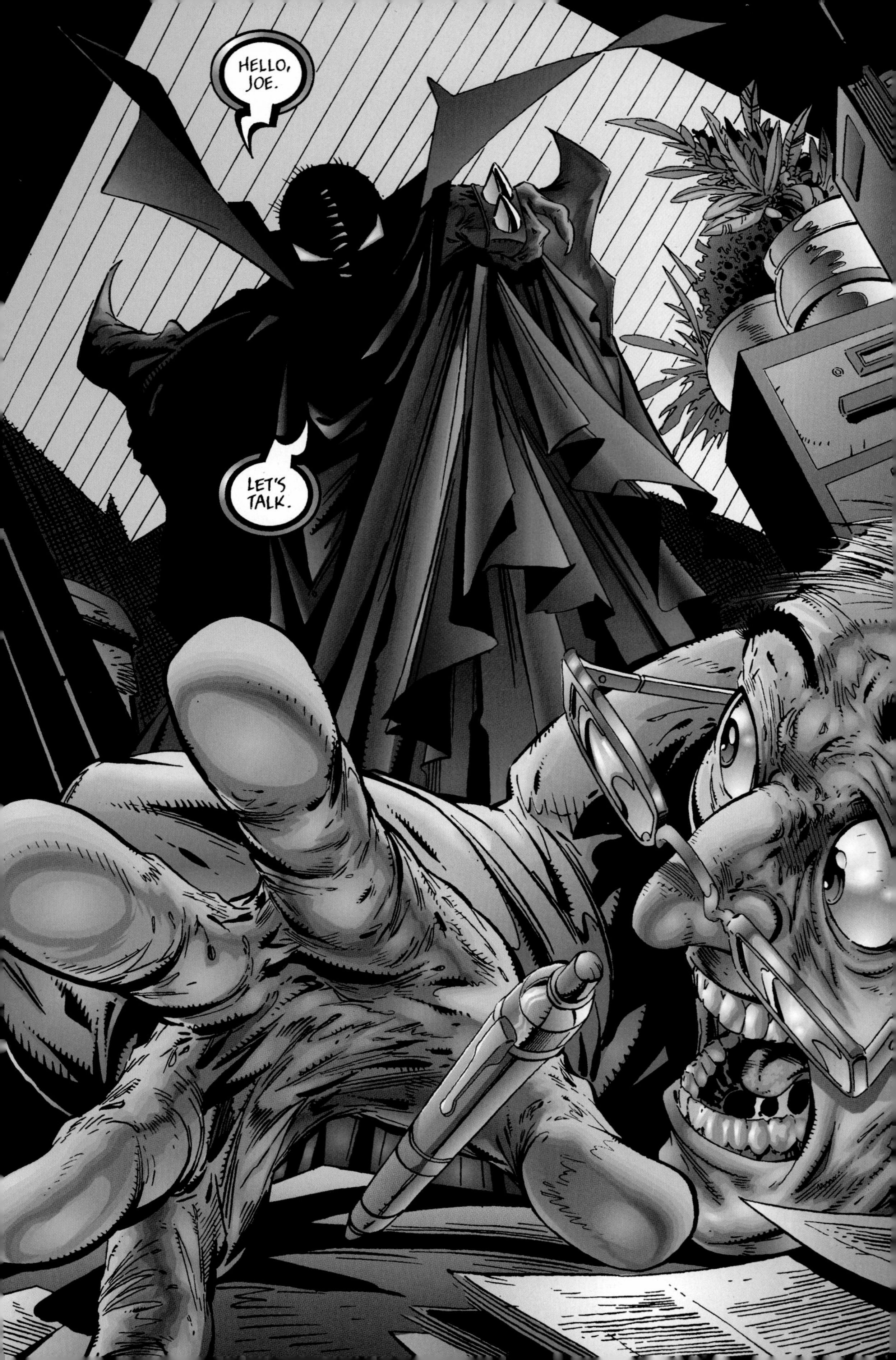
HELLO, JOE.
LET'S TALK.

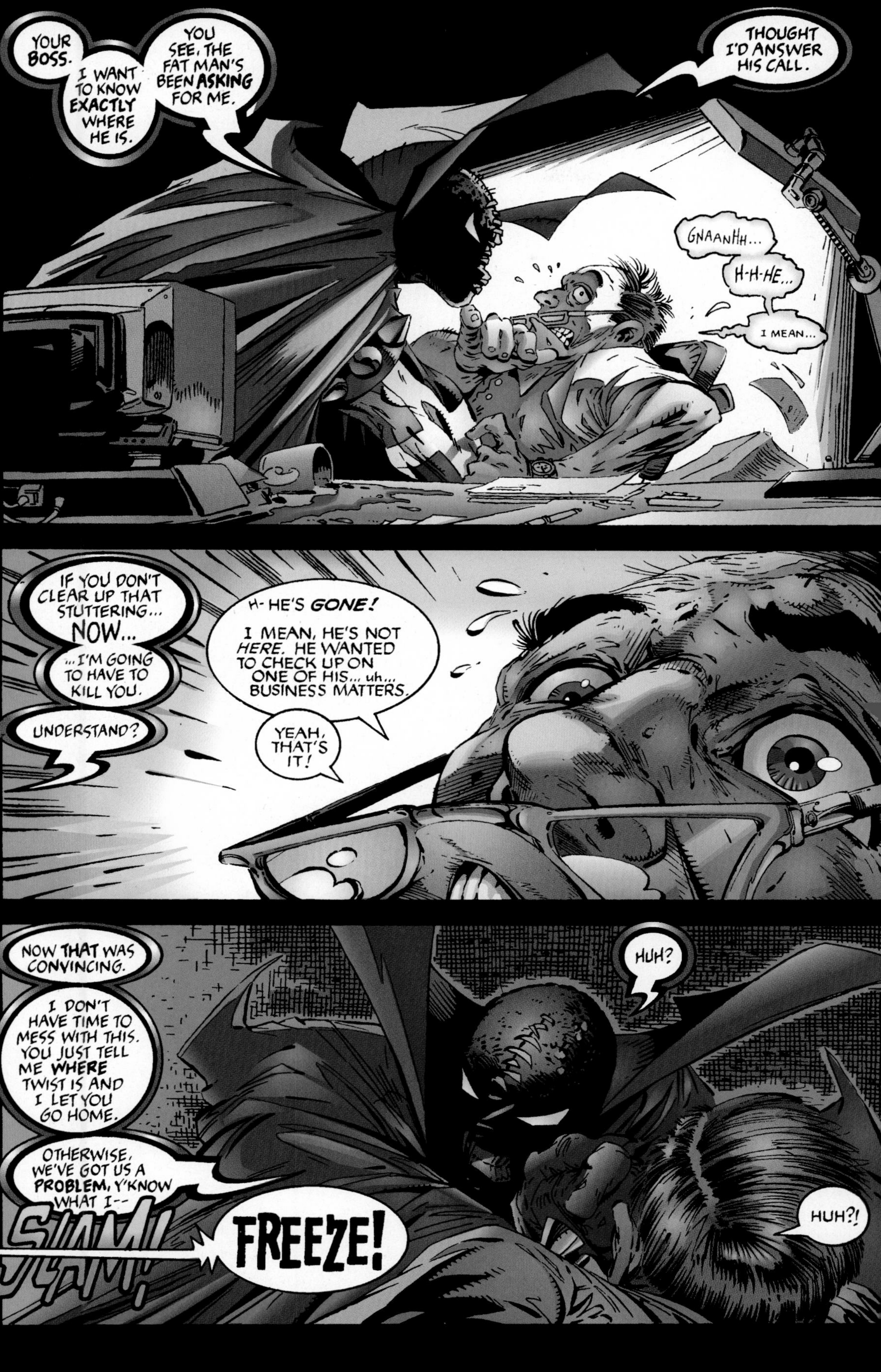

YOUR BOSS.
I WANT TO KNOW EXACTLY WHERE HE IS.
YOU SEE, THE FAT MAN'S BEEN ASKING FOR ME.
THOUGHT I'D ANSWER HIS CALL.
GNAANHH...
H-H-HE...
I MEAN...
IF YOU DON'T CLEAR UP THAT STUTTERING... NOW...
...I'M GOING TO HAVE TO KILL YOU.
UNDERSTAND?
H- HE'S GONE!
I MEAN, HE'S NOT HERE. HE WANTED TO CHECK UP ON ONE OF HIS... uh... BUSINESS MATTERS.
YEAH, THAT'S IT!
NOW THAT WAS CONVINCING.
I DON'T HAVE TIME TO MESS WITH THIS. YOU JUST TELL ME WHERE TWIST IS AND I LET YOU GO HOME.
OTHERWISE, WE'VE GOT US A PROBLEM, Y'KNOW WHAT I--
HUH?
SLAM!
FREEZE!
HUH?!

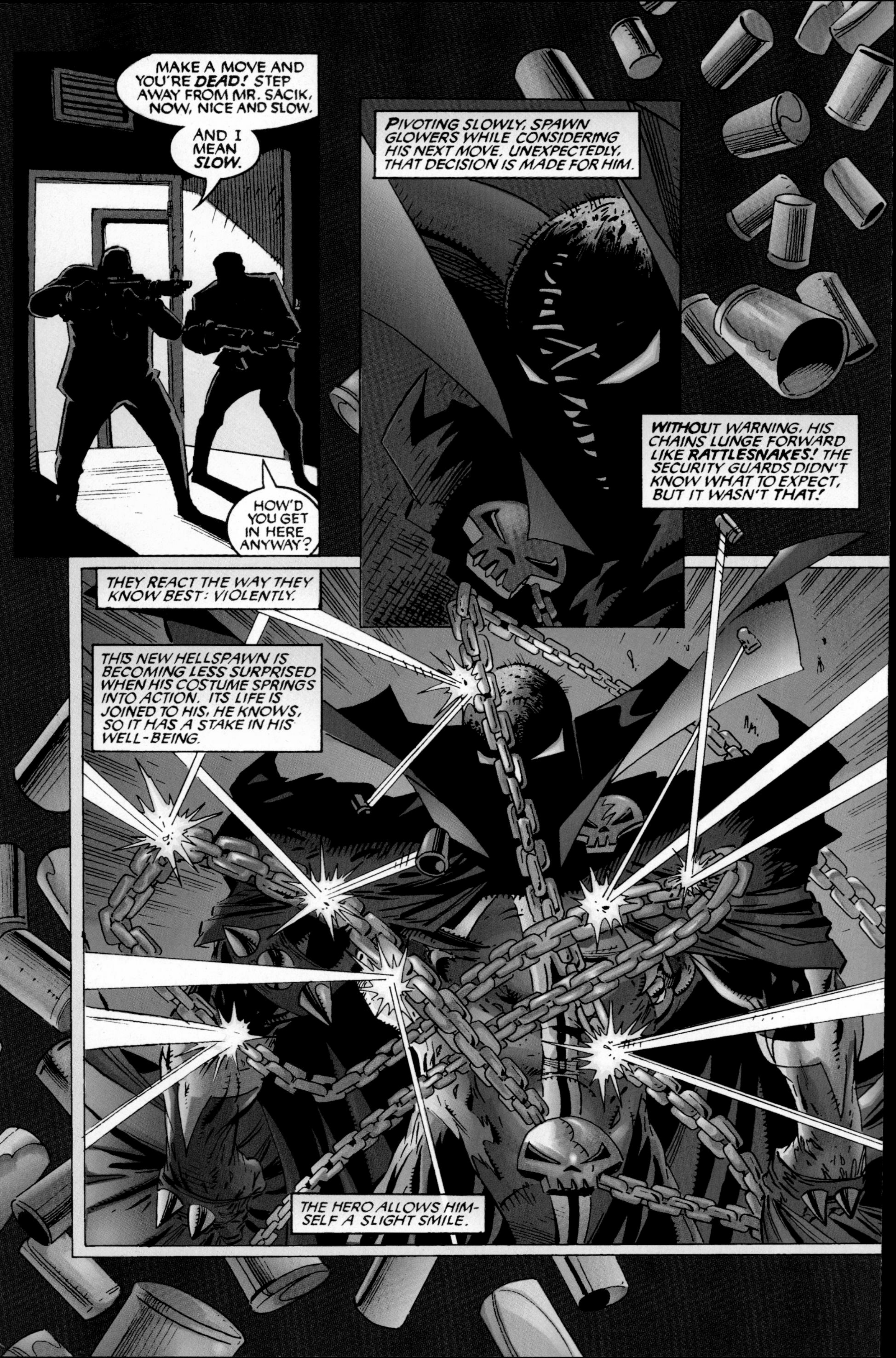
MAKE A MOVE AND YOU'RE DEAD! STEP AWAY FROM MR. SACIK. NOW, NICE AND SLOW.
AND I MEAN SLOW.
HOW'D YOU GET IN HERE ANYWAY?
PIVOTING SLOWLY, SPAWN GLOWERS WHILE CONSIDERING HIS NEXT MOVE. UNEXPECTEDLY, THAT DECISION IS MADE FOR HIM.
WITHOUT WARNING, HIS CHAINS LUNGE FORWARD LIKE RATTLESNAKES! THE SECURITY GUARDS DIDN'T KNOW WHAT TO EXPECT, BUT IT WASN'T THAT!
THEY REACT THE WAY THEY KNOW BEST: VIOLENTLY.
THIS NEW HELLSPAWN IS BECOMING LESS SURPRISED WHEN HIS COSTUME SPRINGS INTO ACTION. ITS LIFE IS JOINED TO HIS, HE KNOWS, SO IT HAS A STAKE IN HIS WELL-BEING.
THE HERO ALLOWS HIMSELF A SLIGHT SMILE.

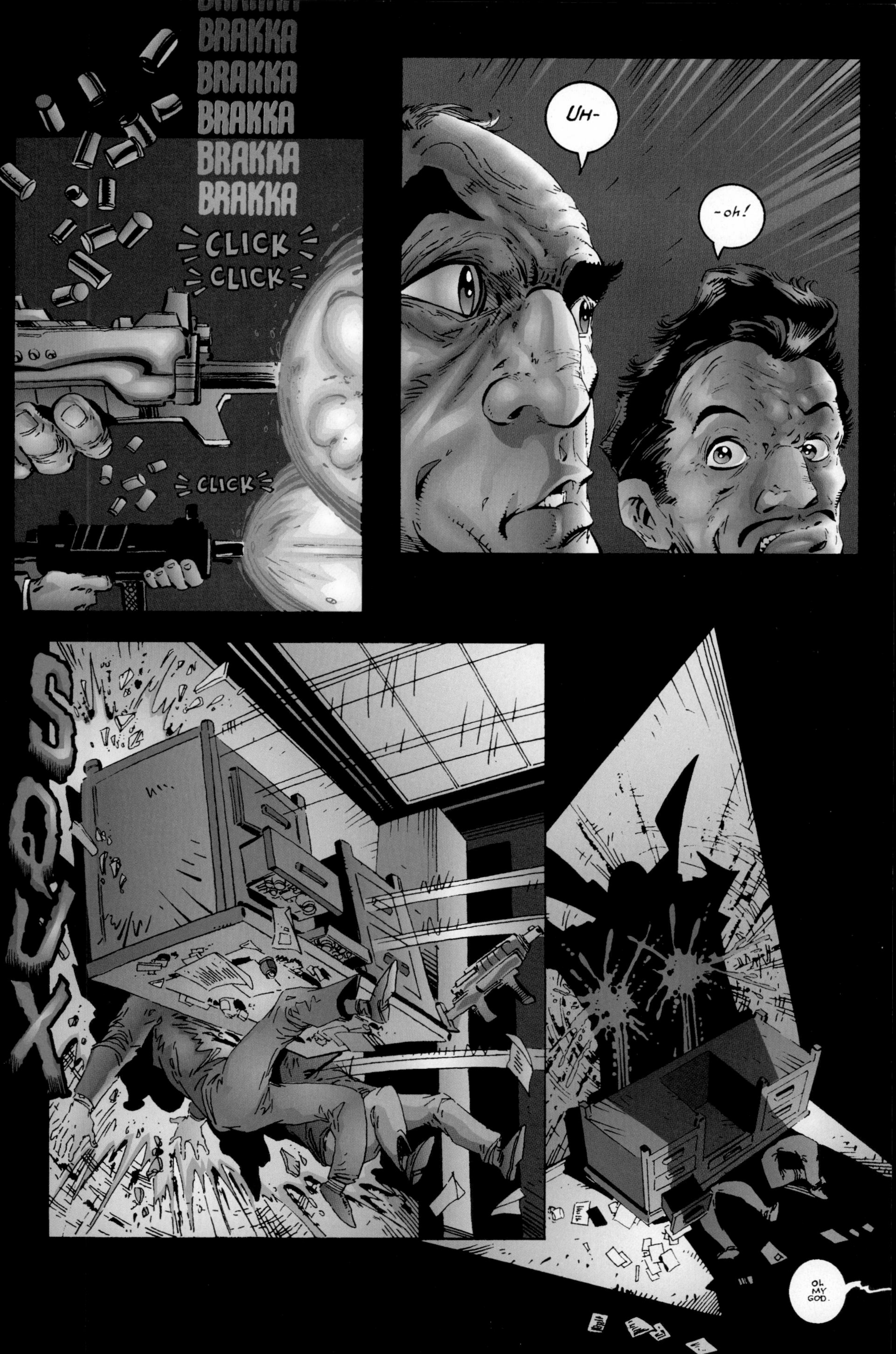
BRAKKA
BRAKKA
BRAKKA
BRAKKA
BRAKKA
CLICK
CLICK
CLICK
UH-
-oh!
OH MY GOD.

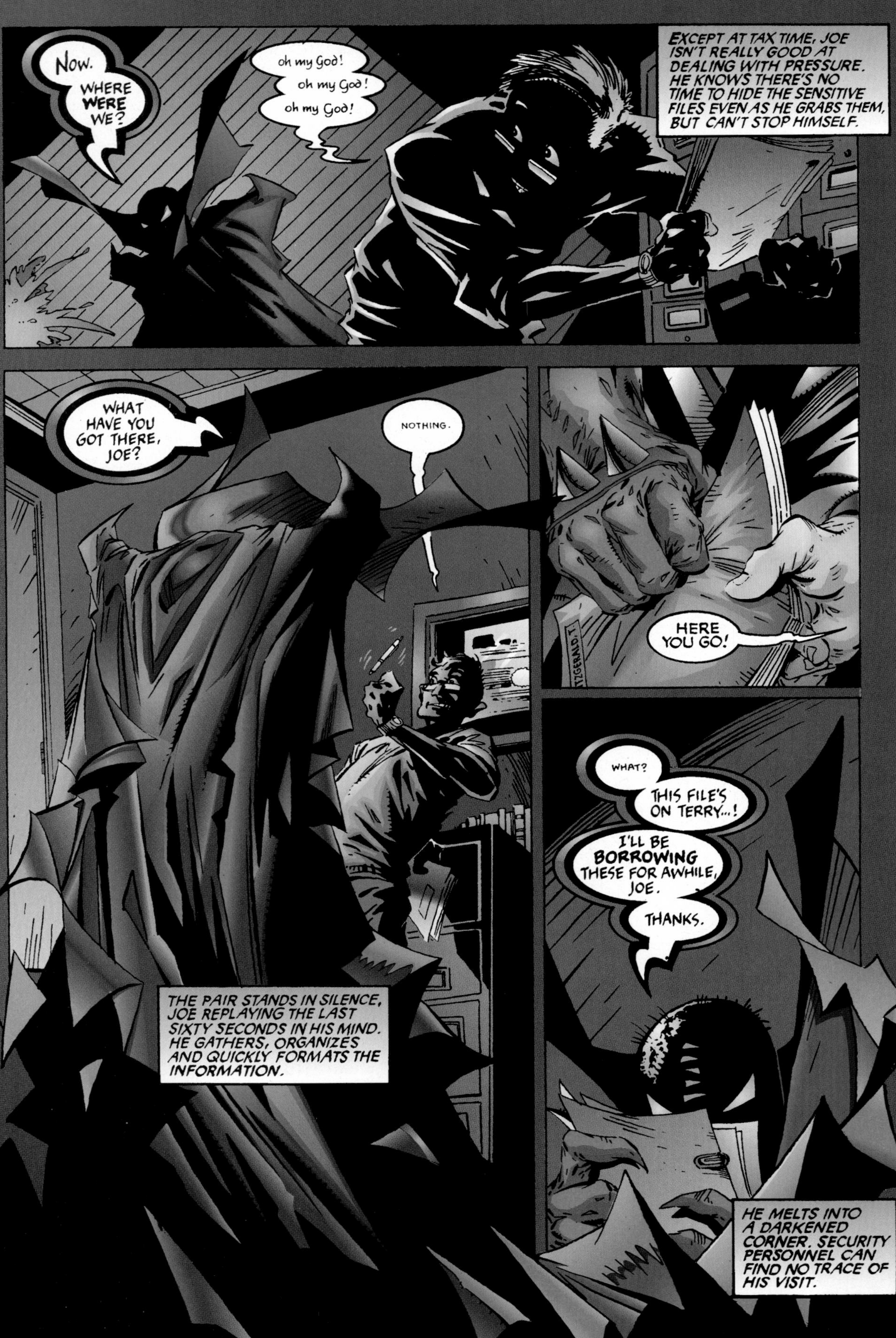

EXCEPT AT TAX TIME, JOE ISN'T REALLY GOOD AT DEALING WITH PRESSURE. HE KNOWS THERE'S NO TIME TO HIDE THE SENSITIVE FILES EVEN AS HE GRABS THEM, BUT CAN'T STOP HIMSELF.
Now. WHERE WERE WE?
oh my God!
oh my God!
oh my God!
WHAT HAVE YOU GOT THERE, JOE?
NOTHING.
HERE YOU GO!
WHAT?
THIS FILE'S ON TERRY...!
I'LL BE BORROWING THESE FOR AWHILE, JOE.
THANKS.
THE PAIR STANDS IN SILENCE, JOE REPLAYING THE LAST SIXTY SECONDS IN HIS MIND. HE GATHERS, ORGANIZES AND QUICKLY FORMATS THE INFORMATION.
HE MELTS INTO A DARKENED CORNER. SECURITY PERSONNEL CAN FIND NO TRACE OF HIS VISIT.

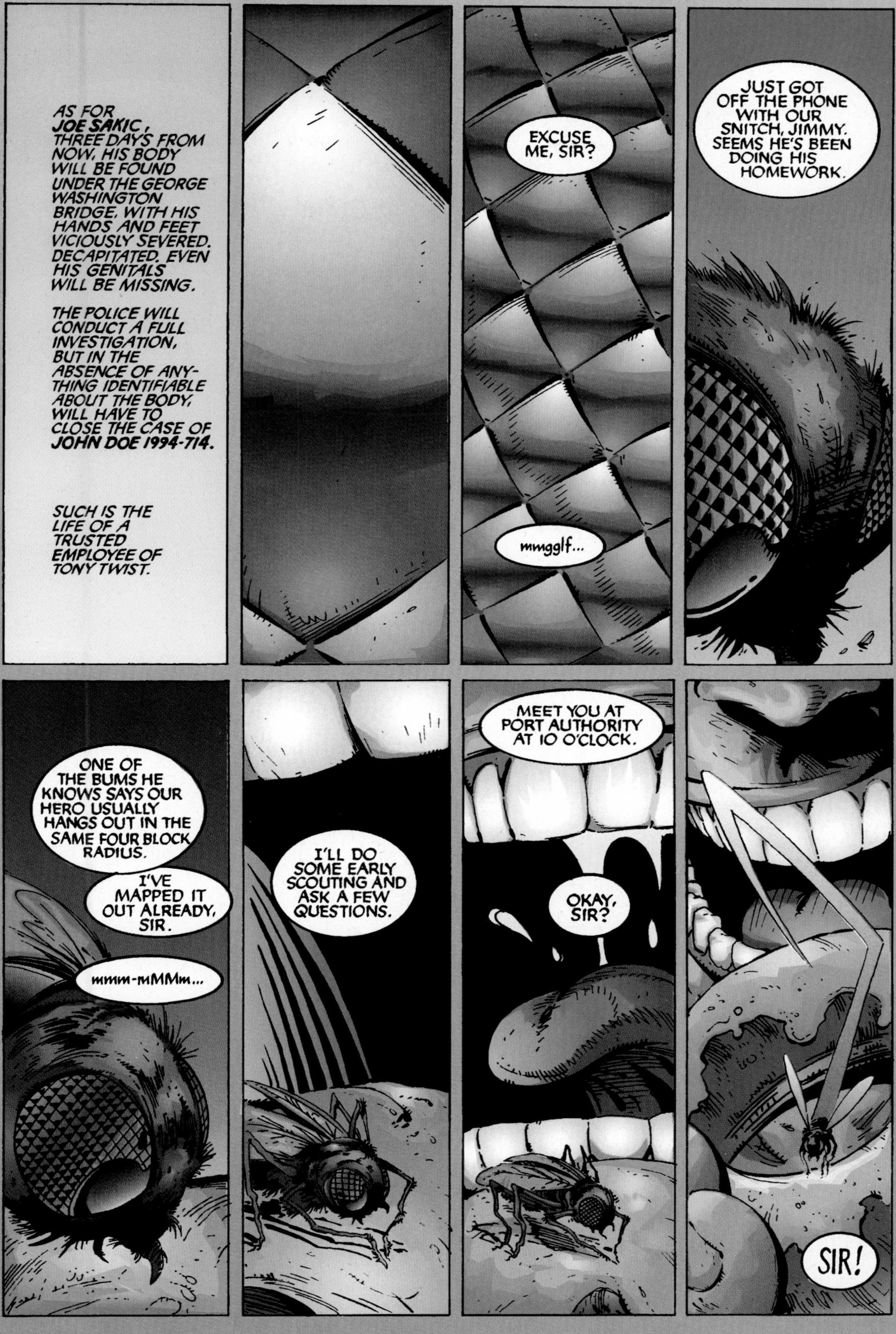

AS FOR JOE SAKIC, THREE DAYS FROM NOW, HIS BODY WILL BE FOUND UNDER THE GEORGE WASHINGTON BRIDGE, WITH HIS HANDS AND FEET VICIOUSLY SEVERED. DECAPITATED. EVEN HIS GENITALS WILL BE MISSING.
THE POLICE WILL CONDUCT A FULL INVESTIGATION, BUT IN THE ABSENCE OF ANYTHING IDENTIFIABLE ABOUT THE BODY, WILL HAVE TO CLOSE THE CASE OF JOHN DOE 1994-714.
SUCH IS THE LIFE OF A TRUSTED EMPLOYEE OF TONY TWIST.
EXCUSE ME, SIR?
mmgglf...
JUST GOT OFF THE PHONE WITH OUR SNITCH, JIMMY. SEEMS HE'S BEEN DOING HIS HOMEWORK.
ONE OF THE BUMS HE KNOWS SAYS OUR HERO USUALLY HANGS OUT IN THE SAME FOUR BLOCK RADIUS.
I'VE MAPPED IT OUT ALREADY, SIR.
mmm-mMMm...
I'LL DO SOME EARLY SCOUTING AND ASK A FEW QUESTIONS.
MEET YOU AT PORT AUTHORITY AT 10 O'CLOCK.
OKAY, SIR?
SIR!

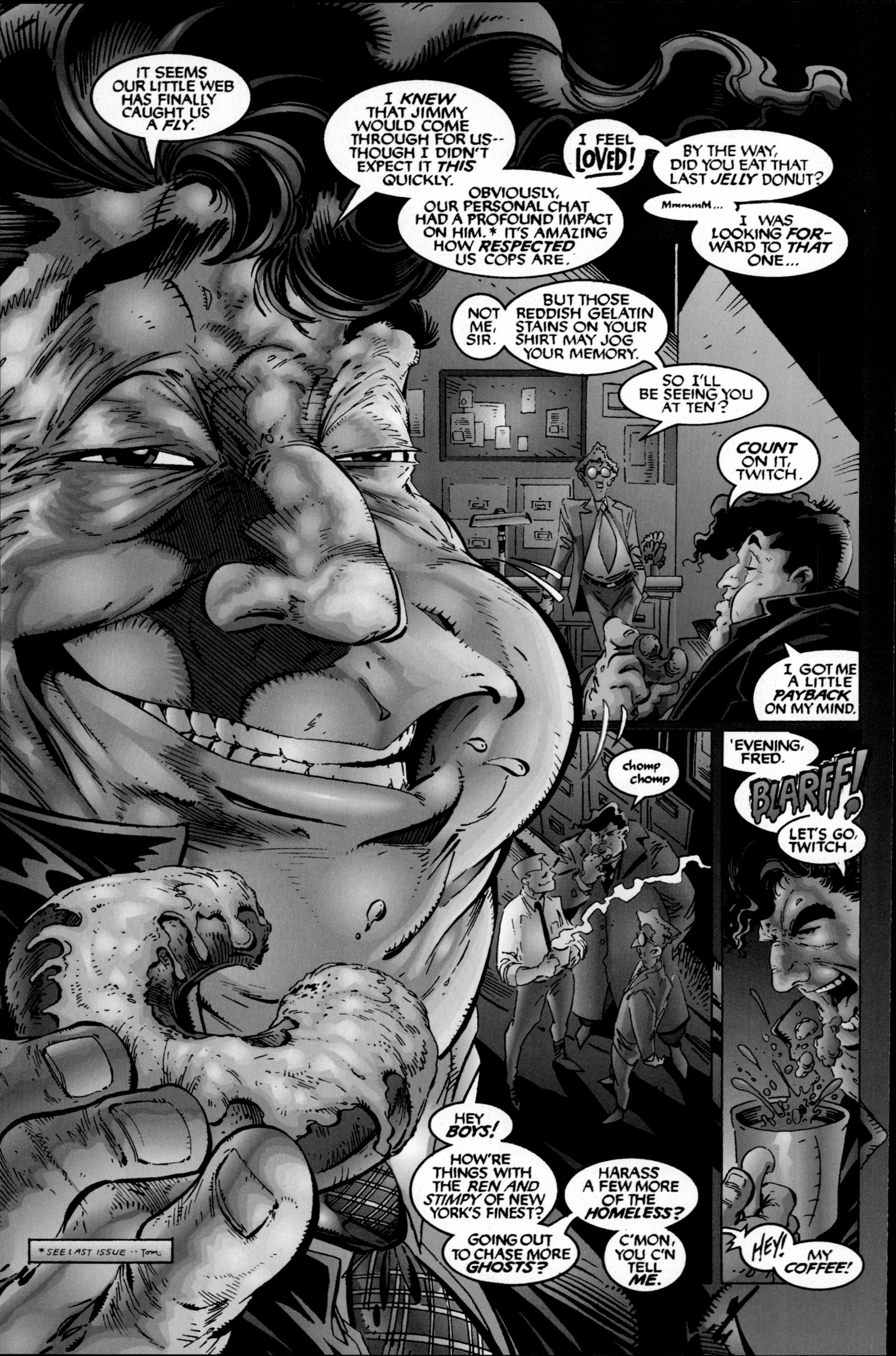
IT SEEMS OUR LITTLE WEB HAS FINALLY CAUGHT US A FLY.
I KNEW THAT JIMMY WOULD COME THROUGH FOR US-- THOUGH I DIDN'T EXPECT IT THIS QUICKLY.
OBVIOUSLY, OUR PERSONAL CHAT HAD A PROFOUND IMPACT ON HIM.* IT'S AMAZING HOW RESPECTED US COPS ARE.
I FEEL LOVED!
BY THE WAY, DID YOU EAT THAT LAST JELLY DONUT?
MmmmM...
I WAS LOOKING FOR-WARD TO THAT ONE...
NOT ME, SIR.
BUT THOSE REDDISH GELATIN STAINS ON YOUR SHIRT MAY JOG YOUR MEMORY.
SO I'LL BE SEEING YOU AT TEN?
COUNT ON IT, TWITCH.
I GOT ME A LITTLE PAYBACK ON MY MIND.
chomp chomp
'EVENING, FRED.
BLARFF!
LET'S GO, TWITCH.
HEY BOYS!
HOW'RE THINGS WITH THE REN AND STIMPY OF NEW YORK'S FINEST?
GOING OUT TO CHASE MORE GHOSTS?
HARASS A FEW MORE OF THE HOMELESS?
C'MON, YOU C'N TELL ME.
HEY!
MY COFFEE!
*SEE LAST ISSUE -- Tom

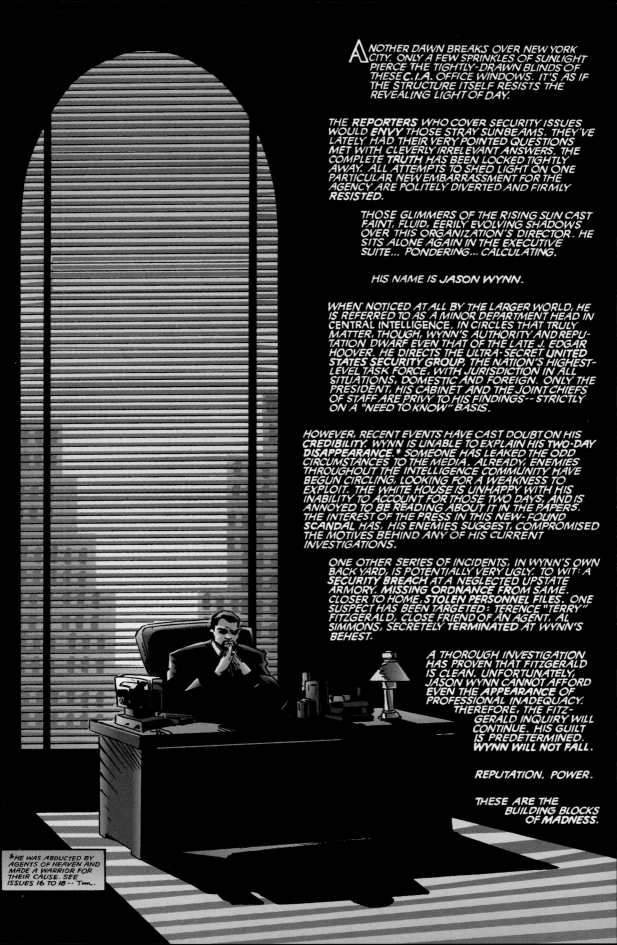

ANOTHER DAWN BREAKS OVER NEW YORK CITY. ONLY A FEW SPRINKLES OF SUNLIGHT PIERCE THE TIGHTLY-DRAWN BLINDS OF THESE **C.I.A.** OFFICE WINDOWS. IT'S AS IF THE STRUCTURE ITSELF RESISTS THE REVEALING LIGHT OF DAY.

THE **REPORTERS** WHO COVER SECURITY ISSUES WOULD **ENVY** THOSE STRAY SUNBEAMS. THEY'VE LATELY HAD THEIR VERY POINTED QUESTIONS MET WITH CLEVERLY IRRELEVANT ANSWERS. THE COMPLETE **TRUTH** HAS BEEN LOCKED TIGHTLY AWAY. ALL ATTEMPTS TO SHED LIGHT ON ONE PARTICULAR NEW EMBARRASSMENT FOR THE AGENCY ARE POLITELY DIVERTED AND FIRMLY RESISTED.

THOSE GLIMMERS OF THE RISING SUN CAST FAINT, FLUID, EERILY EVOLVING SHADOWS OVER THIS ORGANIZATION'S DIRECTOR. HE SITS ALONE AGAIN IN THE EXECUTIVE SUITE... PONDERING... CALCULATING.

HIS NAME IS **JASON WYNN.**

WHEN NOTICED AT ALL BY THE LARGER WORLD, HE IS REFERRED TO AS A MINOR DEPARTMENT HEAD IN CENTRAL INTELLIGENCE. IN CIRCLES THAT TRULY MATTER, THOUGH, WYNN'S AUTHORITY AND REPUTATION DWARF EVEN THAT OF THE LATE J. EDGAR HOOVER. HE DIRECTS THE ULTRA-SECRET **UNITED STATES SECURITY GROUP,** THE NATION'S HIGHEST-LEVEL TASK FORCE, WITH JURISDICTION IN ALL SITUATIONS, DOMESTIC AND FOREIGN. ONLY THE PRESIDENT, HIS CABINET AND THE JOINT CHIEFS OF STAFF ARE PRIVY TO HIS FINDINGS--STRICTLY ON A "NEED TO KNOW" BASIS.

HOWEVER, RECENT EVENTS HAVE CAST DOUBT ON HIS **CREDIBILITY.** WYNN IS UNABLE TO EXPLAIN HIS **TWO-DAY DISAPPEARANCE.*** SOMEONE HAS LEAKED THE ODD CIRCUMSTANCES TO THE MEDIA. ALREADY, ENEMIES THROUGHOUT THE INTELLIGENCE COMMUNITY HAVE BEGUN CIRCLING, LOOKING FOR A WEAKNESS TO EXPLOIT. THE WHITE HOUSE IS UNHAPPY WITH HIS INABILITY TO ACCOUNT FOR THOSE TWO DAYS, AND IS ANNOYED TO BE READING ABOUT IT IN THE PAPERS. THE INTEREST OF THE PRESS IN THIS NEW-FOUND **SCANDAL** HAS, HIS ENEMIES SUGGEST, COMPROMISED THE MOTIVES BEHIND ANY OF HIS CURRENT INVESTIGATIONS.

ONE OTHER SERIES OF INCIDENTS, IN WYNN'S OWN BACK YARD, IS POTENTIALLY VERY UGLY. TO WIT: A **SECURITY BREACH** AT A NEGLECTED UPSTATE ARMORY. MISSING ORDNANCE FROM SAME. CLOSER TO HOME, STOLEN PERSONNEL FILES. ONE SUSPECT HAS BEEN TARGETED: TERENCE "TERRY" FITZGERALD, CLOSE FRIEND OF AN AGENT, AL SIMMONS, SECRETELY **TERMINATED** AT WYNN'S BEHEST.

A THOROUGH INVESTIGATION HAS PROVEN THAT FITZGERALD IS CLEAN. UNFORTUNATELY, JASON WYNN CANNOT AFFORD EVEN THE APPEARANCE OF PROFESSIONAL INADEQUACY. THEREFORE, THE FITZGERALD INQUIRY WILL CONTINUE. HIS GUILT IS PREDETERMINED. **WYNN WILL NOT FALL.**

REPUTATION. POWER.

THESE ARE THE BUILDING BLOCKS OF MADNESS.

*HE WAS ABDUCTED BY AGENTS OF HEAVEN AND MADE A WARRIOR FOR THEIR CAUSE. SEE ISSUES 16 TO 18 -- Tom.

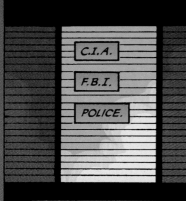

C.I.A.

F.B.I.

POLICE.

ALL HAVE BEEN TOLD THE SAME STORY:

...THAT ONE OF THEIR OWN HAS *TURNED* ON THEM. THE ACCUSATION COMES FROM SO HIGH UP THAT IT GOES *UNCHALLENGED.* MEANWHILE, "CONCRETE EVIDENCE" HAS BEEN MANUFACTURED, APPROPRIATE TO SATISFY ANYONE'S QUESTIONS.

MAN, WHAT A BORE!

I *HATE* FILLING OUT THESE DAMN REPORTS.

ESPECIALLY WHEN I HAVE TO FILL 'EM OUT IN *RUSSIAN.*

WHAT A PAIN.

TERRY FITZGERALD CONCENTRATES ON HIS MONITOR, TRYING TO FORGET THE HARRASSING PHONE CALLS AND FACE-TO-FACE *THREATS.* PRACTICALLY EVERY LAW ENFORCEMENT OR INTELLIGENCE AGENCY IN THE STATE HAS MADE THEIR DISPLEASURE KNOWN.

HE IS GRATEFUL THAT WANDA IS UNAWARE OF THIS WITCH-HUNT. HIS FAMILY'S UNTOUCHED.

HE KNOWS THAT WON'T LAST.

COULD THE DEBACLE AT COLUMBIA UNIVERSITY* HAVE HAD SOMETHING TO DO WITH HIS PREDICAMENT? HE WAS NEVER CONFIDENT IN HIS FIELD ABILITIES-- WAS HE BEING *TESTED?* IF SO, IT WAS *NO* HELP WHEN THAT UKRANIAN NUCLEAR SCIENTIST--

EEEK!

*JEE-*ZUS!

ISSUES 19 AND 20-- NOT OUT YET! -- Tom.

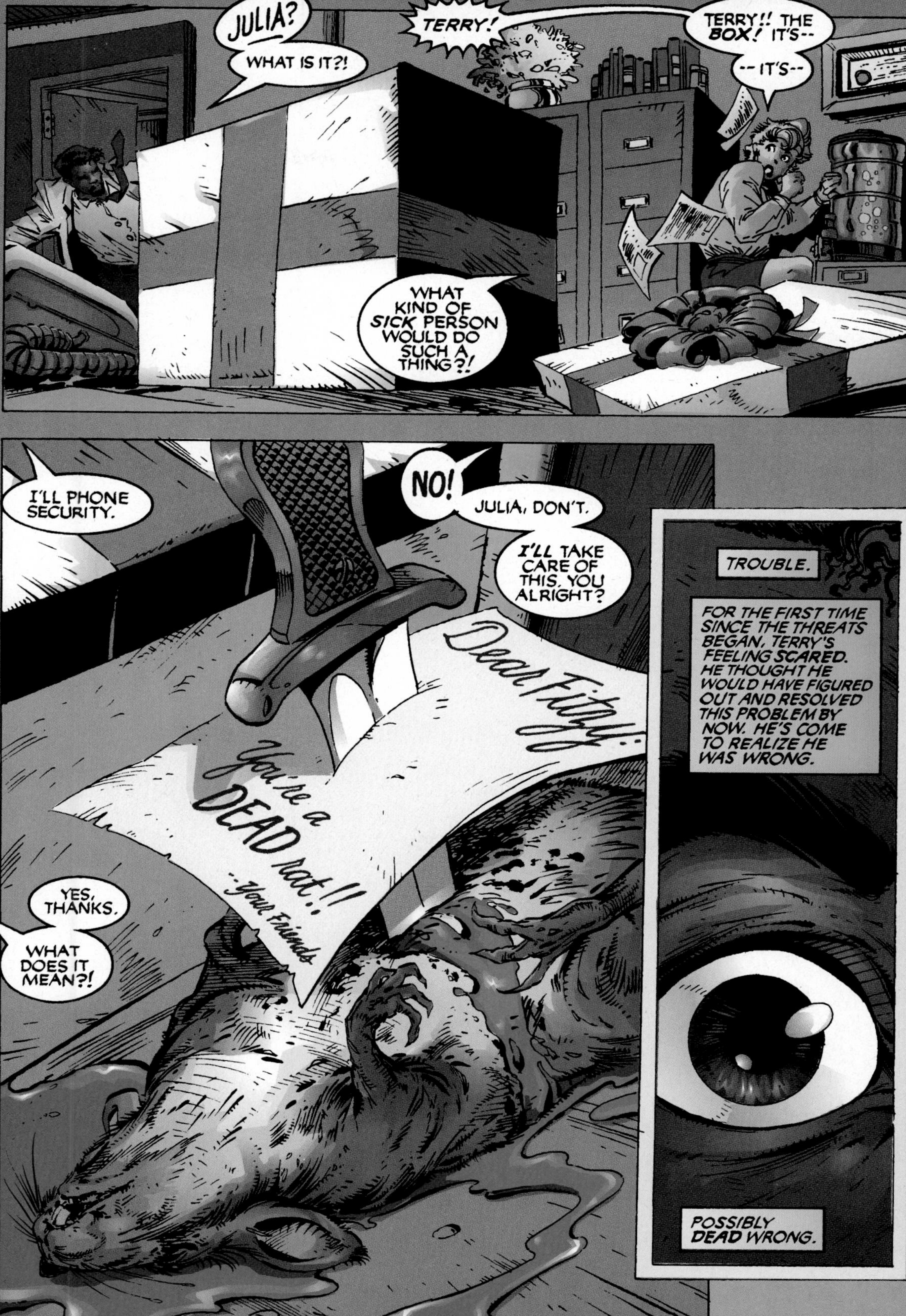
JULIA?
WHAT IS IT?!
TERRY!
TERRY!! THE BOX! IT'S--
-- IT'S--
WHAT KIND OF SICK PERSON WOULD DO SUCH A THING?!
I'LL PHONE SECURITY.
NO!
JULIA, DON'T.
I'LL TAKE CARE OF THIS. YOU ALRIGHT?
Dear Fitzy!
You're a DEAD rat!!
..Your Friends
YES, THANKS.
WHAT DOES IT MEAN?!
TROUBLE.
FOR THE FIRST TIME SINCE THE THREATS BEGAN, TERRY'S FEELING SCARED. HE THOUGHT HE WOULD HAVE FIGURED OUT AND RESOLVED THIS PROBLEM BY NOW. HE'S COME TO REALIZE HE WAS WRONG.
POSSIBLY DEAD WRONG.
*ISSUE 12 -- Tom.

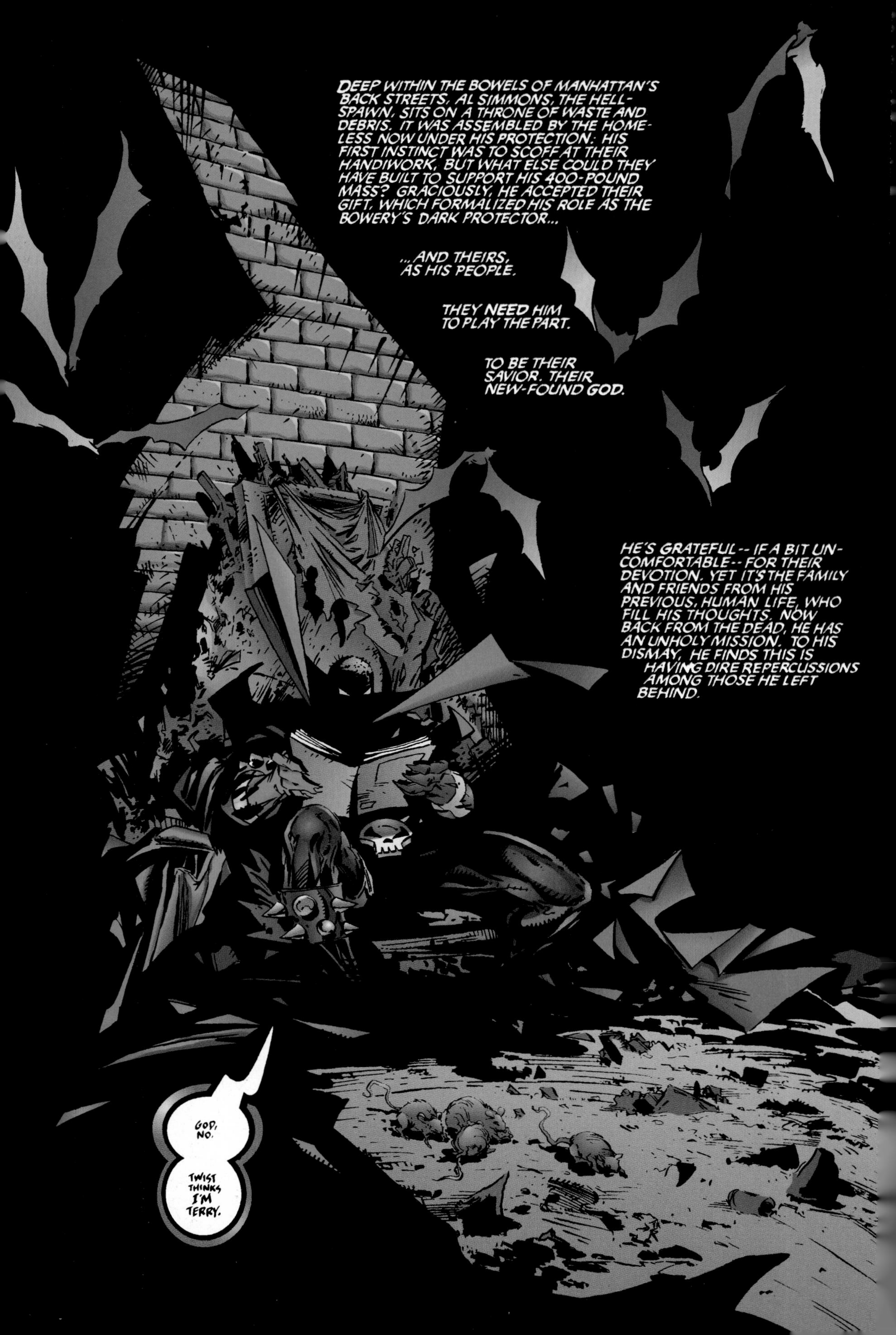
DEEP WITHIN THE BOWELS OF MANHATTAN'S BACK STREETS, AL SIMMONS, THE HELL-SPAWN, SITS ON A THRONE OF WASTE AND DEBRIS. IT WAS ASSEMBLED BY THE HOME-LESS NOW UNDER HIS PROTECTION: HIS FIRST INSTINCT WAS TO SCOFF AT THEIR HANDIWORK, BUT WHAT ELSE COULD THEY HAVE BUILT TO SUPPORT HIS 400-POUND MASS? GRACIOUSLY, HE ACCEPTED THEIR GIFT, WHICH FORMALIZED HIS ROLE AS THE BOWERY'S DARK PROTECTOR...
...AND THEIRS, AS HIS PEOPLE.
THEY NEED HIM TO PLAY THE PART.
TO BE THEIR SAVIOR. THEIR NEW-FOUND GOD.
HE'S GRATEFUL-- IF A BIT UN-COMFORTABLE-- FOR THEIR DEVOTION. YET IT'S THE FAMILY AND FRIENDS FROM HIS PREVIOUS, HUMAN LIFE, WHO FILL HIS THOUGHTS. NOW BACK FROM THE DEAD, HE HAS AN UNHOLY MISSION. TO HIS DISMAY, HE FINDS THIS IS HAVING DIRE REPERCUSSIONS AMONG THOSE HE LEFT BEHIND.
GOD, NO.
TWIST THINKS I'M TERRY.

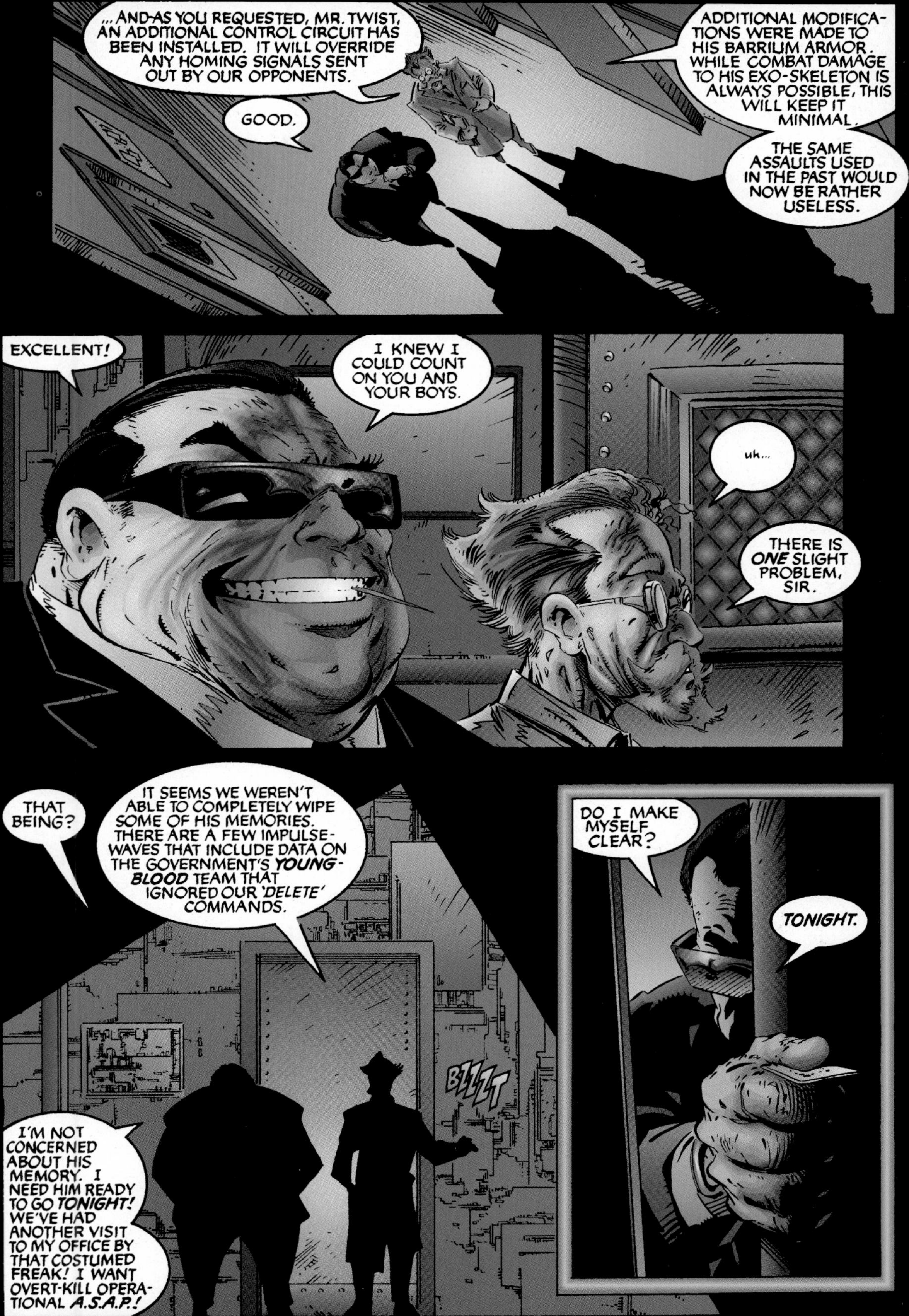
...AND AS YOU REQUESTED, MR. TWIST, AN ADDITIONAL CONTROL CIRCUIT HAS BEEN INSTALLED. IT WILL OVERRIDE ANY HOMING SIGNALS SENT OUT BY OUR OPPONENTS.
GOOD.
ADDITIONAL MODIFICATIONS WERE MADE TO HIS BARRIUM ARMOR. WHILE COMBAT DAMAGE TO HIS EXO-SKELETON IS ALWAYS POSSIBLE, THIS WILL KEEP IT MINIMAL.
THE SAME ASSAULTS USED IN THE PAST WOULD NOW BE RATHER USELESS.
EXCELLENT!
I KNEW I COULD COUNT ON YOU AND YOUR BOYS.
uh...
THERE IS ONE SLIGHT PROBLEM, SIR.
THAT BEING?
IT SEEMS WE WEREN'T ABLE TO COMPLETELY WIPE SOME OF HIS MEMORIES. THERE ARE A FEW IMPULSE-WAVES THAT INCLUDE DATA ON THE GOVERNMENT'S YOUNGBLOOD TEAM THAT IGNORED OUR 'DELETE' COMMANDS.
BZZZT
I'M NOT CONCERNED ABOUT HIS MEMORY. I NEED HIM READY TO GO TONIGHT! WE'VE HAD ANOTHER VISIT TO MY OFFICE BY THAT COSTUMED FREAK! I WANT OVERT-KILL OPERATIONAL A.S.A.P.!
DO I MAKE MYSELF CLEAR?
TONIGHT.

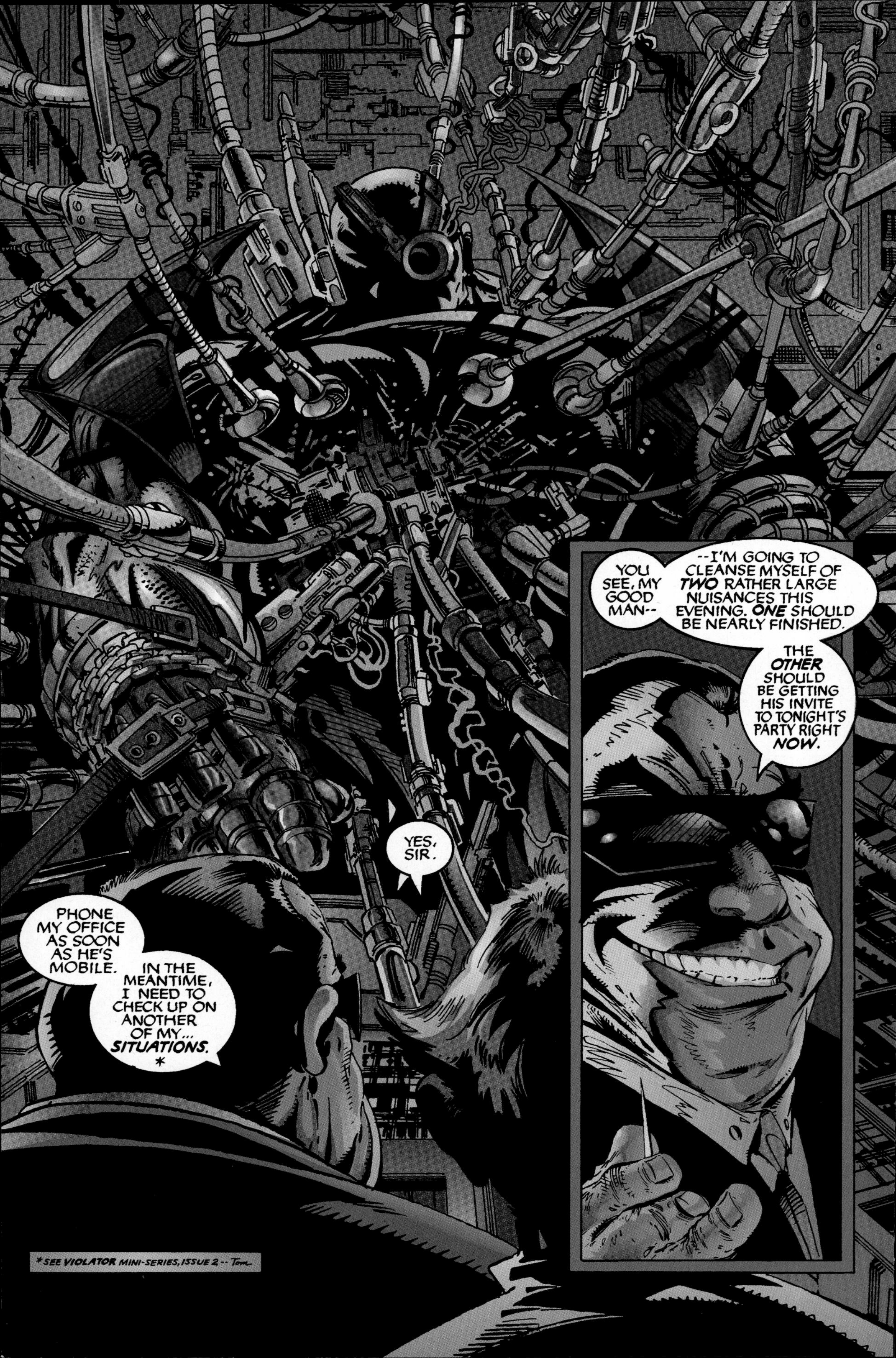
YOU SEE, MY GOOD MAN--
--I'M GOING TO CLEANSE MYSELF OF TWO RATHER LARGE NUISANCES THIS EVENING. ONE SHOULD BE NEARLY FINISHED.
THE OTHER SHOULD BE GETTING HIS INVITE TO TONIGHT'S PARTY RIGHT NOW.
YES, SIR.
PHONE MY OFFICE AS SOON AS HE'S MOBILE.
IN THE MEANTIME, I NEED TO CHECK UP ON ANOTHER OF MY... SITUATIONS. *
*SEE VIOLATOR MINI-SERIES, ISSUE 2 -- Tom

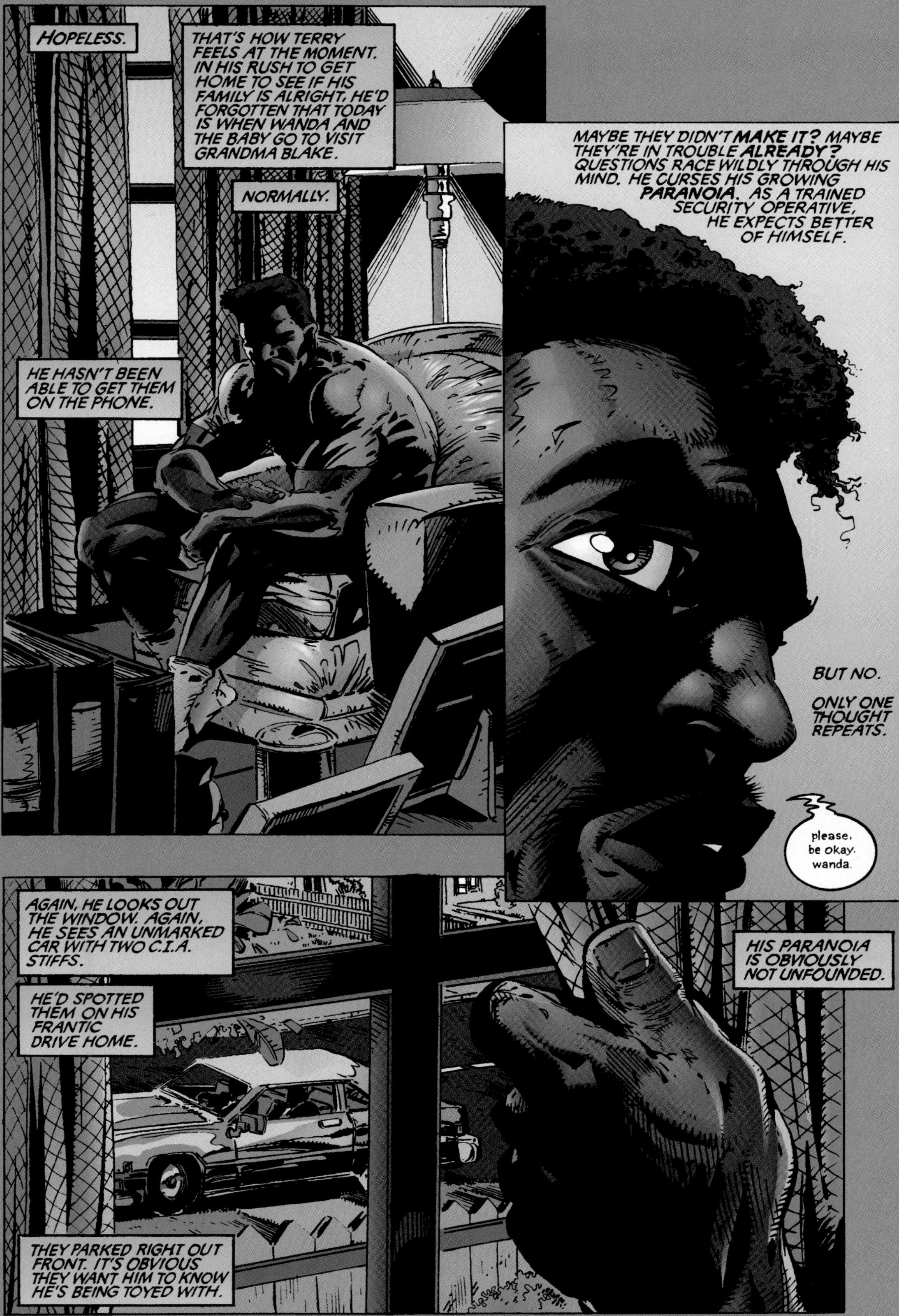
HOPELESS.
THAT'S HOW TERRY FEELS AT THE MOMENT. IN HIS RUSH TO GET HOME TO SEE IF HIS FAMILY IS ALRIGHT, HE'D FORGOTTEN THAT TODAY IS WHEN WANDA AND THE BABY GO TO VISIT GRANDMA BLAKE.
NORMALLY.
HE HASN'T BEEN ABLE TO GET THEM ON THE PHONE.
MAYBE THEY DIDN'T MAKE IT? MAYBE THEY'RE IN TROUBLE ALREADY? QUESTIONS RACE WILDLY THROUGH HIS MIND. HE CURSES HIS GROWING PARANOIA. AS A TRAINED SECURITY OPERATIVE, HE EXPECTS BETTER OF HIMSELF.
BUT NO.
ONLY ONE THOUGHT REPEATS.
please, be okay. wanda.
AGAIN, HE LOOKS OUT THE WINDOW. AGAIN, HE SEES AN UNMARKED CAR WITH TWO C.I.A. STIFFS.
HE'D SPOTTED THEM ON HIS FRANTIC DRIVE HOME.
THEY PARKED RIGHT OUT FRONT. IT'S OBVIOUS THEY WANT HIM TO KNOW HE'S BEING TOYED WITH.
HIS PARANOIA IS OBVIOUSLY NOT UNFOUNDED.

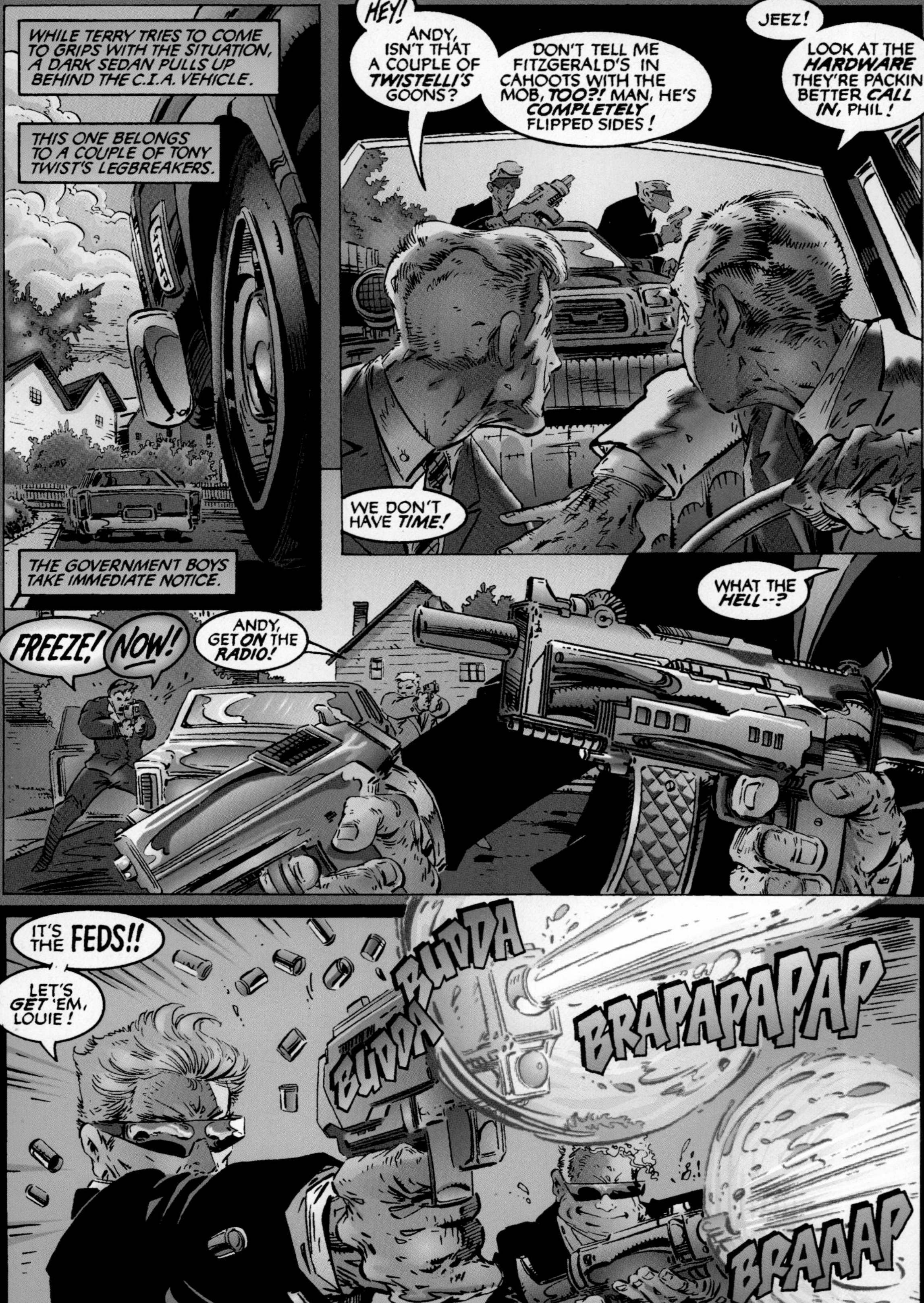
WHILE TERRY TRIES TO COME TO GRIPS WITH THE SITUATION, A DARK SEDAN PULLS UP BEHIND THE C.I.A. VEHICLE.
THIS ONE BELONGS TO A COUPLE OF TONY TWIST'S LEGBREAKERS.
HEY!
ANDY, ISN'T THAT A COUPLE OF TWISTELLI'S GOONS?
DON'T TELL ME FITZGERALD'S IN CAHOOTS WITH THE MOB, TOO?! MAN, HE'S COMPLETELY FLIPPED SIDES!
JEEZ!
LOOK AT THE HARDWARE THEY'RE PACKIN'! BETTER CALL IN, PHIL!
WE DON'T HAVE TIME!
THE GOVERNMENT BOYS TAKE IMMEDIATE NOTICE.
FREEZE!
NOW!!
ANDY, GET ON THE RADIO!
WHAT THE HELL--?
IT'S THE FEDS!!
LET'S GET 'EM, LOUIE!
BUDDA BUDDA
BRAPAPAPAPAP
BRAAAP

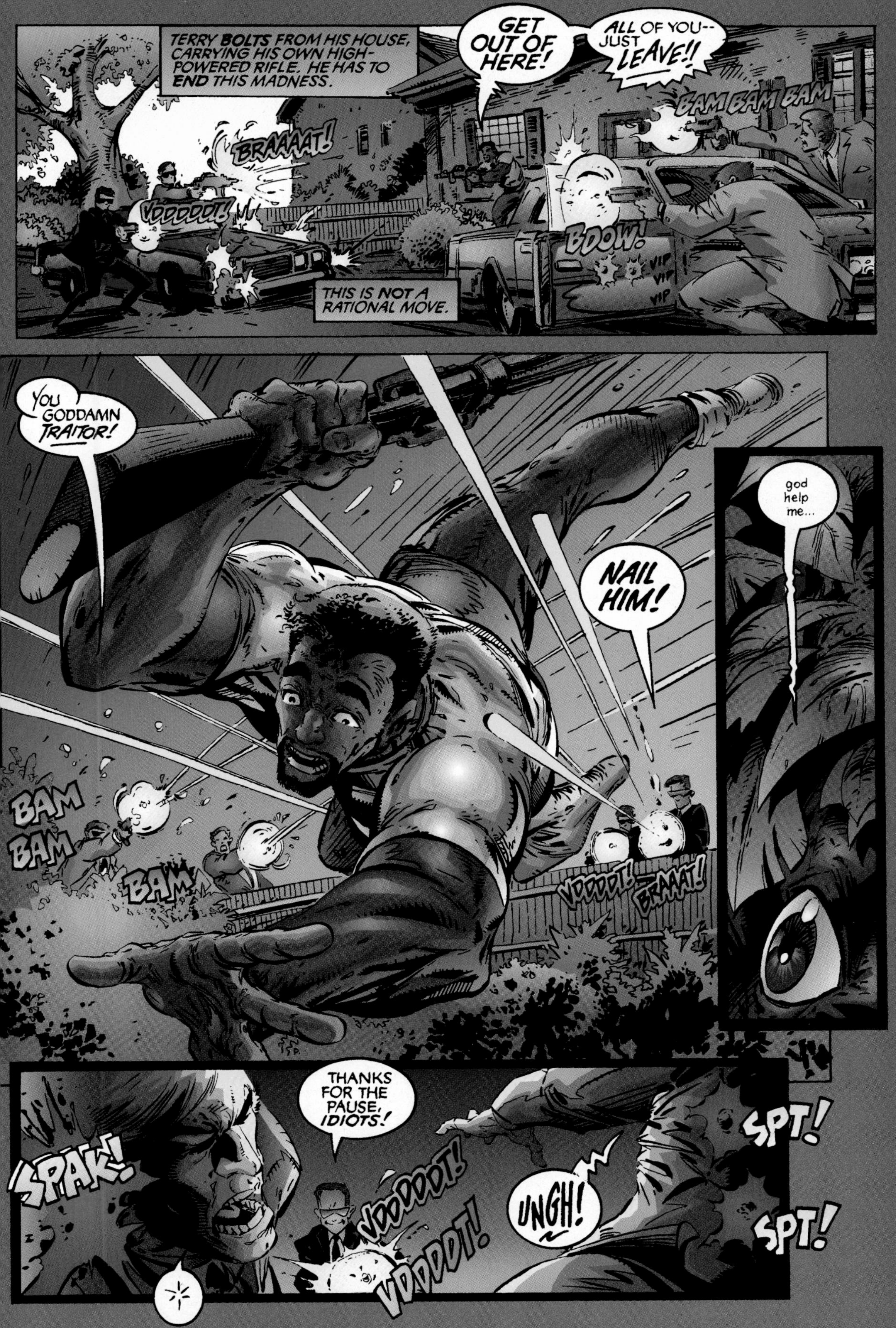
TERRY BOLTS FROM HIS HOUSE, CARRYING HIS OWN HIGH-POWERED RIFLE. HE HAS TO END THIS MADNESS.
GET OUT OF HERE!
ALL OF YOU-- JUST LEAVE!!
BAM BAM BAM
BRAAAAT!
VDDDDDT!
BDOW!
VIP VIP VIP
THIS IS NOT A RATIONAL MOVE.
YOU GODDAMN TRAITOR!
NAIL HIM!
god help me...
BAM BAM
BAM
VDDDDT!
BRAAAT!
THANKS FOR THE PAUSE, IDIOTS!
SPAK!
VDDDDDT!
VDDDDT!
UNGH!
SPT!
SPT!

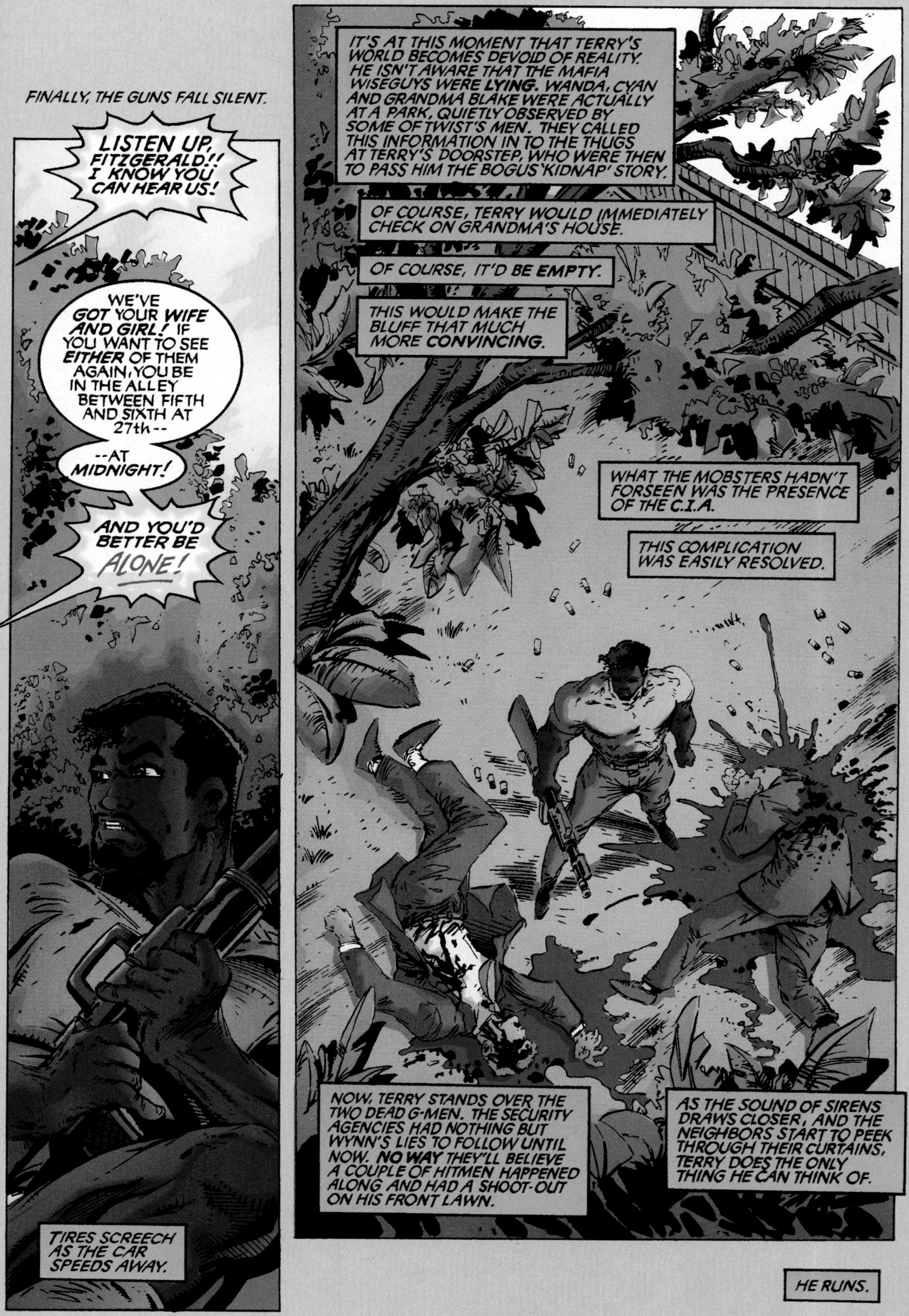

FINALLY, THE GUNS FALL SILENT.
LISTEN UP, FITZGERALD!! I KNOW YOU CAN HEAR US!
WE'VE GOT YOUR WIFE AND GIRL! IF YOU WANT TO SEE EITHER OF THEM AGAIN, YOU BE IN THE ALLEY BETWEEN FIFTH AND SIXTH AT 27th--
--AT MIDNIGHT!
AND YOU'D BETTER BE ALONE!
TIRES SCREECH AS THE CAR SPEEDS AWAY.
IT'S AT THIS MOMENT THAT TERRY'S WORLD BECOMES DEVOID OF REALITY. HE ISN'T AWARE THAT THE MAFIA WISEGUYS WERE LYING. WANDA, CYAN AND GRANDMA BLAKE WERE ACTUALLY AT A PARK, QUIETLY OBSERVED BY SOME OF TWIST'S MEN. THEY CALLED THIS INFORMATION IN TO THE THUGS AT TERRY'S DOORSTEP, WHO WERE THEN TO PASS HIM THE BOGUS 'KIDNAP' STORY.
OF COURSE, TERRY WOULD IMMEDIATELY CHECK ON GRANDMA'S HOUSE.
OF COURSE, IT'D BE EMPTY.
THIS WOULD MAKE THE BLUFF THAT MUCH MORE CONVINCING.
WHAT THE MOBSTERS HADN'T FORSEEN WAS THE PRESENCE OF THE C.I.A.
THIS COMPLICATION WAS EASILY RESOLVED.
NOW, TERRY STANDS OVER THE TWO DEAD G-MEN. THE SECURITY AGENCIES HAD NOTHING BUT WYNN'S LIES TO FOLLOW UNTIL NOW. NO WAY THEY'LL BELIEVE A COUPLE OF HITMEN HAPPENED ALONG AND HAD A SHOOT-OUT ON HIS FRONT LAWN.
AS THE SOUND OF SIRENS DRAWS CLOSER, AND THE NEIGHBORS START TO PEEK THROUGH THEIR CURTAINS, TERRY DOES THE ONLY THING HE CAN THINK OF.
HE RUNS.

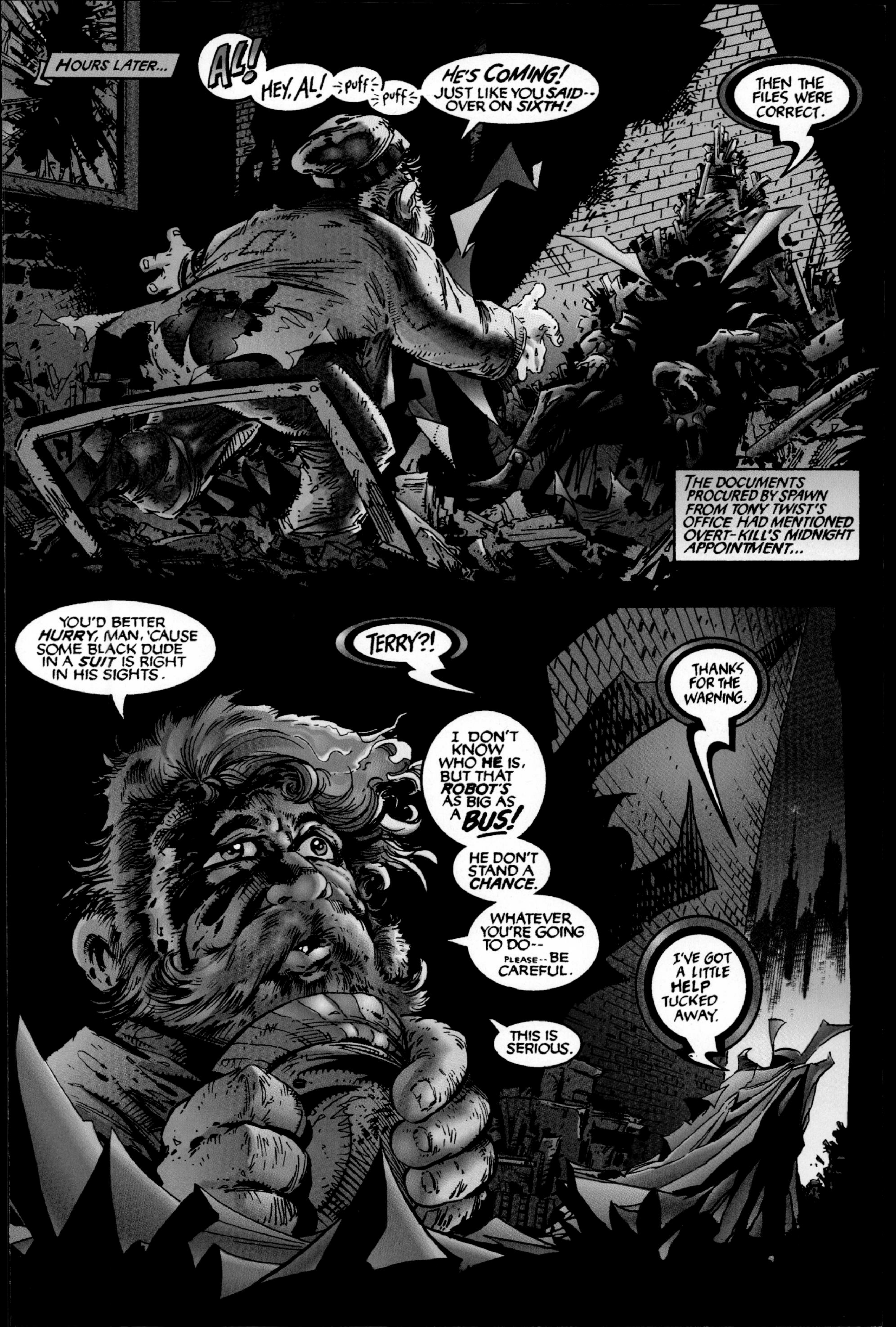

HOURS LATER...
AL!
HEY, AL!
puff
puff
HE'S COMING! JUST LIKE YOU SAID-- OVER ON SIXTH!
THEN THE FILES WERE CORRECT.
THE DOCUMENTS PROCURED BY SPAWN FROM TONY TWIST'S OFFICE HAD MENTIONED OVERT-KILL'S MIDNIGHT APPOINTMENT...
YOU'D BETTER HURRY, MAN, 'CAUSE SOME BLACK DUDE IN A SUIT IS RIGHT IN HIS SIGHTS.
TERRY?!
THANKS FOR THE WARNING.
I DON'T KNOW WHO HE IS, BUT THAT ROBOT'S AS BIG AS A BUS!
HE DON'T STAND A CHANCE.
WHATEVER YOU'RE GOING TO DO-- PLEASE-- BE CAREFUL.
I'VE GOT A LITTLE HELP TUCKED AWAY.
THIS IS SERIOUS.

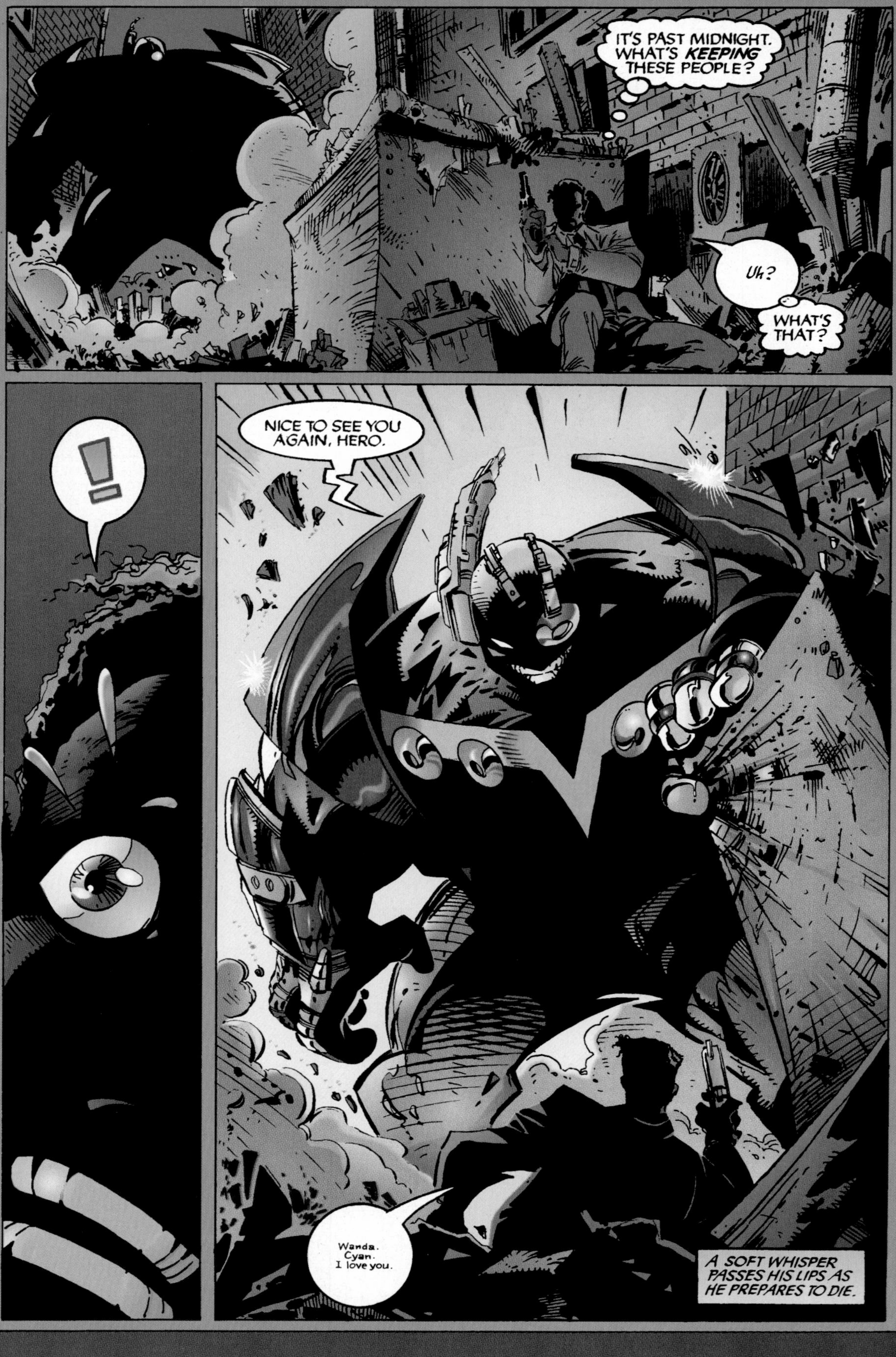
IT'S PAST MIDNIGHT. WHAT'S KEEPING THESE PEOPLE?
Uh?
WHAT'S THAT?
!
NICE TO SEE YOU AGAIN, HERO.
Wanda. Cyan. I love you.
A SOFT WHISPER PASSES HIS LIPS AS HE PREPARES TO DIE.

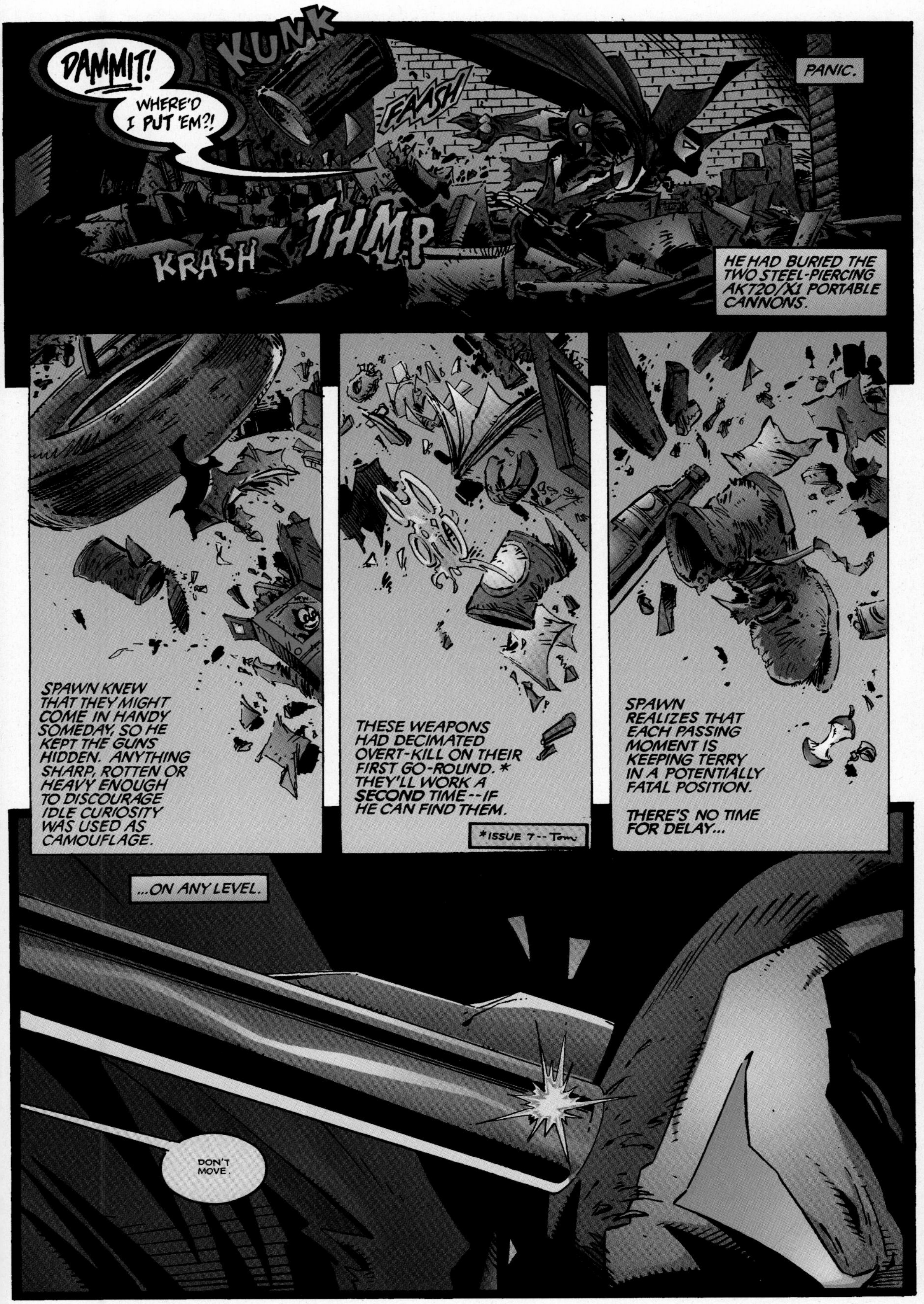
KUNK
DAMMIT!
WHERE'D I PUT 'EM?!
PANIC.
FAASH
KRASH
THMP
HE HAD BURIED THE TWO STEEL-PIERCING AK720/X1 PORTABLE CANNONS.
SPAWN KNEW THAT THEY MIGHT COME IN HANDY SOMEDAY, SO HE KEPT THE GUNS HIDDEN. ANYTHING SHARP, ROTTEN OR HEAVY ENOUGH TO DISCOURAGE IDLE CURIOSITY WAS USED AS CAMOUFLAGE.
THESE WEAPONS HAD DECIMATED OVERT-KILL ON THEIR FIRST GO-ROUND. * THEY'LL WORK A SECOND TIME--IF HE CAN FIND THEM.
*ISSUE 7--Tom
SPAWN REALIZES THAT EACH PASSING MOMENT IS KEEPING TERRY IN A POTENTIALLY FATAL POSITION.
THERE'S NO TIME FOR DELAY...
...ON ANY LEVEL.
DON'T MOVE.

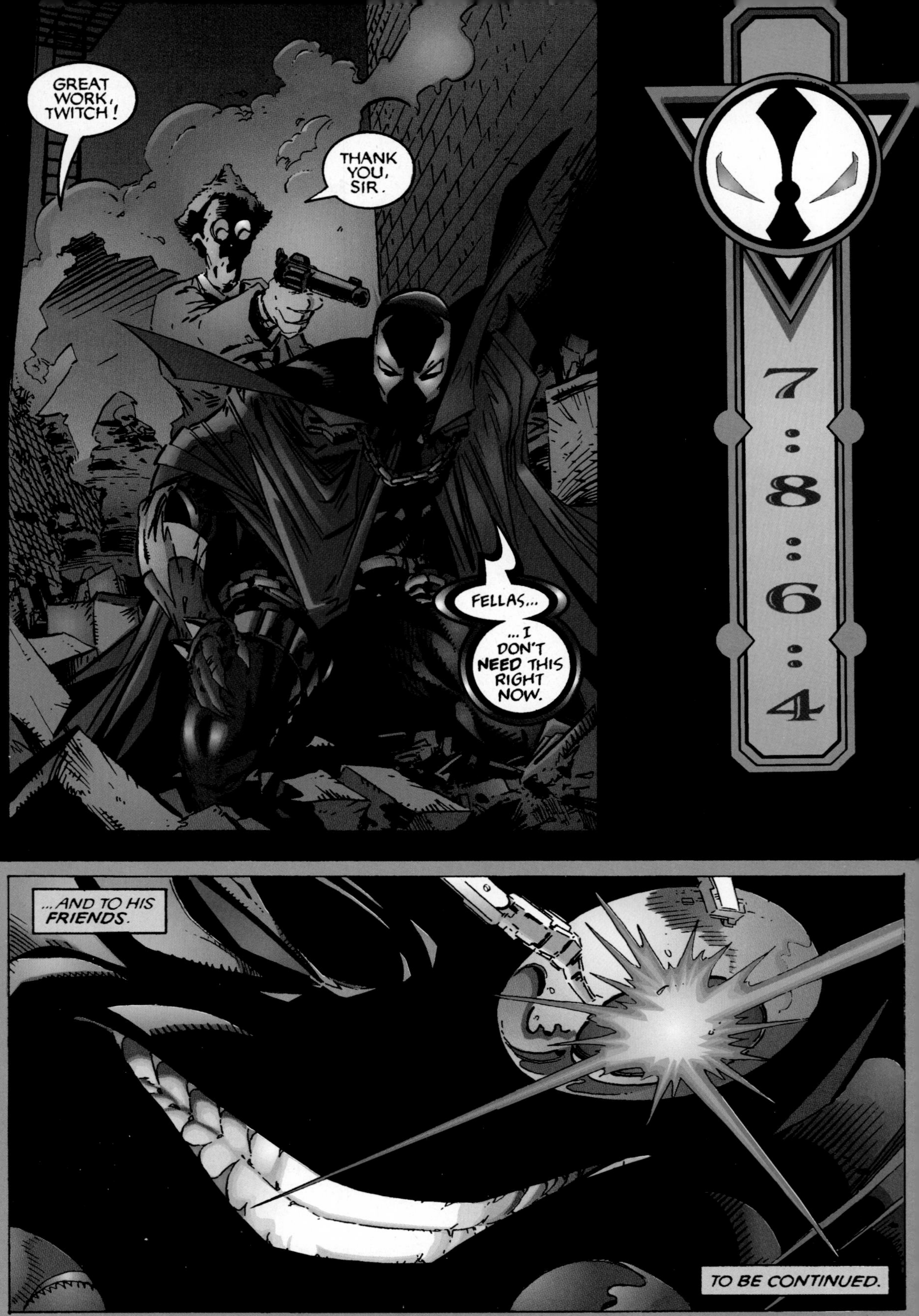
GREAT WORK, TWITCH!
THANK YOU, SIR.
FELLAS...
...I DON'T NEED THIS RIGHT NOW.
7:8:6:4
...AND TO HIS FRIENDS.
TO BE CONTINUED.

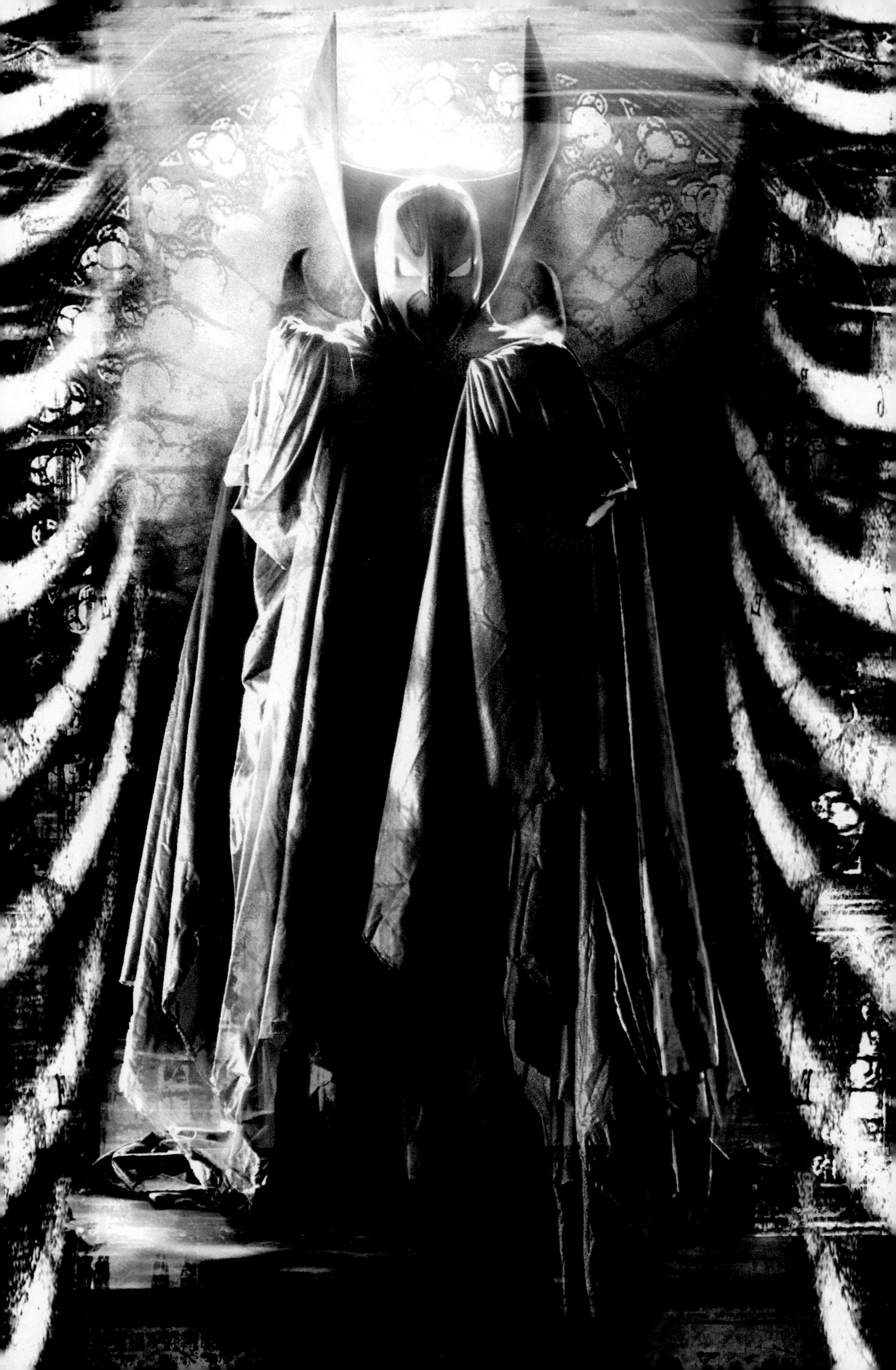

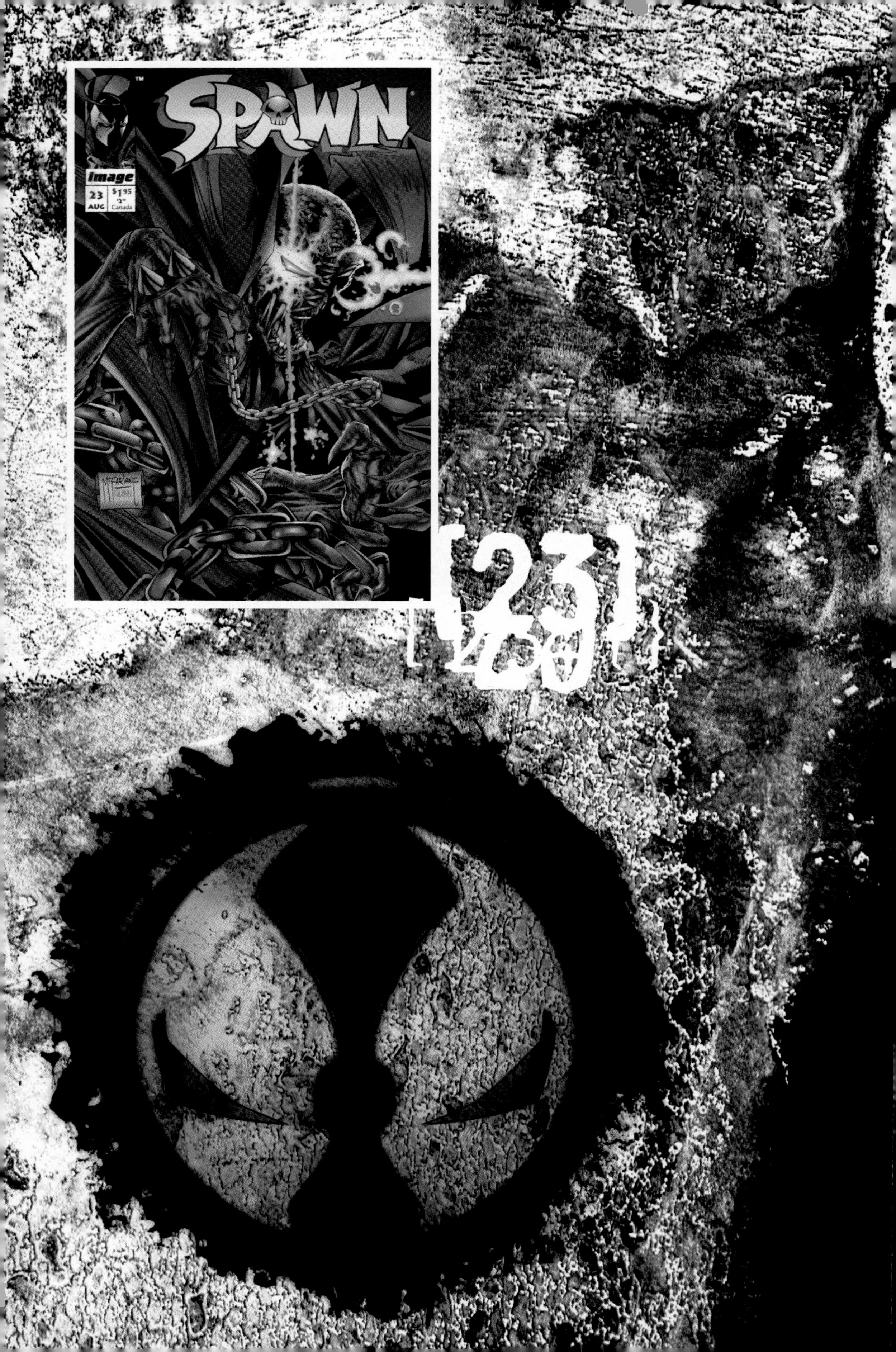
SPAWN
image
23
AUG
$1.95
Canada

23

JASON WYNN: HEAD OF THE UNITED STATES SECURITY GROUP, THE HIGHEST-LEVEL INTELLIGENCE AGENCY.

HIS SECURITY STATUS HAS BEEN COMPROMISED, AND THE PRESIDENT'S OFFICE IS NOT PLEASED. WYNN IS UNDER PRESSURE TO RESTORE HIS REPUTATION IN THE INTELLIGENCE COMMUNITY. TERRY FITZGERALD, A VICTIM OF CIRCUMSTANCE, HAS BEEN IDENTIFIED AS THE SOURCE OF THE TENSION... AND IS NOW IN DANGER OF HIS LIFE, AT WYNN'S DIRECTION.

SPAWN: AGENT OF HELL.

HIS VERY EXISTENCE HAS SET INTO MOTION A CRAZY RIPPLE EFFECT, WITH INCREASINGLY DANGEROUS CONSEQUENCES FOR THOSE AROUND HIM. SPAWN SIMPLY WANTS TO CREATE AND NURTURE A FAMILY, BUT THAT DESIRE HAS ALREADY DAMNED HIM AND NOW INADVERTANTLY THREATENS ALL WHO TRUST HIM.

TONY TWIST: MAFIA DON.

HIS OPERATIONS HAD RUN SMOOTHLY FOR YEARS, BUT LATELY AN UNKNOWN ATTACKER HAS SLAUGHTERED A NUMBER OF HIS MEN. TWIST HAS FOCUSED ON REMOVING THIS BLEMISH... SPAWN, HE BELIEVES... FROM THE FACE OF HIS CITY. HE IS UNAWARE THAT SOME OF THE INFORMATION DRIVING HIS HUNT IS INACCURATE.

WANDA BLAKE: WIDOW OF LT. COL. AL SIMMONS, A.K.A. SPAWN.

WANDA IS NOW HAPPILY MARRIED TO HER LATE HUSBAND'S BEST FRIEND, TERRY FITZGERALD, WITH WHOM SHE HAS A DAUGHTER, CYAN. SHE IS CURRENTLY UNAWARE OF AL'S LIFE STATUS, OR OF THE VICIOUS WEB IN WHICH TERRY IS RAPIDLY FINDING HIMSELF ENSNARED.

SAM BURKE: DETECTIVE, N.Y.P.D.

NOW CLEARED OF WRONGDOING IN THE DEATH OF CHILDKILLER BILLY KINCAID, BURKE IS ALLOWING HIMSELF THE LUXURY OF BRUTALITY IN THE NAME OF FACT GATHERING. SOMEONE (OR SOMETHING) CAUSED HIS SUPERIORS TO QUESTION HIS LOYALTY, AND HE WANTS TO HAVE WORDS WITH THIS INDIVIDUAL.

"TWITCH" WILLIAMS: DETECTIVE, N.Y.P.D.

THIS FATHER OF SEVEN IS ONE OF THE STATE'S TOP SHARPSHOOTERS. HIS SENSE OF FAIRNESS WORKS COUNTERPOINT TO HIS PARTNER BURKE'S OCCASIONAL LAPSES. METHODOLOGY AND ARM-TWISTING HAVE LED THE PAIR TO THEIR QUARRY-- THE COSTUMED MYSTERY MAN WHO HAS A FEW SERIOUS QUESTIONS TO ANSWER.

THESE ARE THE MAJOR PLAYERS IN AN INCREASINGLY TWISTED GAME OF CAT AND MOUSE. EACH IS SOMEHOW CONNECTED TO THE STRANGE EXISTENCE OF A *DEAD MAN* BROUGHT BACK TO *LIFE*. STRIPPED OF HIS IDENTITY... CHARGED WITH TREMENDOUS BUT EXHAUSTABLE *POWER*... AWAKENED FIVE YEARS AFTER HIS TIME TO FIND HIS WIFE REMARRIED... THESE WERE THE REALITIES AWAITING A MAN IN LOVE--

--*GIFTS* GIVEN BY SOME UNHOLY *CREATURE OF HELL*.

A PRISONER OF HIS NEW LIFE ON EARTH, SPAWN'S ACTIONS HAVE TRIGGERED SEVERAL *MANHUNTS* BY VERY INFLUENTIAL PEOPLE. NONE IS PREPARED FOR WHAT *TRUTH* MAY EMERGE FROM THEIR INVESTIGATIONS...

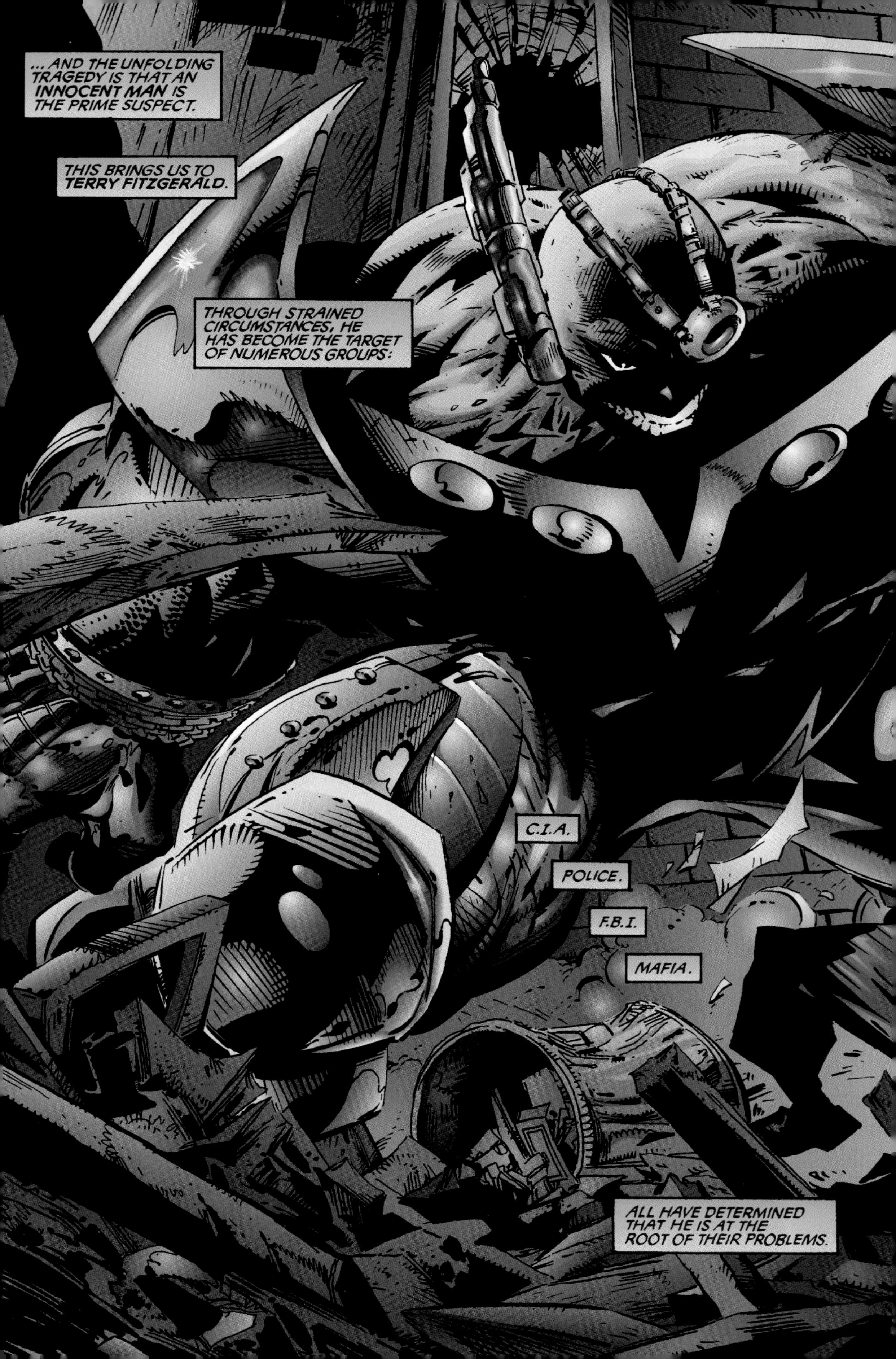
...AND THE UNFOLDING TRAGEDY IS THAT AN INNOCENT MAN IS THE PRIME SUSPECT.
THIS BRINGS US TO TERRY FITZGERALD.
THROUGH STRAINED CIRCUMSTANCES, HE HAS BECOME THE TARGET OF NUMEROUS GROUPS:
C.I.A.
POLICE.
F.B.I.
MAFIA.
ALL HAVE DETERMINED THAT HE IS AT THE ROOT OF THEIR PROBLEMS.

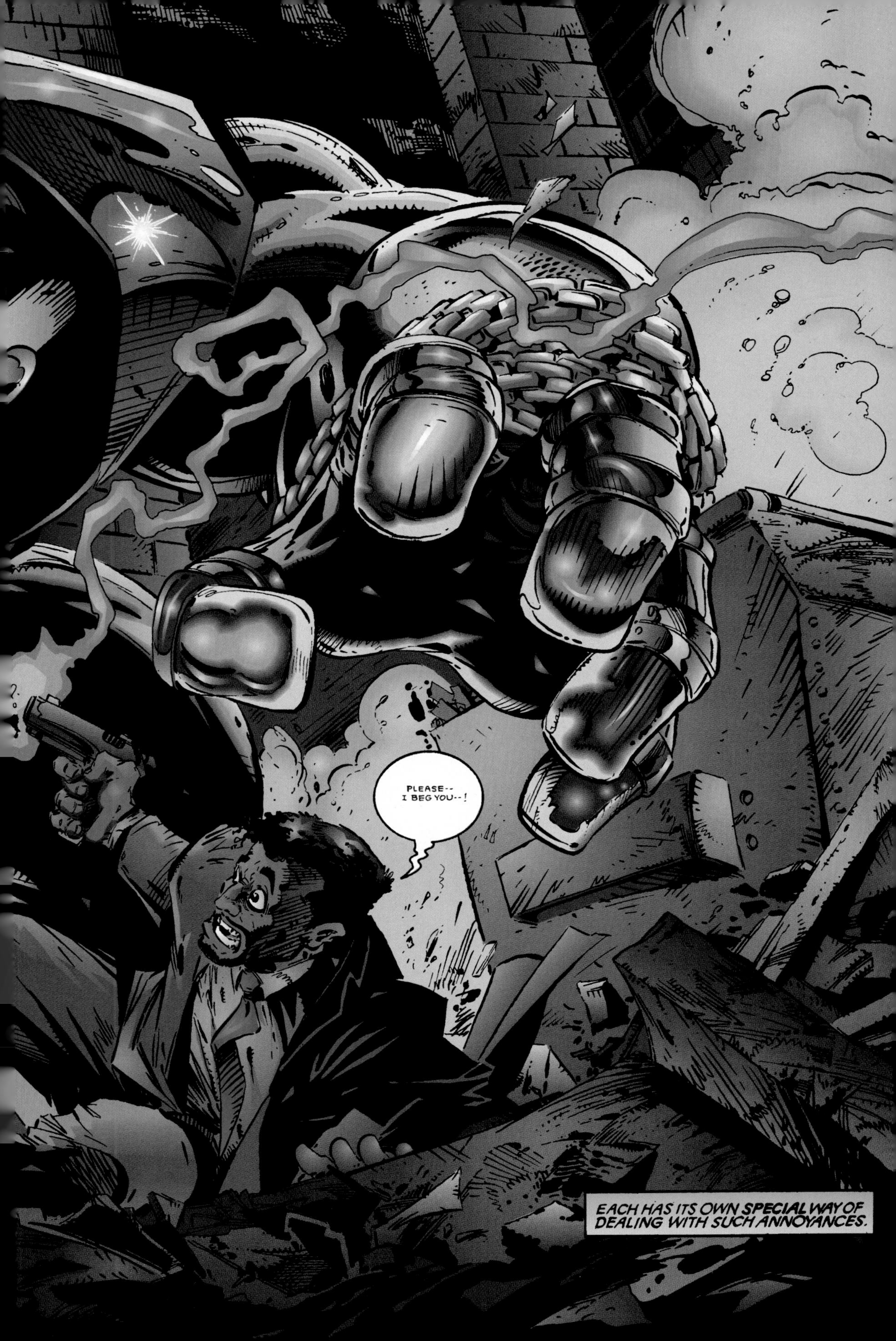
PLEASE--
I BEG YOU--!
EACH HAS ITS OWN SPECIAL WAY OF DEALING WITH SUCH ANNOYANCES.

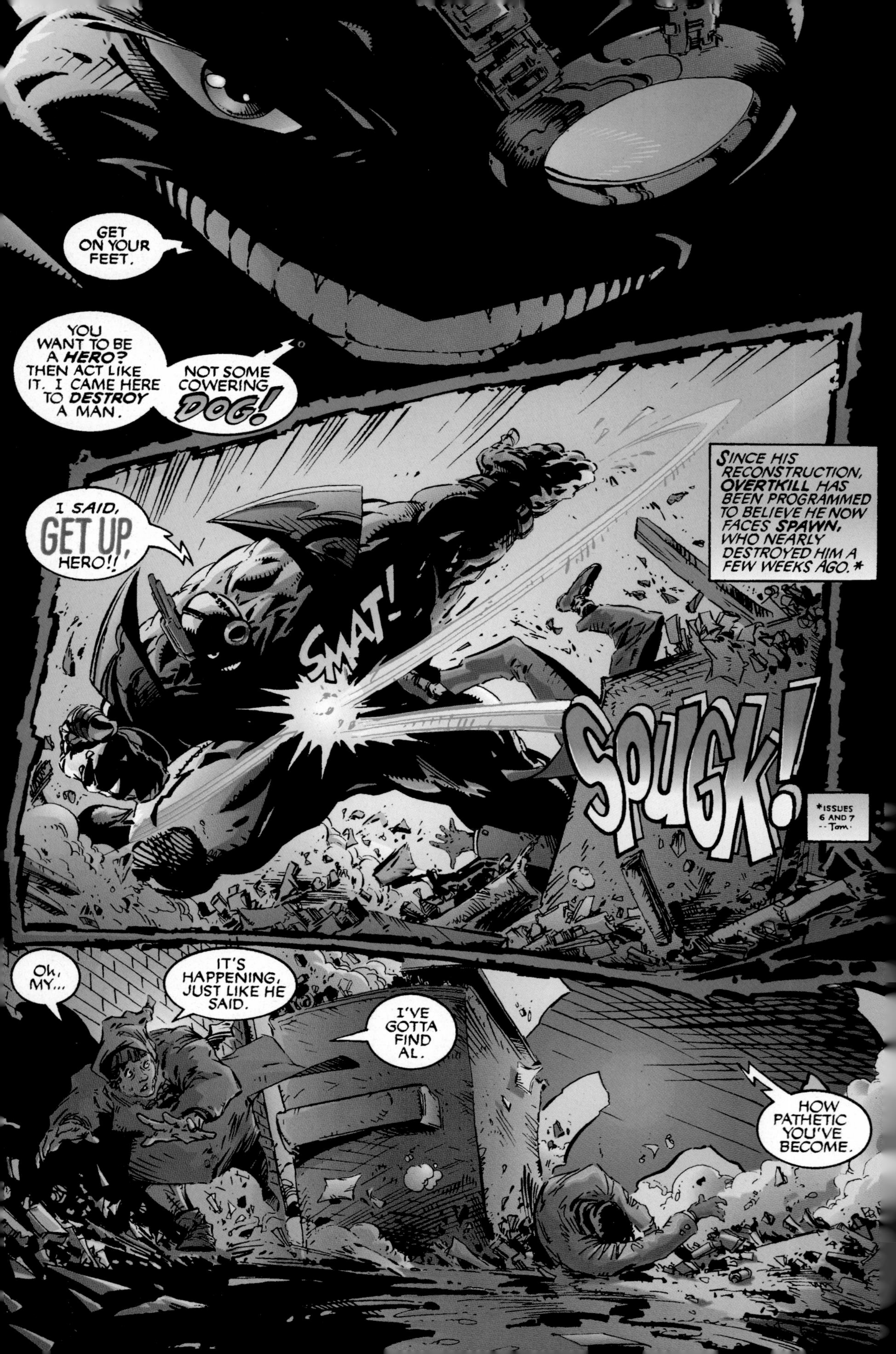
GET ON YOUR FEET.
YOU WANT TO BE A HERO? THEN ACT LIKE IT. I CAME HERE TO DESTROY A MAN.
NOT SOME COWERING DOG!
I SAID, GET UP, HERO!!
SINCE HIS RECONSTRUCTION, OVERTKILL HAS BEEN PROGRAMMED TO BELIEVE HE NOW FACES SPAWN, WHO NEARLY DESTROYED HIM A FEW WEEKS AGO.*
SMAT!
SPUGK!
*ISSUES 6 AND 7 --Tom.
Oh, MY...
IT'S HAPPENING, JUST LIKE HE SAID.
I'VE GOTTA FIND AL.
HOW PATHETIC YOU'VE BECOME.

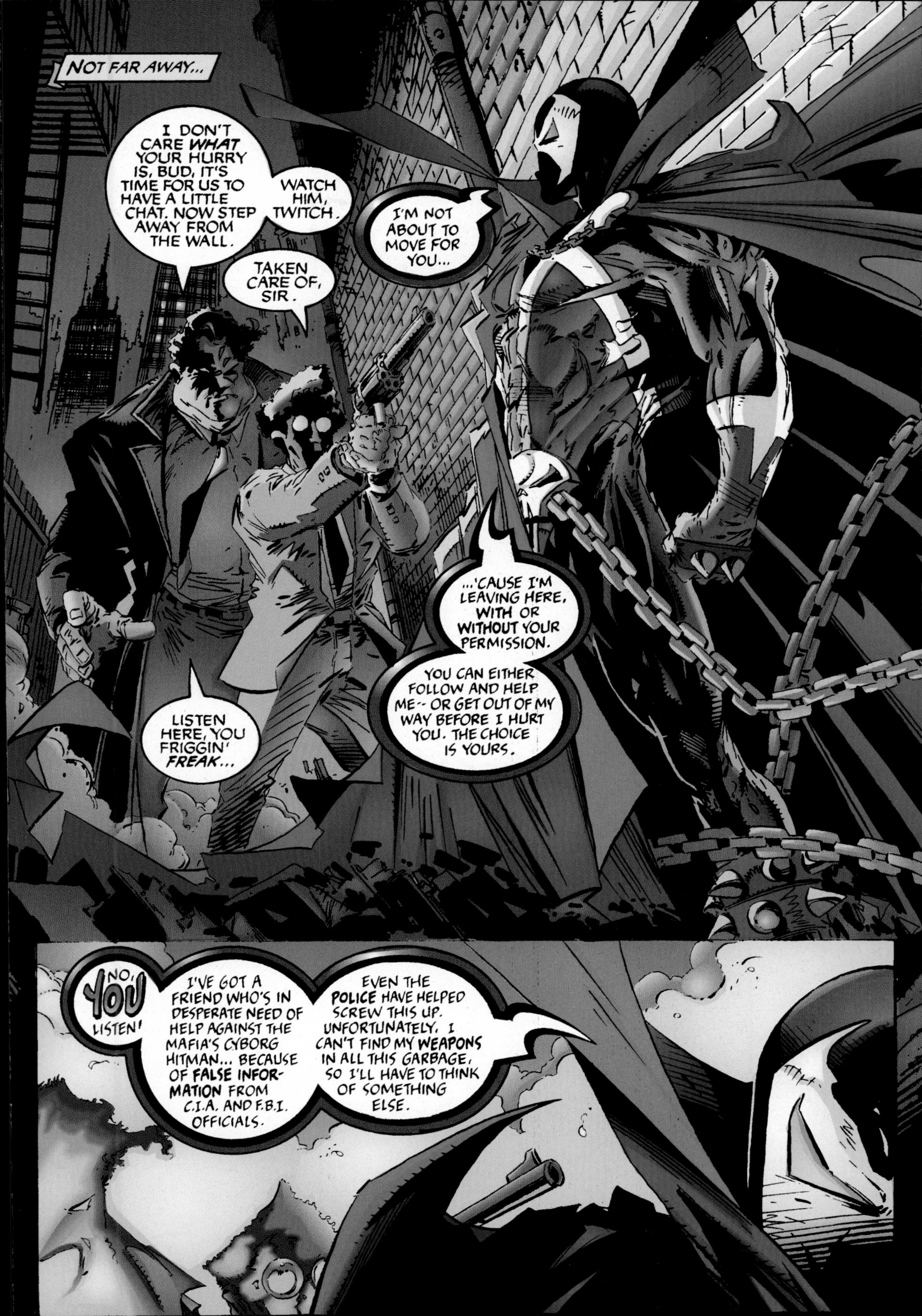
NOT FAR AWAY...
I DON'T CARE WHAT YOUR HURRY IS, BUD, IT'S TIME FOR US TO HAVE A LITTLE CHAT. NOW STEP AWAY FROM THE WALL.
WATCH HIM, TWITCH.
TAKEN CARE OF, SIR.
I'M NOT ABOUT TO MOVE FOR YOU...
...'CAUSE I'M LEAVING HERE, WITH OR WITHOUT YOUR PERMISSION.
YOU CAN EITHER FOLLOW AND HELP ME-- OR GET OUT OF MY WAY BEFORE I HURT YOU. THE CHOICE IS YOURS.
LISTEN HERE, YOU FRIGGIN' FREAK...
NO, YOU LISTEN!
I'VE GOT A FRIEND WHO'S IN DESPERATE NEED OF HELP AGAINST THE MAFIA'S CYBORG HITMAN... BECAUSE OF FALSE INFORMATION FROM C.I.A. AND F.B.I. OFFICIALS.
EVEN THE POLICE HAVE HELPED SCREW THIS UP. UNFORTUNATELY, I CAN'T FIND MY WEAPONS IN ALL THIS GARBAGE, SO I'LL HAVE TO THINK OF SOMETHING ELSE.

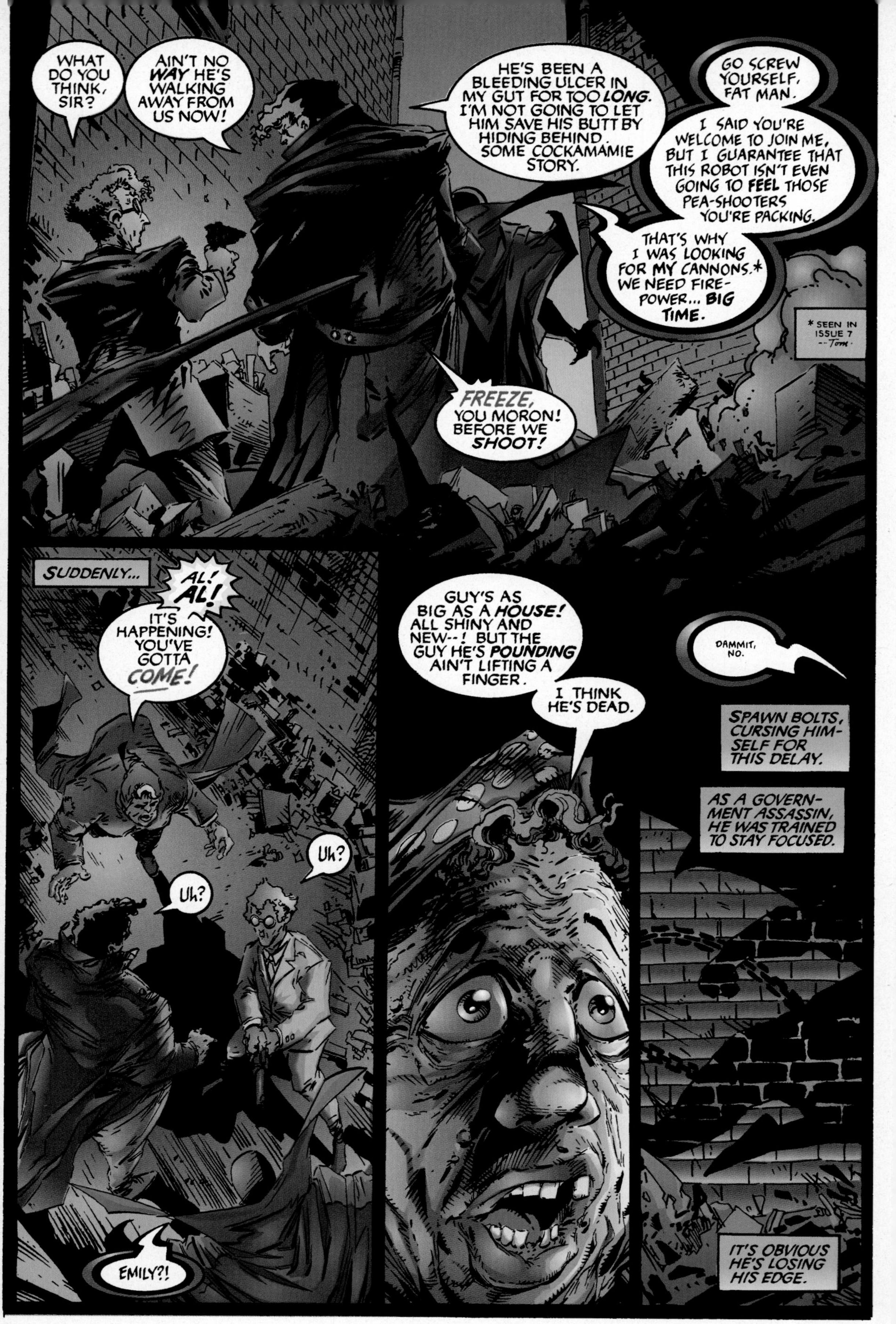
WHAT DO YOU THINK, SIR?
AIN'T NO WAY HE'S WALKING AWAY FROM US NOW!
HE'S BEEN A BLEEDING ULCER IN MY GUT FOR TOO LONG. I'M NOT GOING TO LET HIM SAVE HIS BUTT BY HIDING BEHIND SOME COCKAMAMIE STORY.
GO SCREW YOURSELF, FAT MAN.
I SAID YOU'RE WELCOME TO JOIN ME, BUT I GUARANTEE THAT THIS ROBOT ISN'T EVEN GOING TO FEEL THOSE PEA-SHOOTERS YOU'RE PACKING.
THAT'S WHY I WAS LOOKING FOR MY CANNONS.* WE NEED FIRE-POWER... BIG TIME.
* SEEN IN ISSUE 7 --Tom.
FREEZE, YOU MORON! BEFORE WE SHOOT!
SUDDENLY...
AL! AL!
IT'S HAPPENING! YOU'VE GOTTA COME!
Uh?
Uh?
EMILY?!
GUY'S AS BIG AS A HOUSE! ALL SHINY AND NEW--! BUT THE GUY HE'S POUNDING AIN'T LIFTING A FINGER.
I THINK HE'S DEAD.
DAMMIT, NO.
SPAWN BOLTS, CURSING HIMSELF FOR THIS DELAY.
AS A GOVERNMENT ASSASSIN, HE WAS TRAINED TO STAY FOCUSED.
IT'S OBVIOUS HE'S LOSING HIS EDGE.

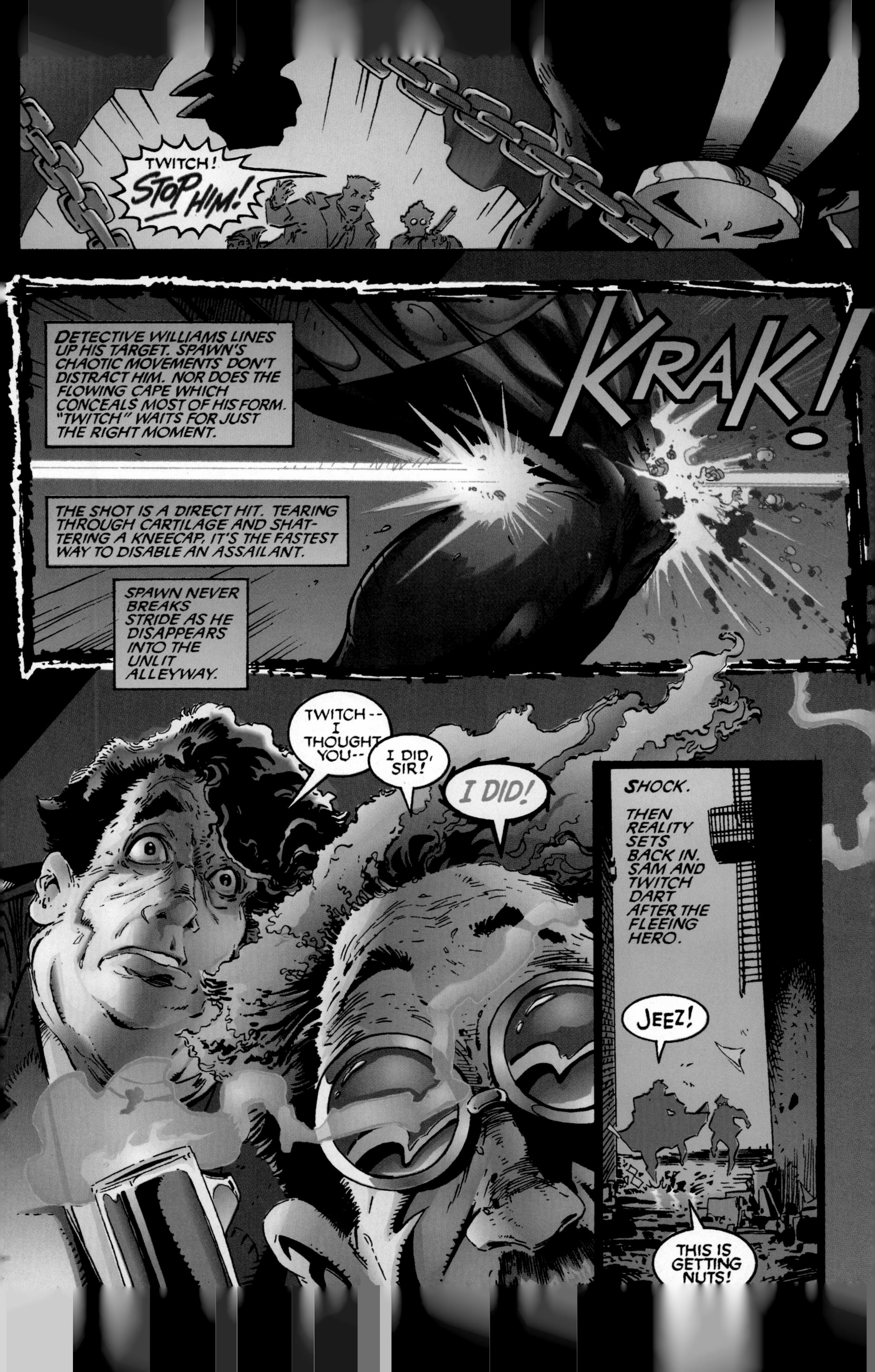
TWITCH! STOP HIM!
DETECTIVE WILLIAMS LINES UP HIS TARGET. SPAWN'S CHAOTIC MOVEMENTS DON'T DISTRACT HIM. NOR DOES THE FLOWING CAPE WHICH CONCEALS MOST OF HIS FORM. "TWITCH" WAITS FOR JUST THE RIGHT MOMENT.
KRAK!
THE SHOT IS A DIRECT HIT. TEARING THROUGH CARTILAGE AND SHATTERING A KNEECAP. IT'S THE FASTEST WAY TO DISABLE AN ASSAILANT.
SPAWN NEVER BREAKS STRIDE AS HE DISAPPEARS INTO THE UNLIT ALLEYWAY.
TWITCH -- I THOUGHT YOU--
I DID, SIR!
I DID!
SHOCK.
THEN REALITY SETS BACK IN. SAM AND TWITCH DART AFTER THE FLEEING HERO.
JEEZ!
THIS IS GETTING NUTS!

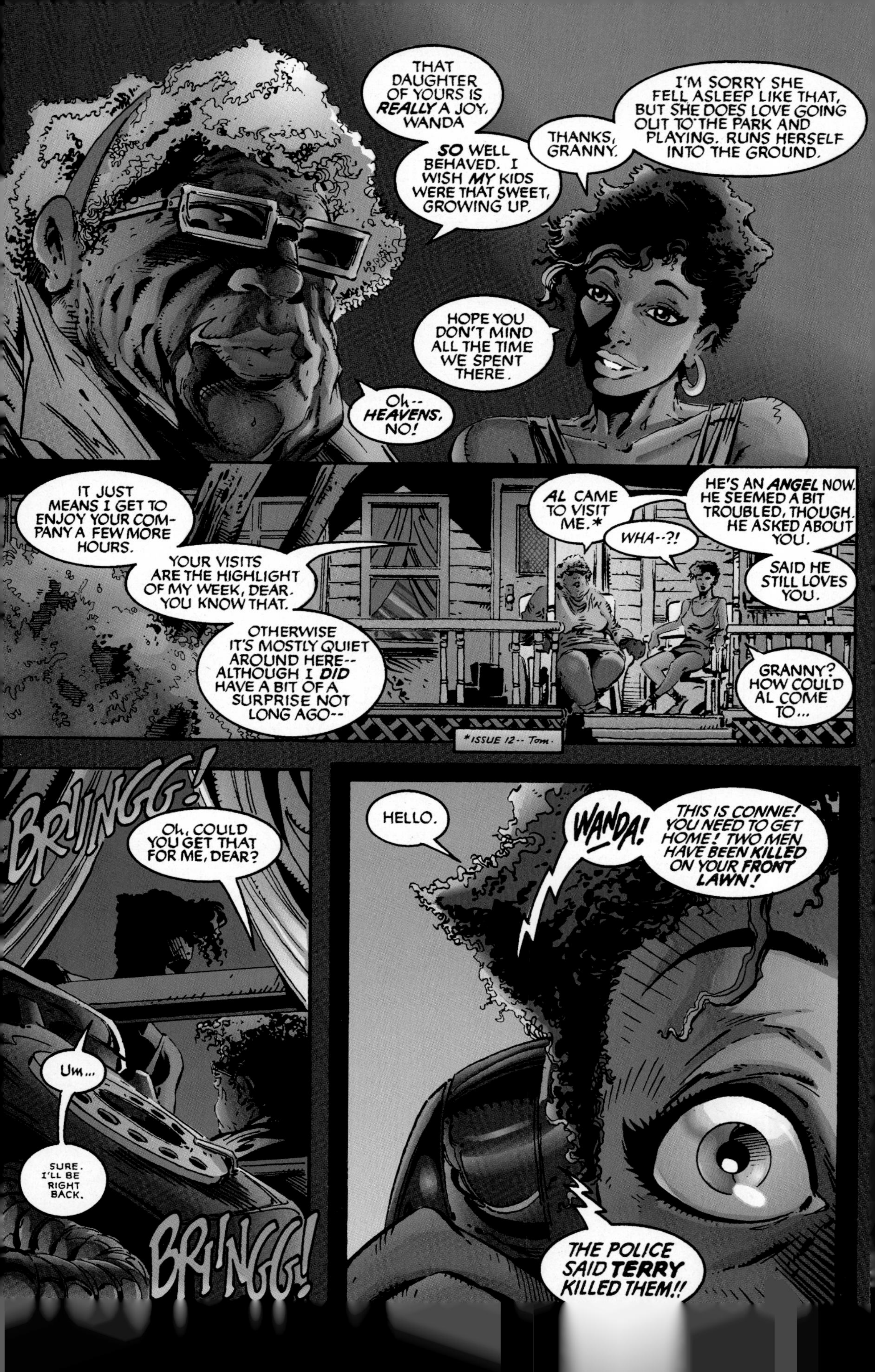
THAT DAUGHTER OF YOURS IS REALLY A JOY, WANDA
SO WELL BEHAVED. I WISH MY KIDS WERE THAT SWEET, GROWING UP.
THANKS, GRANNY.
I'M SORRY SHE FELL ASLEEP LIKE THAT, BUT SHE DOES LOVE GOING OUT TO THE PARK AND PLAYING. RUNS HERSELF INTO THE GROUND.
HOPE YOU DON'T MIND ALL THE TIME WE SPENT THERE.
Oh-- HEAVENS, NO!
IT JUST MEANS I GET TO ENJOY YOUR COMPANY A FEW MORE HOURS.
YOUR VISITS ARE THE HIGHLIGHT OF MY WEEK, DEAR. YOU KNOW THAT.
OTHERWISE IT'S MOSTLY QUIET AROUND HERE-- ALTHOUGH I DID HAVE A BIT OF A SURPRISE NOT LONG AGO--
AL CAME TO VISIT ME.*
WHA--?!
HE'S AN ANGEL NOW. HE SEEMED A BIT TROUBLED, THOUGH. HE ASKED ABOUT YOU.
SAID HE STILL LOVES YOU.
GRANNY? HOW COULD AL COME TO...
*ISSUE 12 -- Tom.
BRINGG!
Oh, COULD YOU GET THAT FOR ME, DEAR?
Um...
SURE. I'LL BE RIGHT BACK.
BRINGG!
HELLO.
WANDA!
THIS IS CONNIE! YOU NEED TO GET HOME! TWO MEN HAVE BEEN KILLED ON YOUR FRONT LAWN!
THE POLICE SAID TERRY KILLED THEM!!

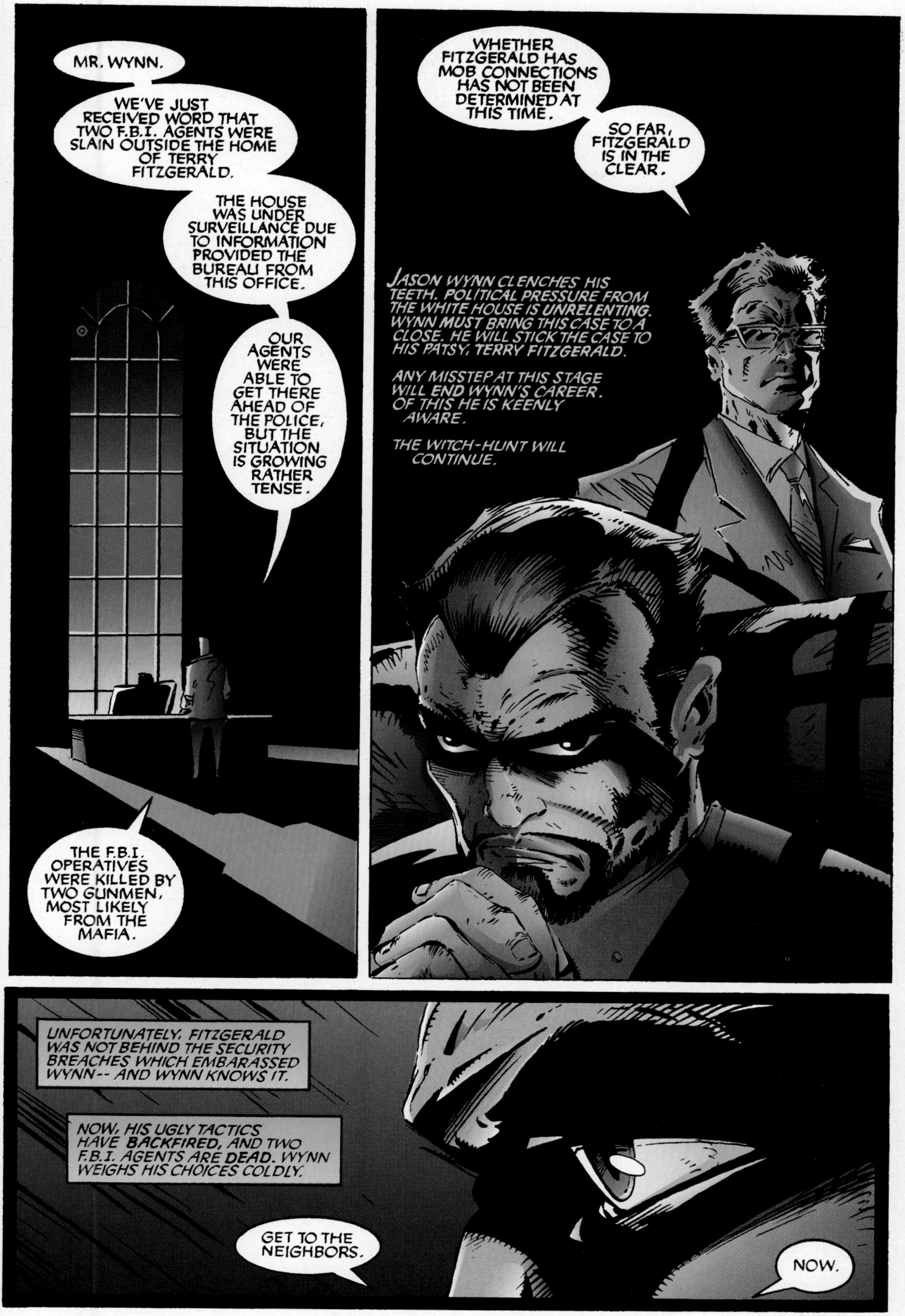
MR. WYNN.
WE'VE JUST RECEIVED WORD THAT TWO F.B.I. AGENTS WERE SLAIN OUTSIDE THE HOME OF TERRY FITZGERALD.
THE HOUSE WAS UNDER SURVEILLANCE DUE TO INFORMATION PROVIDED THE BUREAU FROM THIS OFFICE.
OUR AGENTS WERE ABLE TO GET THERE AHEAD OF THE POLICE, BUT THE SITUATION IS GROWING RATHER TENSE.
THE F.B.I. OPERATIVES WERE KILLED BY TWO GUNMEN, MOST LIKELY FROM THE MAFIA.
WHETHER FITZGERALD HAS MOB CONNECTIONS HAS NOT BEEN DETERMINED AT THIS TIME.
SO FAR, FITZGERALD IS IN THE CLEAR.
JASON WYNN CLENCHES HIS TEETH. POLITICAL PRESSURE FROM THE WHITE HOUSE IS UNRELENTING. WYNN MUST BRING THIS CASE TO A CLOSE. HE WILL STICK THE CASE TO HIS PATSY, TERRY FITZGERALD.
ANY MISSTEP AT THIS STAGE WILL END WYNN'S CAREER. OF THIS HE IS KEENLY AWARE.
THE WITCH-HUNT WILL CONTINUE.
UNFORTUNATELY, FITZGERALD WAS NOT BEHIND THE SECURITY BREACHES WHICH EMBARASSED WYNN-- AND WYNN KNOWS IT.
NOW, HIS UGLY TACTICS HAVE BACKFIRED, AND TWO F.B.I. AGENTS ARE DEAD. WYNN WEIGHS HIS CHOICES COLDLY.
GET TO THE NEIGHBORS.
NOW.

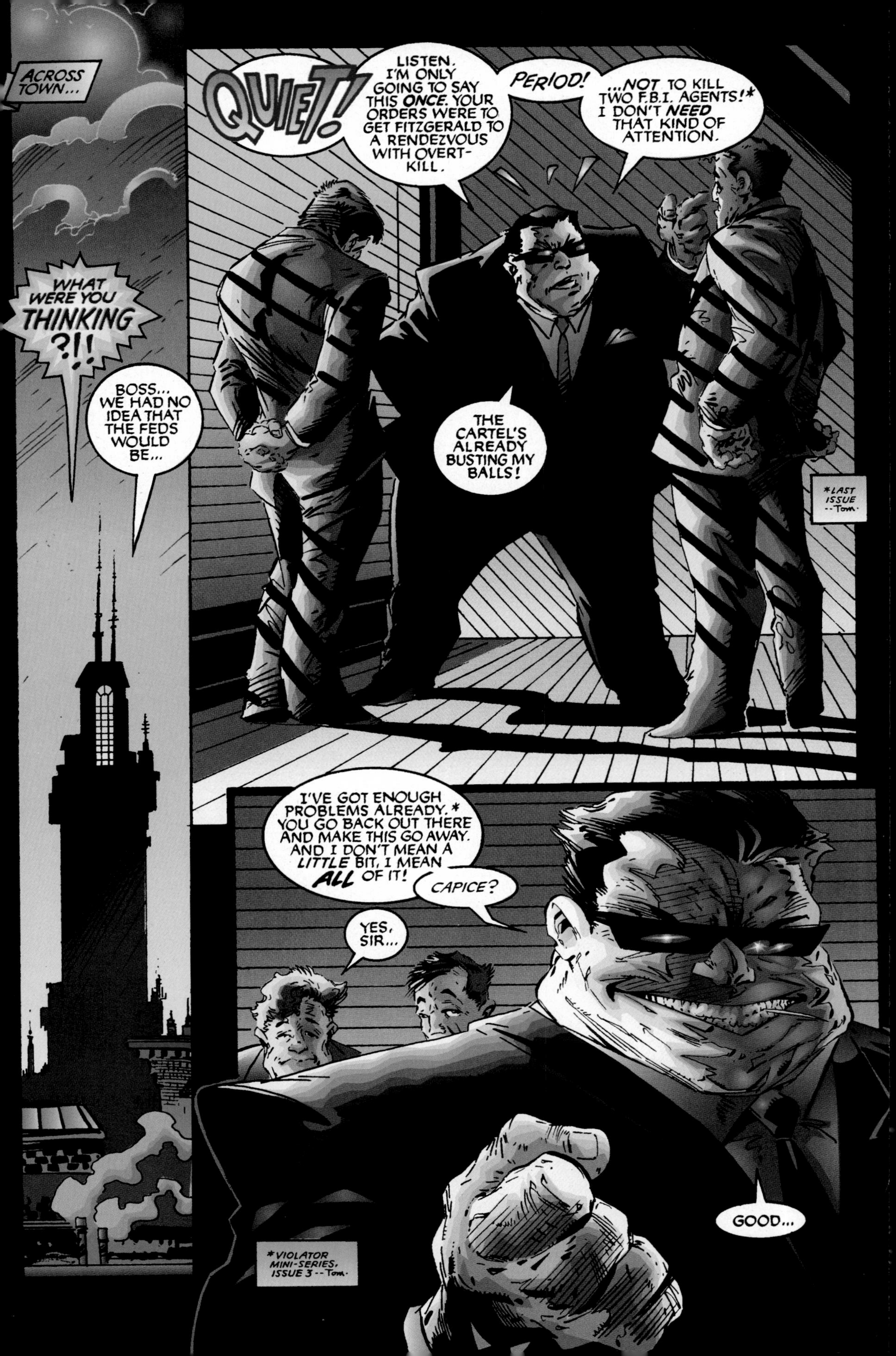
ACROSS TOWN...
QUIET!
LISTEN. I'M ONLY GOING TO SAY THIS ONCE. YOUR ORDERS WERE TO GET FITZGERALD TO A RENDEZVOUS WITH OVERT-KILL.
PERIOD!
...NOT TO KILL TWO F.B.I. AGENTS!* I DON'T NEED THAT KIND OF ATTENTION.
WHAT WERE YOU THINKING ?!!
BOSS... WE HAD NO IDEA THAT THE FEDS WOULD BE...
THE CARTEL'S ALREADY BUSTING MY BALLS!
*LAST ISSUE --Tom.
I'VE GOT ENOUGH PROBLEMS ALREADY.* YOU GO BACK OUT THERE AND MAKE THIS GO AWAY. AND I DON'T MEAN A LITTLE BIT, I MEAN ALL OF IT!
CAPICE?
YES, SIR...
GOOD...
*VIOLATOR MINI-SERIES, ISSUE 3 --Tom.

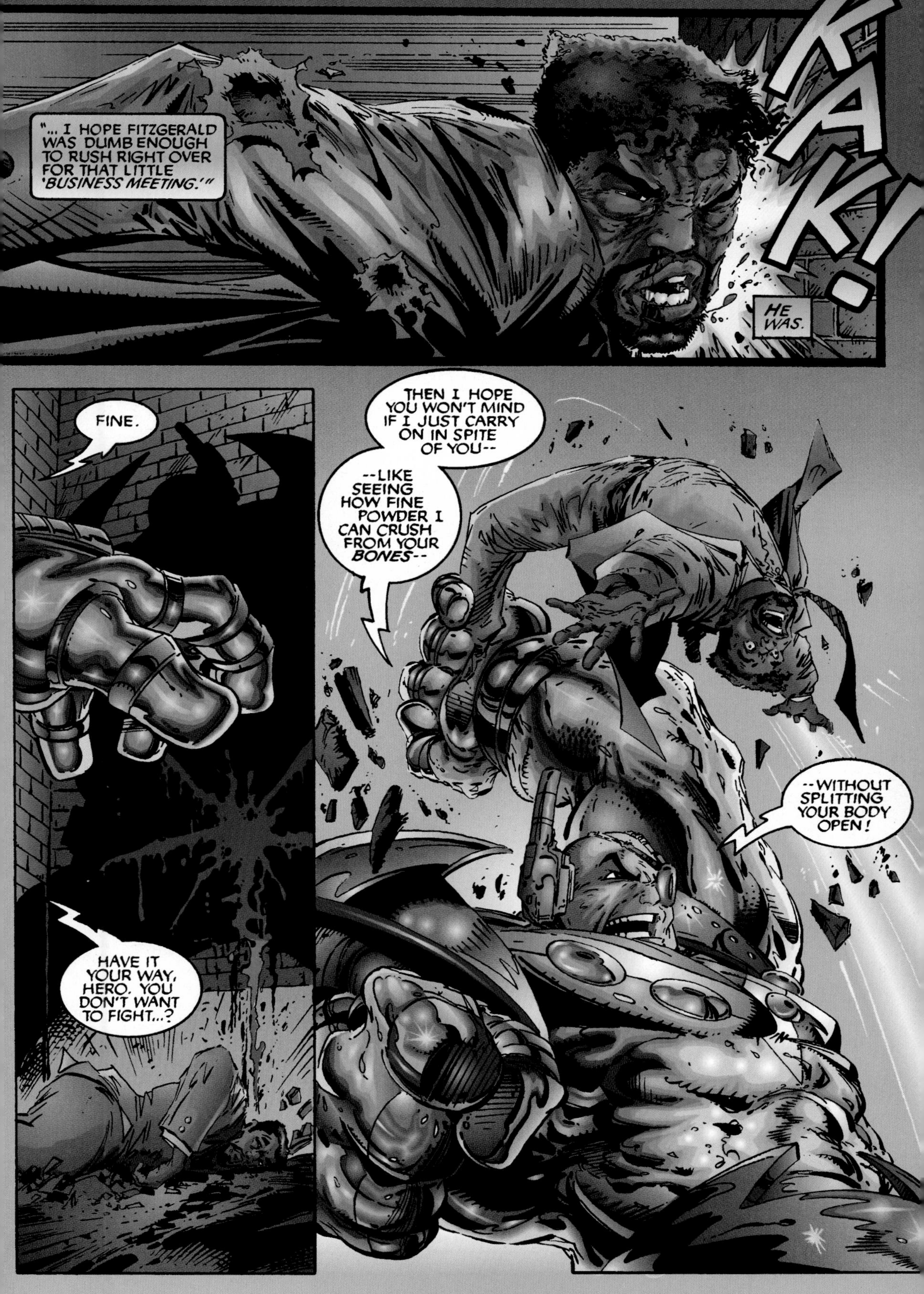
"... I HOPE FITZGERALD WAS DUMB ENOUGH TO RUSH RIGHT OVER FOR THAT LITTLE 'BUSINESS MEETING.'"
KAK!
HE WAS.
FINE.
THEN I HOPE YOU WON'T MIND IF I JUST CARRY ON IN SPITE OF YOU--
--LIKE SEEING HOW FINE POWDER I CAN CRUSH FROM YOUR BONES--
--WITHOUT SPLITTING YOUR BODY OPEN!
HAVE IT YOUR WAY, HERO. YOU DON'T WANT TO FIGHT...?

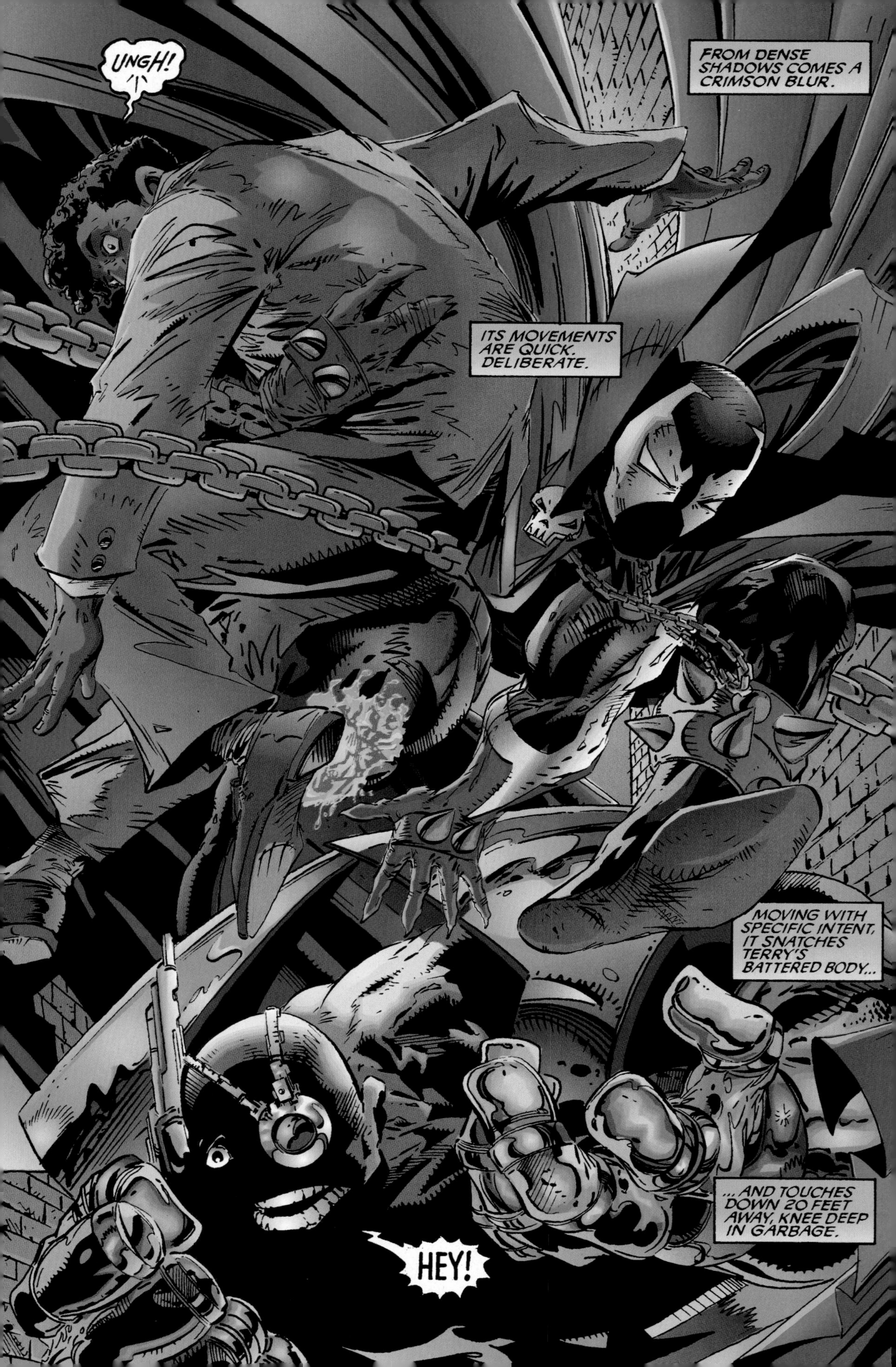
UNGH!
FROM DENSE SHADOWS COMES A CRIMSON BLUR.
ITS MOVEMENTS ARE QUICK. DELIBERATE.
MOVING WITH SPECIFIC INTENT, IT SNATCHES TERRY'S BATTERED BODY...
...AND TOUCHES DOWN 20 FEET AWAY, KNEE DEEP IN GARBAGE.
HEY!

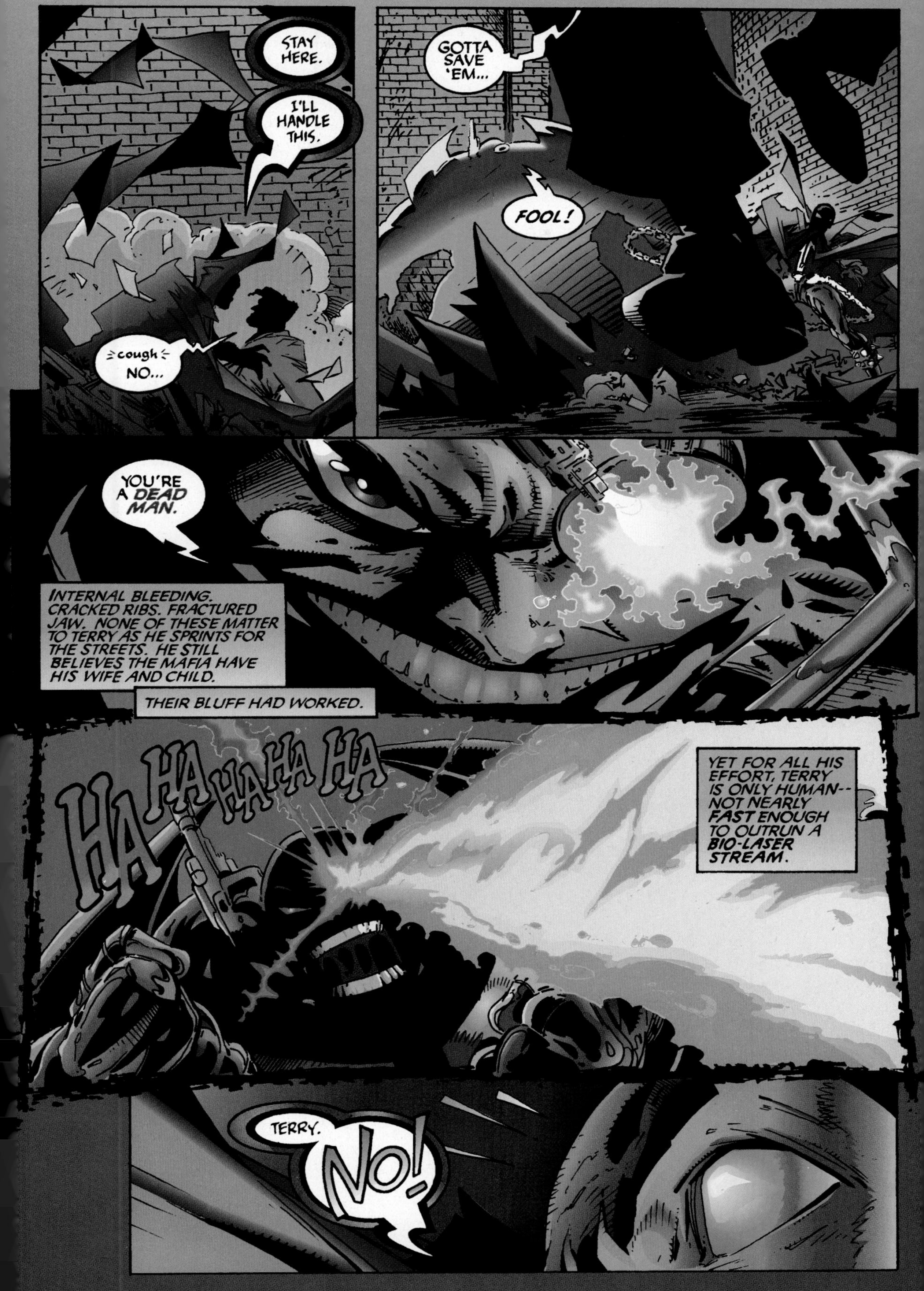
STAY HERE.
I'LL HANDLE THIS.
cough
NO...
GOTTA SAVE 'EM...
FOOL!
YOU'RE A DEAD MAN.
INTERNAL BLEEDING. CRACKED RIBS. FRACTURED JAW. NONE OF THESE MATTER TO TERRY AS HE SPRINTS FOR THE STREETS. HE STILL BELIEVES THE MAFIA HAVE HIS WIFE AND CHILD.
THEIR BLUFF HAD WORKED.
HA HA HA HA HA HA
YET FOR ALL HIS EFFORT, TERRY IS ONLY HUMAN-- NOT NEARLY FAST ENOUGH TO OUTRUN A BIO-LASER STREAM.
TERRY.
NO!

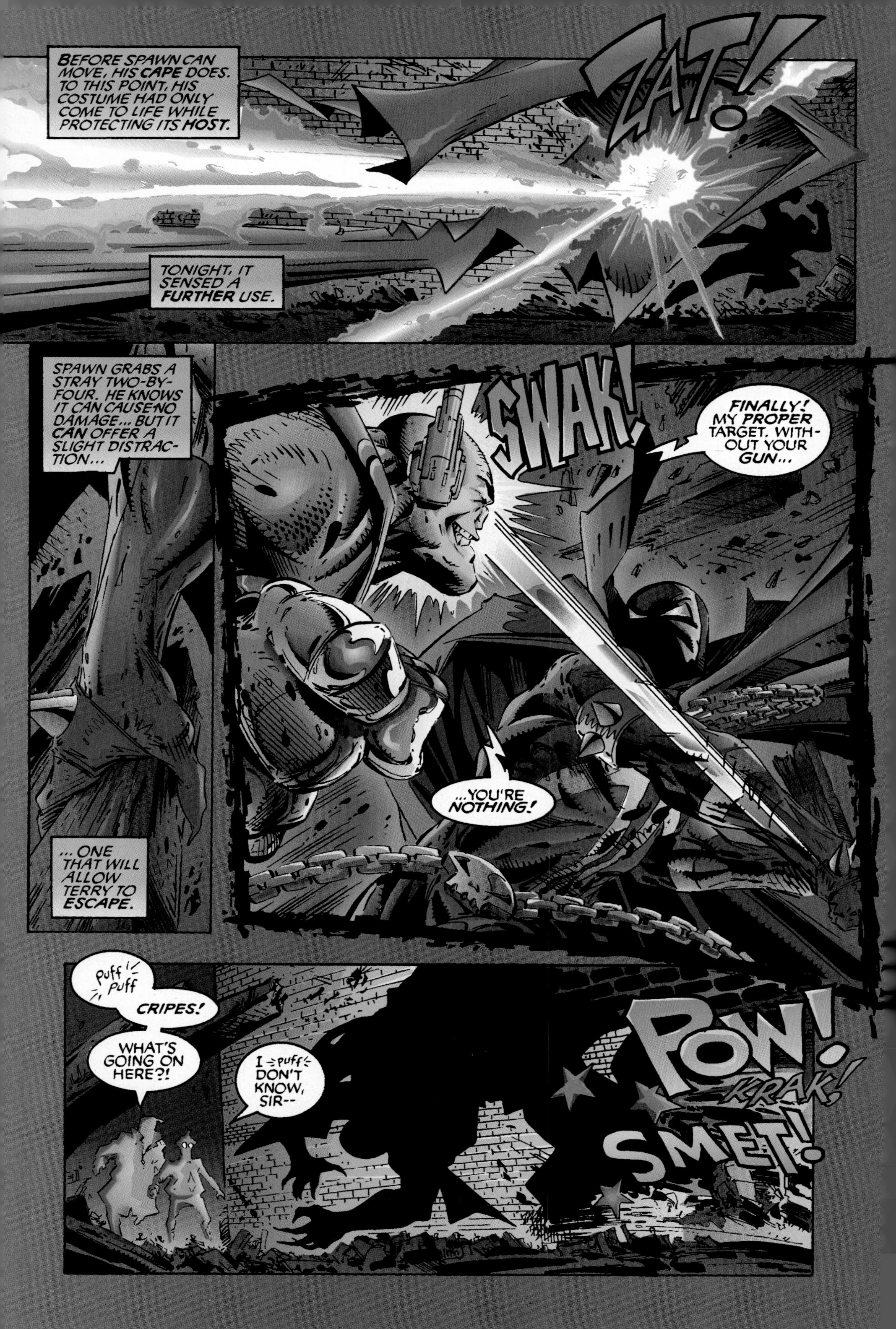
BEFORE SPAWN CAN MOVE, HIS CAPE DOES. TO THIS POINT, HIS COSTUME HAD ONLY COME TO LIFE WHILE PROTECTING ITS HOST.
ZAT!
TONIGHT, IT SENSED A FURTHER USE.
SPAWN GRABS A STRAY TWO-BY-FOUR. HE KNOWS IT CAN CAUSE NO DAMAGE... BUT IT CAN OFFER A SLIGHT DISTRACTION...
SWAK!
FINALLY! MY PROPER TARGET. WITHOUT YOUR GUN...
...YOU'RE NOTHING!
...ONE THAT WILL ALLOW TERRY TO ESCAPE.
puff puff
CRIPES!
WHAT'S GOING ON HERE?!
I puff DON'T KNOW, SIR--
POW!
KRAK!
SMET!

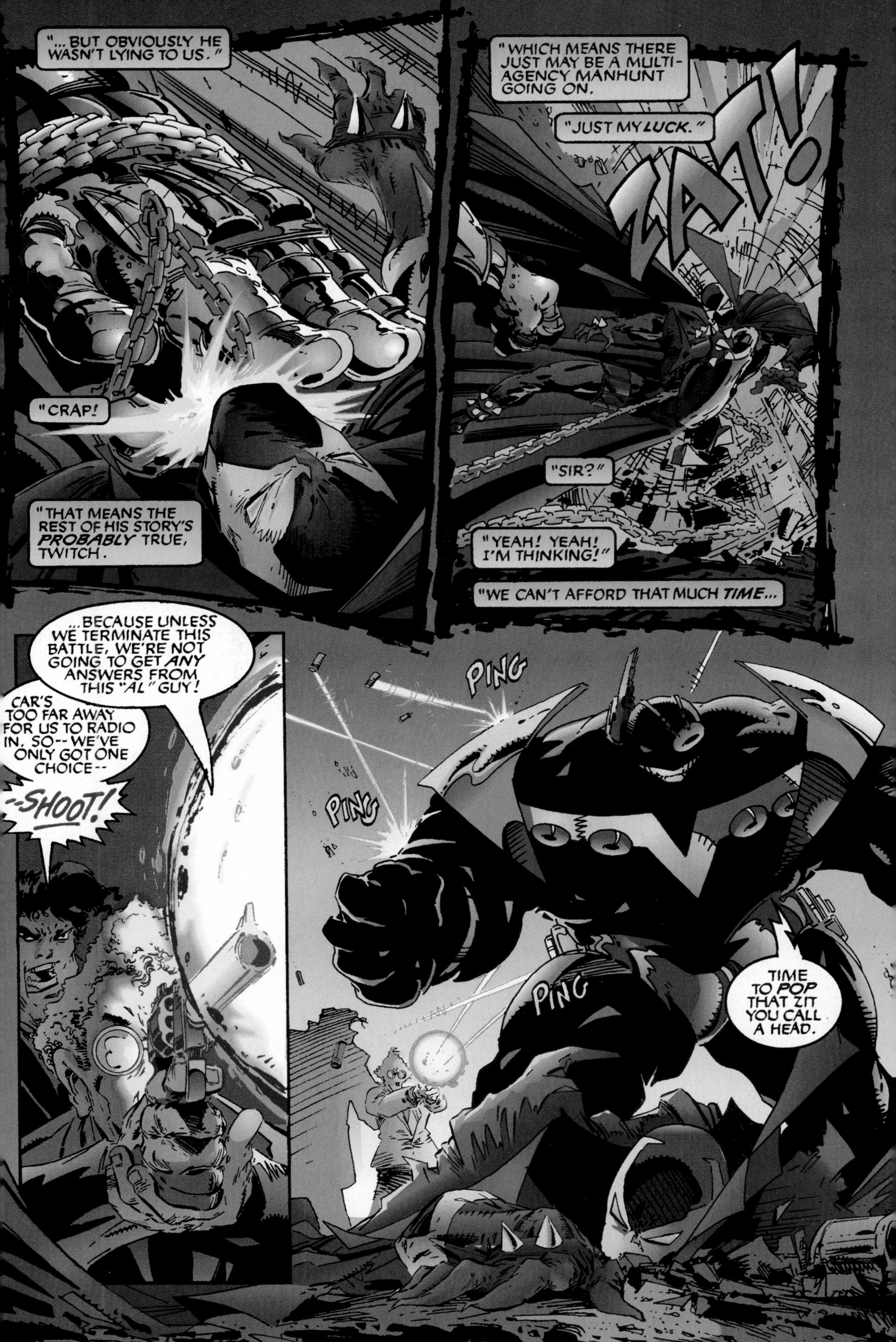
"...BUT OBVIOUSLY HE WASN'T LYING TO US."
"CRAP!
"THAT MEANS THE REST OF HIS STORY'S *PROBABLY* TRUE, TWITCH.
"WHICH MEANS THERE JUST MAY BE A MULTI-AGENCY MANHUNT GOING ON.
"JUST MY *LUCK*."
ZAT!
"SIR?"
"YEAH! YEAH! I'M THINKING!"
"WE CAN'T AFFORD THAT MUCH *TIME*...
...BECAUSE UNLESS WE TERMINATE THIS BATTLE, WE'RE NOT GOING TO GET *ANY* ANSWERS FROM THIS "*AL*" GUY!
CAR'S TOO FAR AWAY FOR US TO RADIO IN. SO-- WE'VE ONLY GOT ONE CHOICE--
--SHOOT!
PING
PING
PING
TIME TO *POP* THAT ZIT YOU CALL A HEAD.

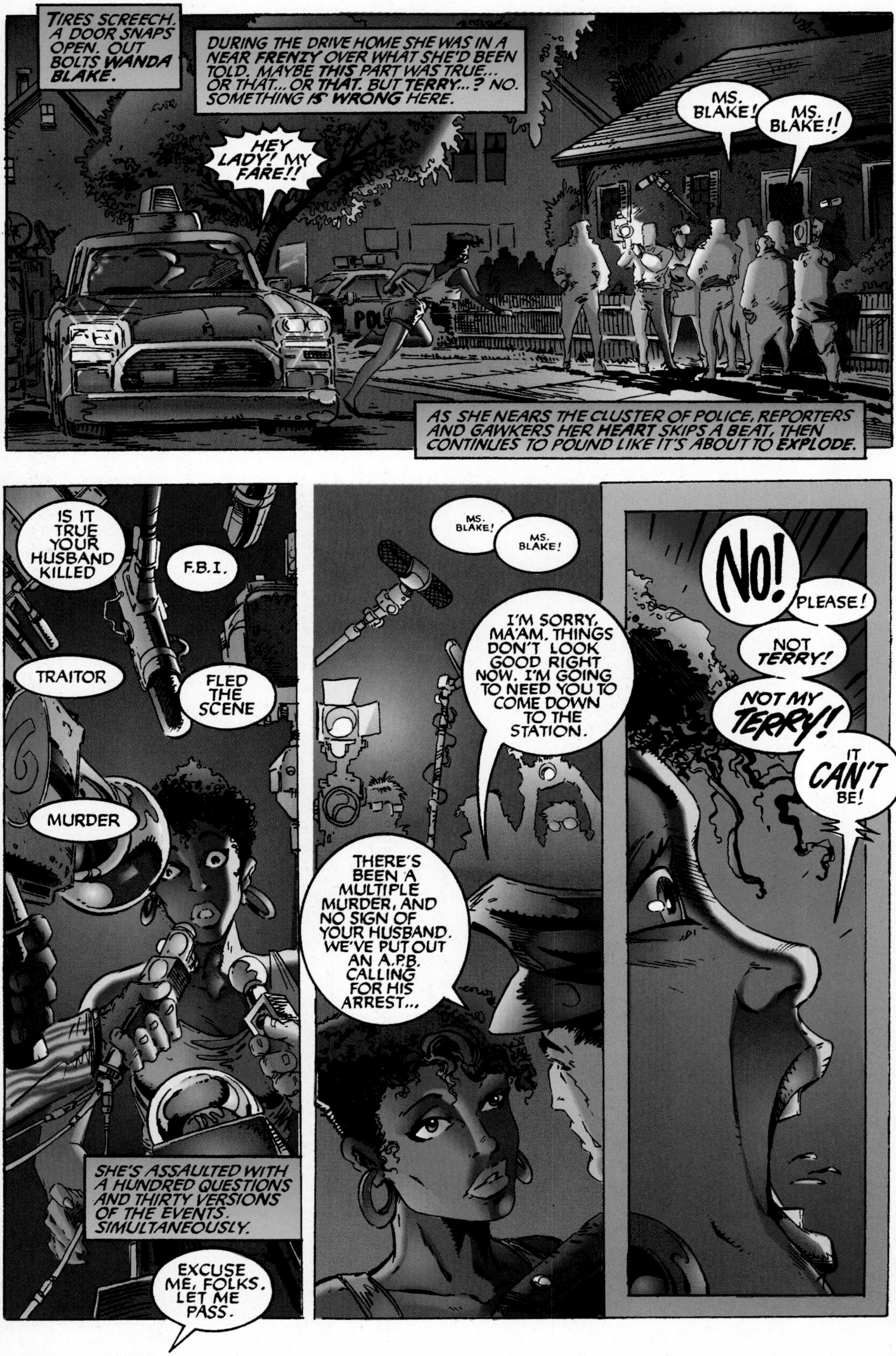
TIRES SCREECH. A DOOR SNAPS OPEN. OUT BOLTS WANDA BLAKE.
DURING THE DRIVE HOME SHE WAS IN A NEAR FRENZY OVER WHAT SHE'D BEEN TOLD. MAYBE THIS PART WAS TRUE... OR THAT... OR THAT. BUT TERRY...? NO. SOMETHING IS WRONG HERE.
HEY LADY! MY FARE!!
MS. BLAKE!
MS. BLAKE!!
AS SHE NEARS THE CLUSTER OF POLICE, REPORTERS AND GAWKERS HER HEART SKIPS A BEAT, THEN CONTINUES TO POUND LIKE IT'S ABOUT TO EXPLODE.
IS IT TRUE YOUR HUSBAND KILLED
F.B.I.
TRAITOR
FLED THE SCENE
MURDER
SHE'S ASSAULTED WITH A HUNDRED QUESTIONS AND THIRTY VERSIONS OF THE EVENTS. SIMULTANEOUSLY.
EXCUSE ME, FOLKS. LET ME PASS.
MS. BLAKE!
MS. BLAKE!
I'M SORRY, MA'AM. THINGS DON'T LOOK GOOD RIGHT NOW. I'M GOING TO NEED YOU TO COME DOWN TO THE STATION.
THERE'S BEEN A MULTIPLE MURDER, AND NO SIGN OF YOUR HUSBAND. WE'VE PUT OUT AN A.P.B. CALLING FOR HIS ARREST...
No!
PLEASE!
NOT TERRY!
NOT MY TERRY!
IT CAN'T BE!

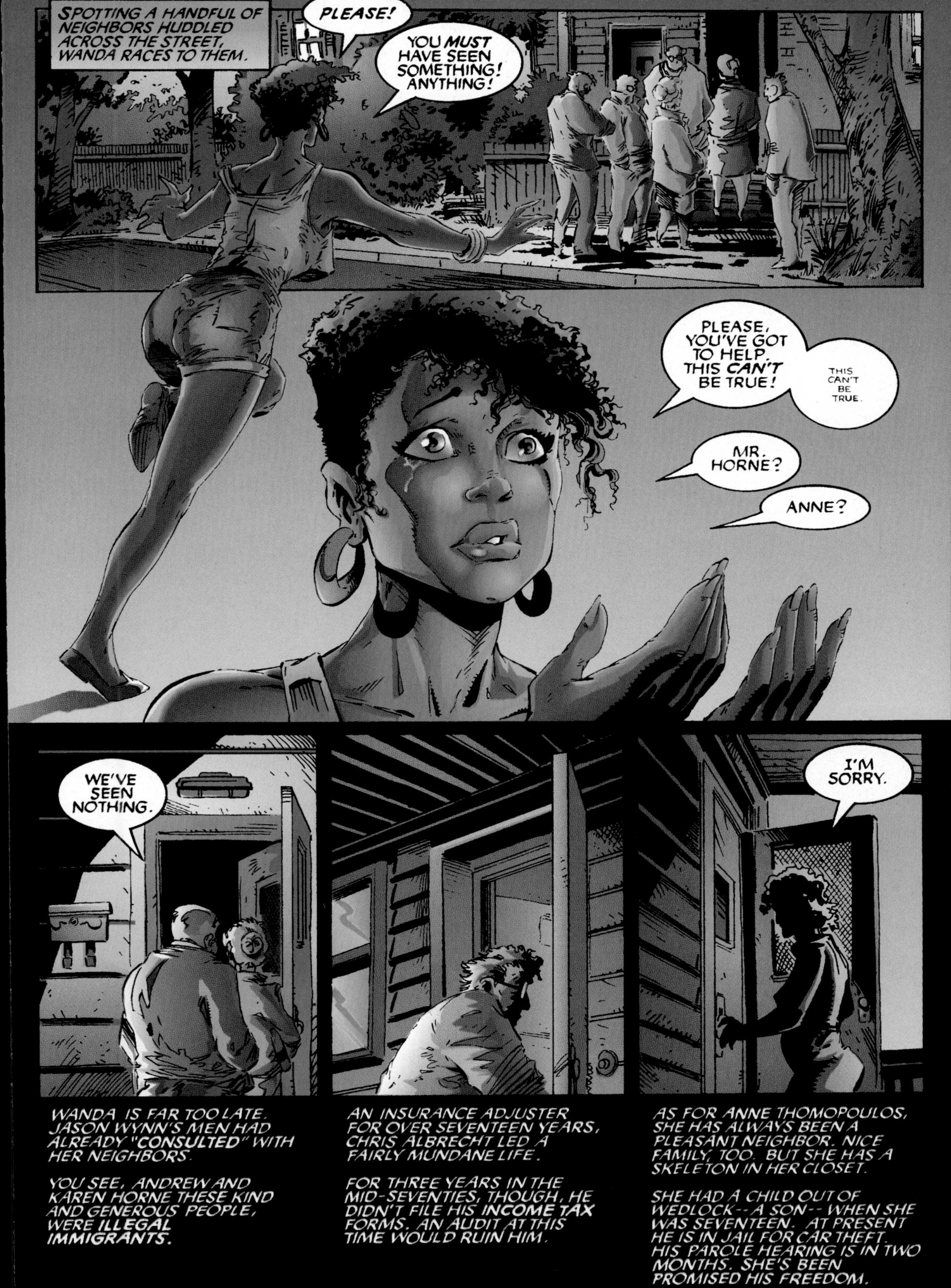
SPOTTING A HANDFUL OF NEIGHBORS HUDDLED ACROSS THE STREET, WANDA RACES TO THEM.
PLEASE!
YOU MUST HAVE SEEN SOMETHING! ANYTHING!
PLEASE, YOU'VE GOT TO HELP. THIS CAN'T BE TRUE!
THIS CAN'T BE TRUE.
MR. HORNE?
ANNE?
WE'VE SEEN NOTHING.
I'M SORRY.

WANDA IS FAR TOO LATE. JASON WYNN'S MEN HAD ALREADY "**CONSULTED**" WITH HER NEIGHBORS.

YOU SEE, ANDREW AND KAREN HORNE THESE KIND AND GENEROUS PEOPLE, WERE **ILLEGAL IMMIGRANTS.**

AN INSURANCE ADJUSTER FOR OVER SEVENTEEN YEARS, CHRIS ALBRECHT LED A FAIRLY MUNDANE LIFE.

FOR THREE YEARS IN THE MID-SEVENTIES, THOUGH, HE DIDN'T FILE HIS **INCOME TAX** FORMS. AN AUDIT AT THIS TIME WOULD RUIN HIM.

AS FOR ANNE THOMOPOULOS, SHE HAS ALWAYS BEEN A PLEASANT NEIGHBOR. NICE FAMILY, TOO. BUT SHE HAS A SKELETON IN HER CLOSET.

SHE HAD A CHILD OUT OF WEDLOCK-- A SON-- WHEN SHE WAS SEVENTEEN. AT PRESENT HE IS IN JAIL FOR CAR THEFT. HIS PAROLE HEARING IS IN TWO MONTHS. SHE'S BEEN PROMISED HIS FREEDOM.

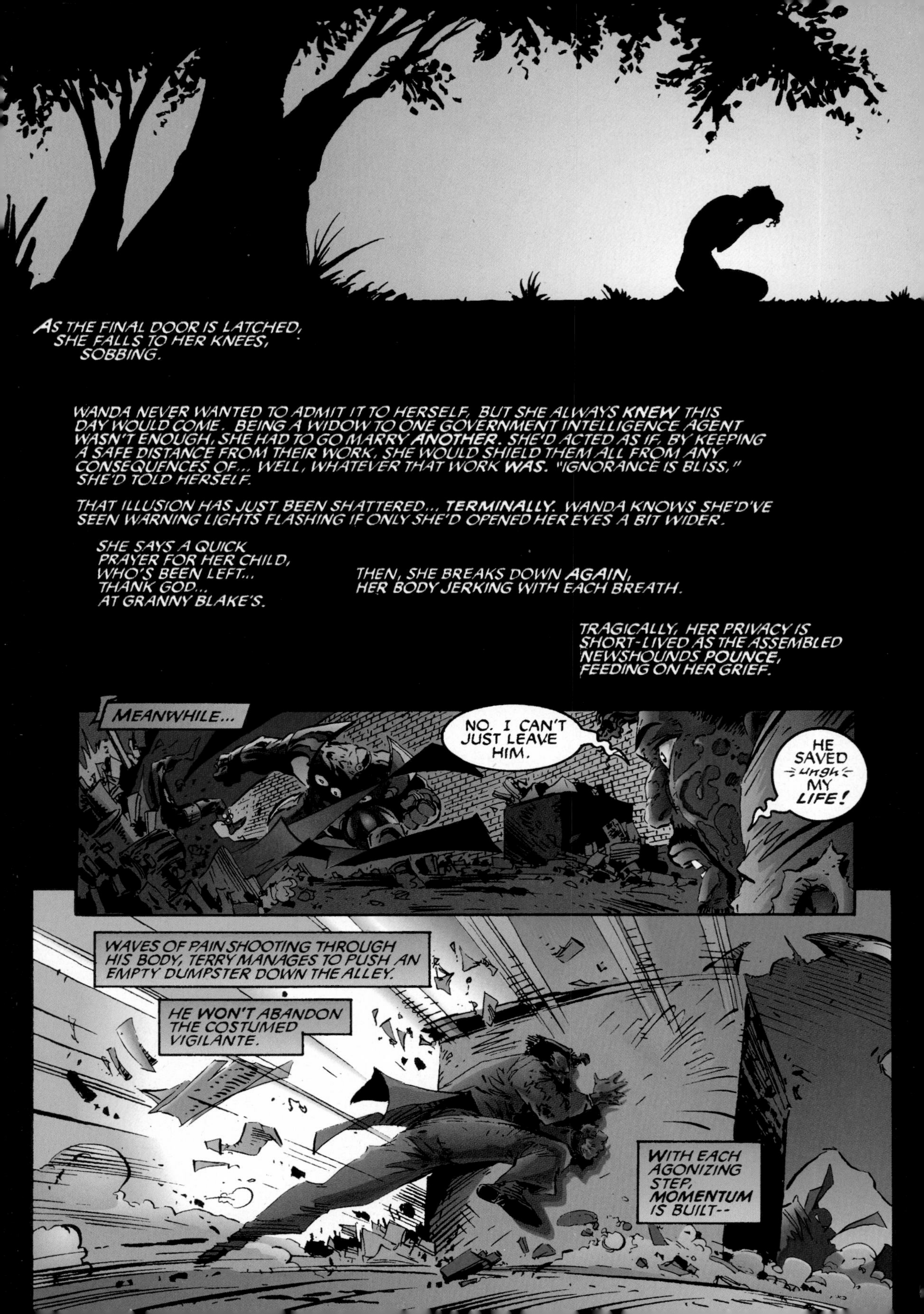

AS THE FINAL DOOR IS LATCHED, SHE FALLS TO HER KNEES, SOBBING.
WANDA NEVER WANTED TO ADMIT IT TO HERSELF, BUT SHE ALWAYS KNEW THIS DAY WOULD COME. BEING A WIDOW TO ONE GOVERNMENT INTELLIGENCE AGENT WASN'T ENOUGH, SHE HAD TO GO MARRY ANOTHER. SHE'D ACTED AS IF, BY KEEPING A SAFE DISTANCE FROM THEIR WORK, SHE WOULD SHIELD THEM ALL FROM ANY CONSEQUENCES OF... WELL, WHATEVER THAT WORK WAS. "IGNORANCE IS BLISS," SHE'D TOLD HERSELF.
THAT ILLUSION HAS JUST BEEN SHATTERED... TERMINALLY. WANDA KNOWS SHE'D'VE SEEN WARNING LIGHTS FLASHING IF ONLY SHE'D OPENED HER EYES A BIT WIDER.
SHE SAYS A QUICK PRAYER FOR HER CHILD, WHO'S BEEN LEFT... THANK GOD... AT GRANNY BLAKE'S.
THEN, SHE BREAKS DOWN AGAIN, HER BODY JERKING WITH EACH BREATH.
TRAGICALLY, HER PRIVACY IS SHORT-LIVED AS THE ASSEMBLED NEWSHOUNDS POUNCE, FEEDING ON HER GRIEF.
MEANWHILE...
NO. I CAN'T JUST LEAVE HIM.
HE SAVED -ungh- MY LIFE!
WAVES OF PAIN SHOOTING THROUGH HIS BODY, TERRY MANAGES TO PUSH AN EMPTY DUMPSTER DOWN THE ALLEY.
HE WON'T ABANDON THE COSTUMED VIGILANTE.
WITH EACH AGONIZING STEP, MOMENTUM IS BUILT--

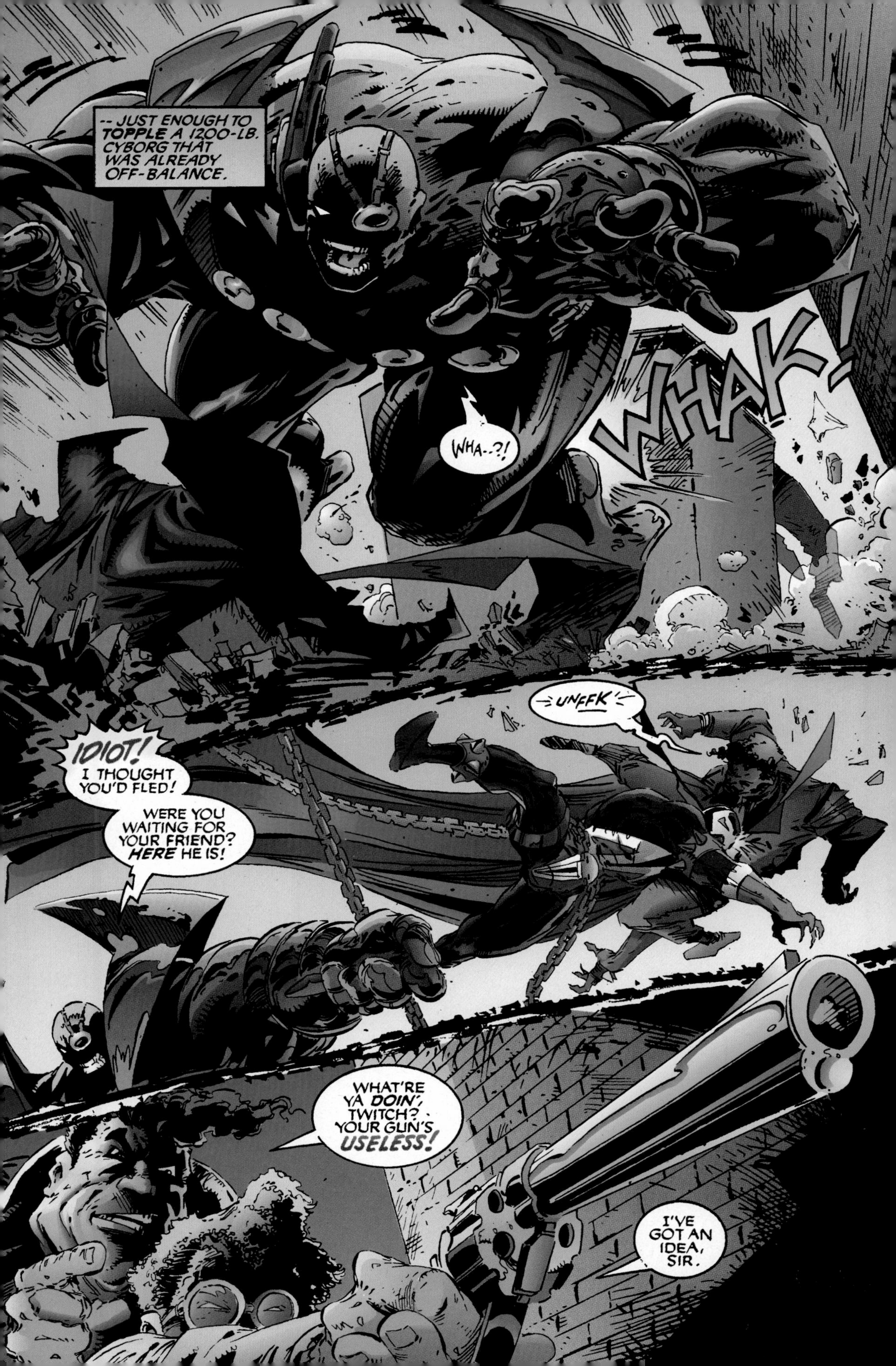
--JUST ENOUGH TO TOPPLE A 1200-LB. CYBORG THAT WAS ALREADY OFF-BALANCE.
WHA--?!
WHAK!
UNFFK
IDIOT! I THOUGHT YOU'D FLED!
WERE YOU WAITING FOR YOUR FRIEND? HERE HE IS!
WHAT'RE YA DOIN', TWITCH? YOUR GUN'S USELESS!
I'VE GOT AN IDEA, SIR.

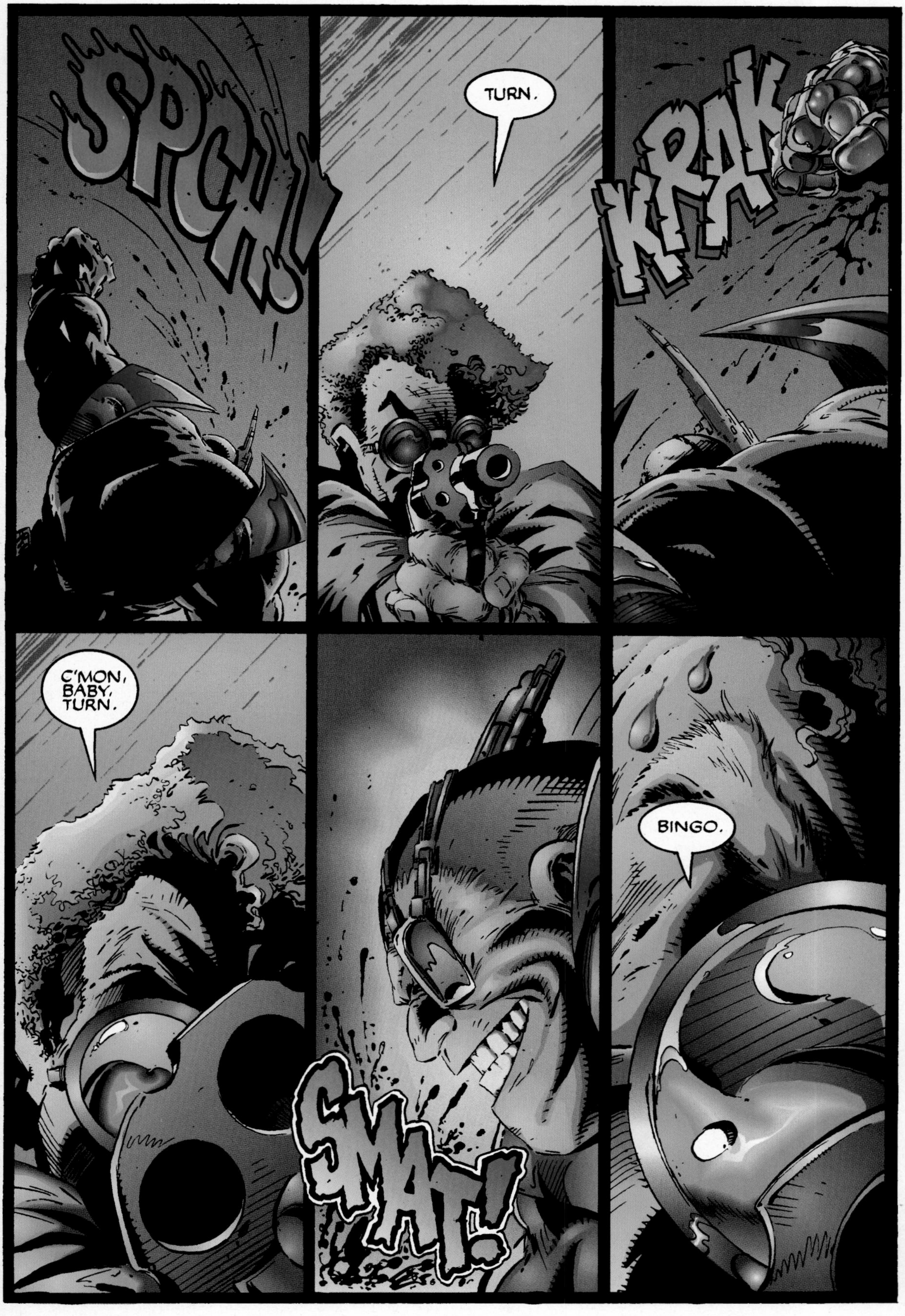
SPCH!
TURN.
KRAK
C'MON, BABY, TURN.
SMAT!
BINGO.

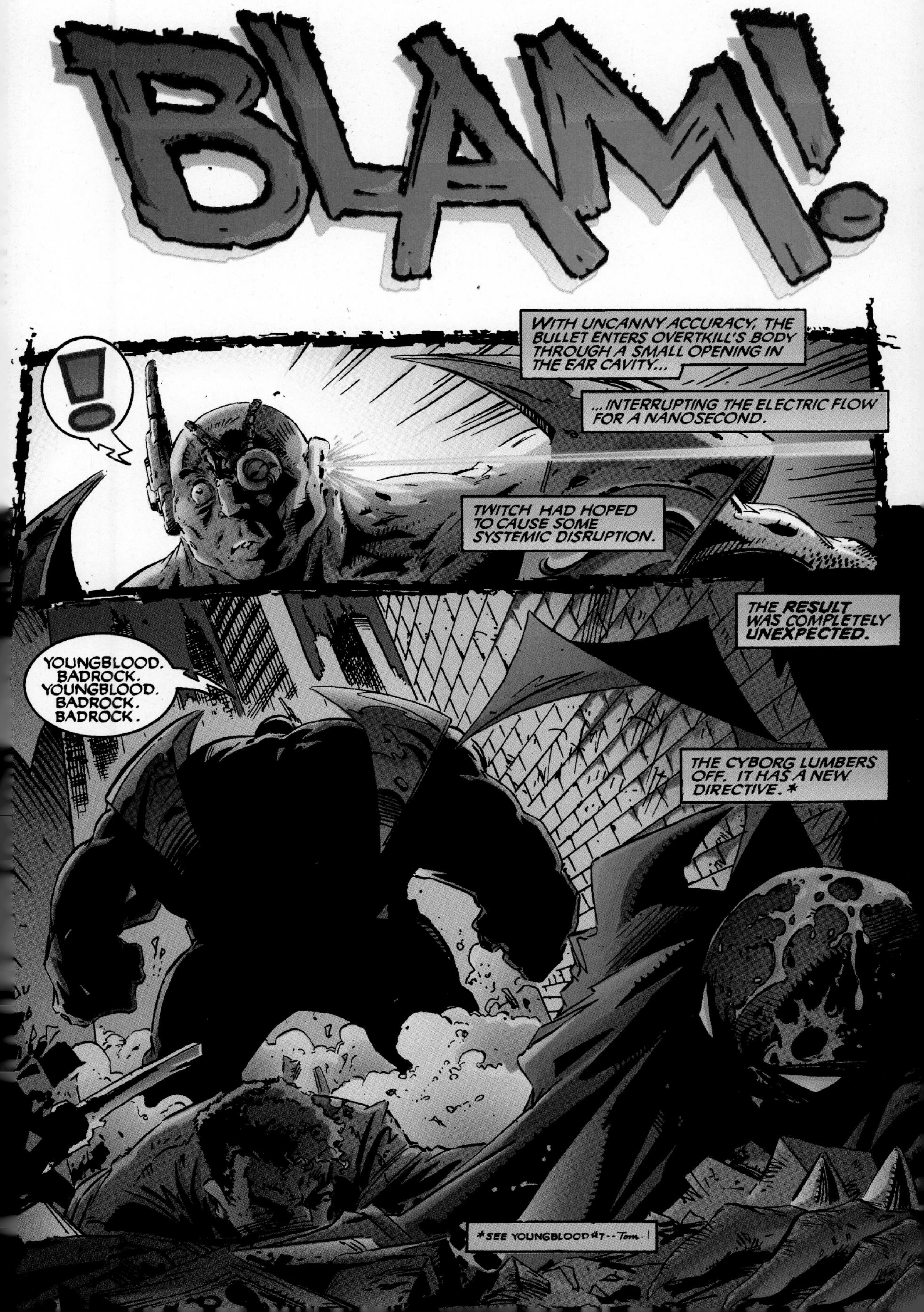
BLAM!
!
WITH UNCANNY ACCURACY, THE BULLET ENTERS OVERTKILL'S BODY THROUGH A SMALL OPENING IN THE EAR CAVITY...
...INTERRUPTING THE ELECTRIC FLOW FOR A NANOSECOND.
TWITCH HAD HOPED TO CAUSE SOME SYSTEMIC DISRUPTION.
THE RESULT WAS COMPLETELY UNEXPECTED.
YOUNGBLOOD. BADROCK. YOUNGBLOOD. BADROCK. BADROCK.
THE CYBORG LUMBERS OFF. IT HAS A NEW DIRECTIVE.*
*SEE YOUNGBLOOD #7--Tom.!

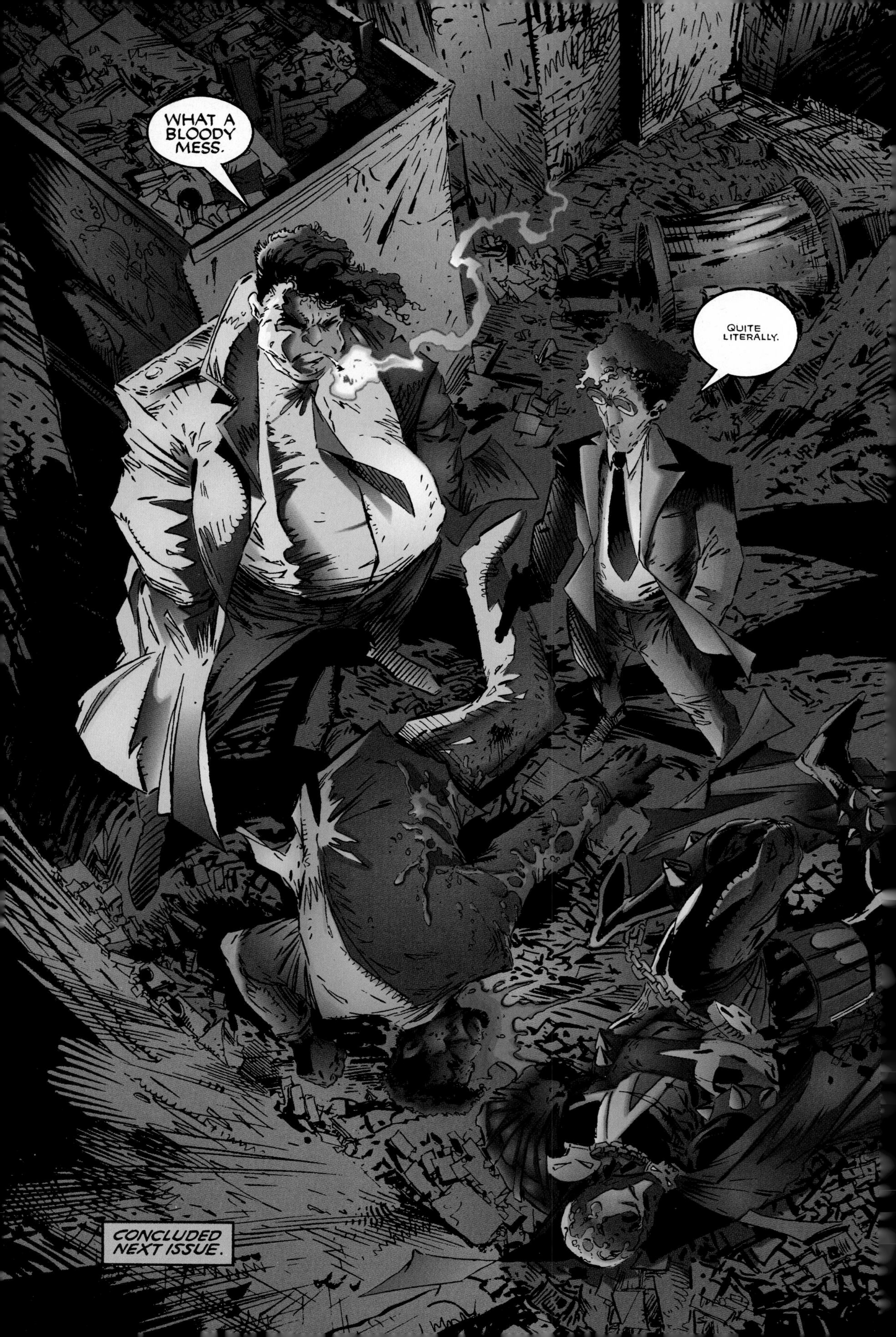
WHAT A BLOODY MESS.
QUITE LITERALLY.
CONCLUDED NEXT ISSUE.

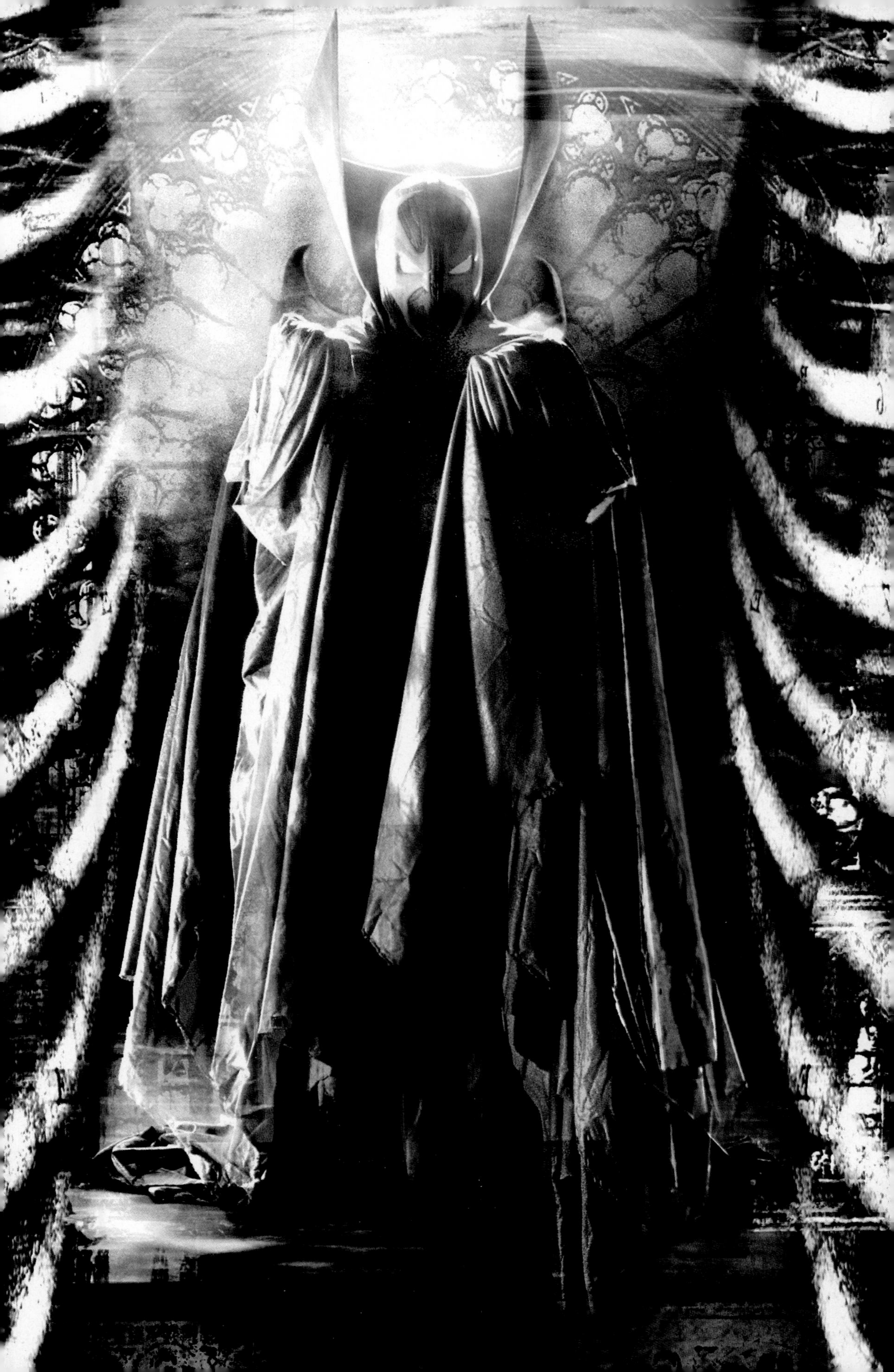

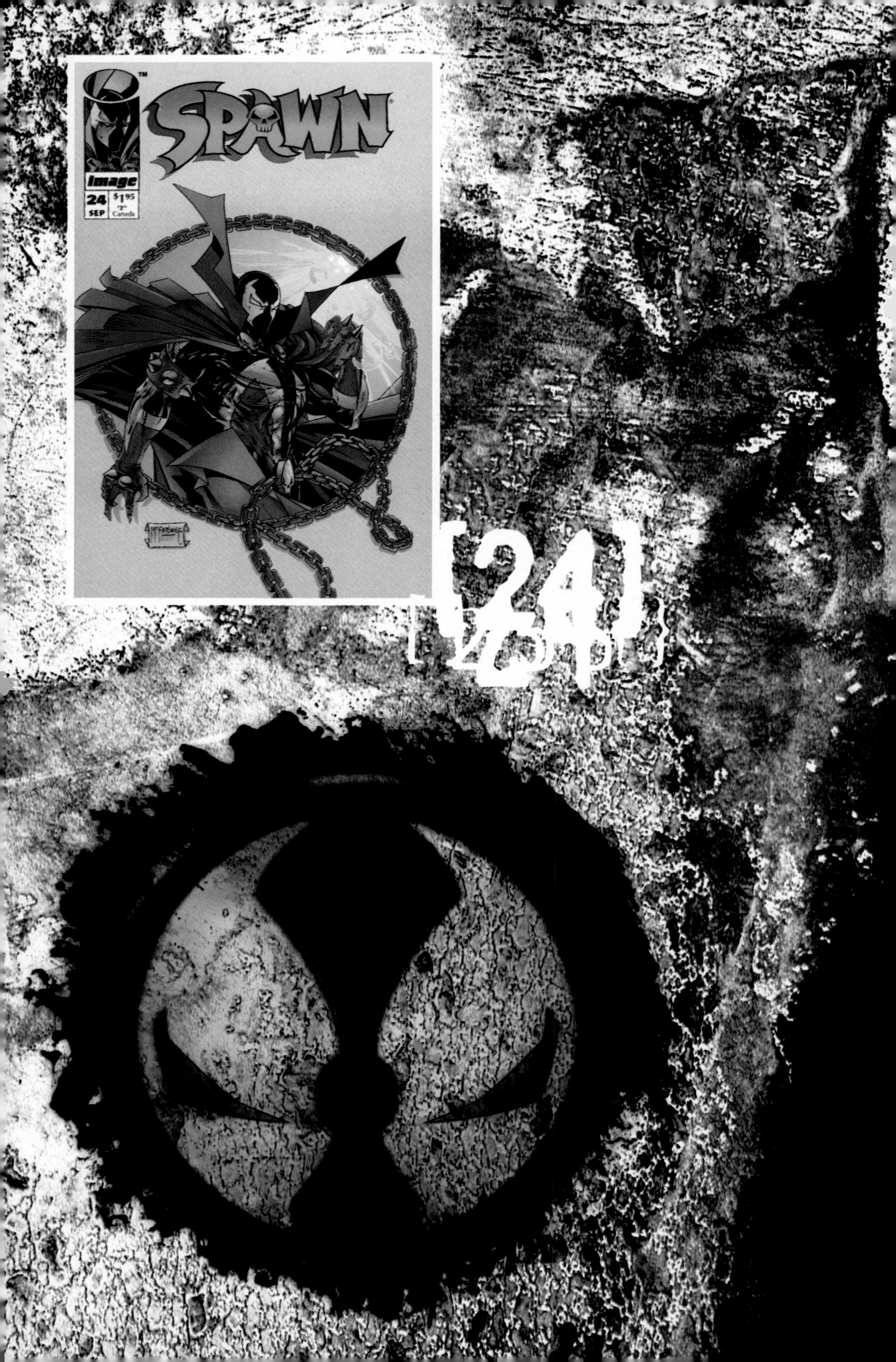
SPAWN
image
24
SEP
$1.95
[24]

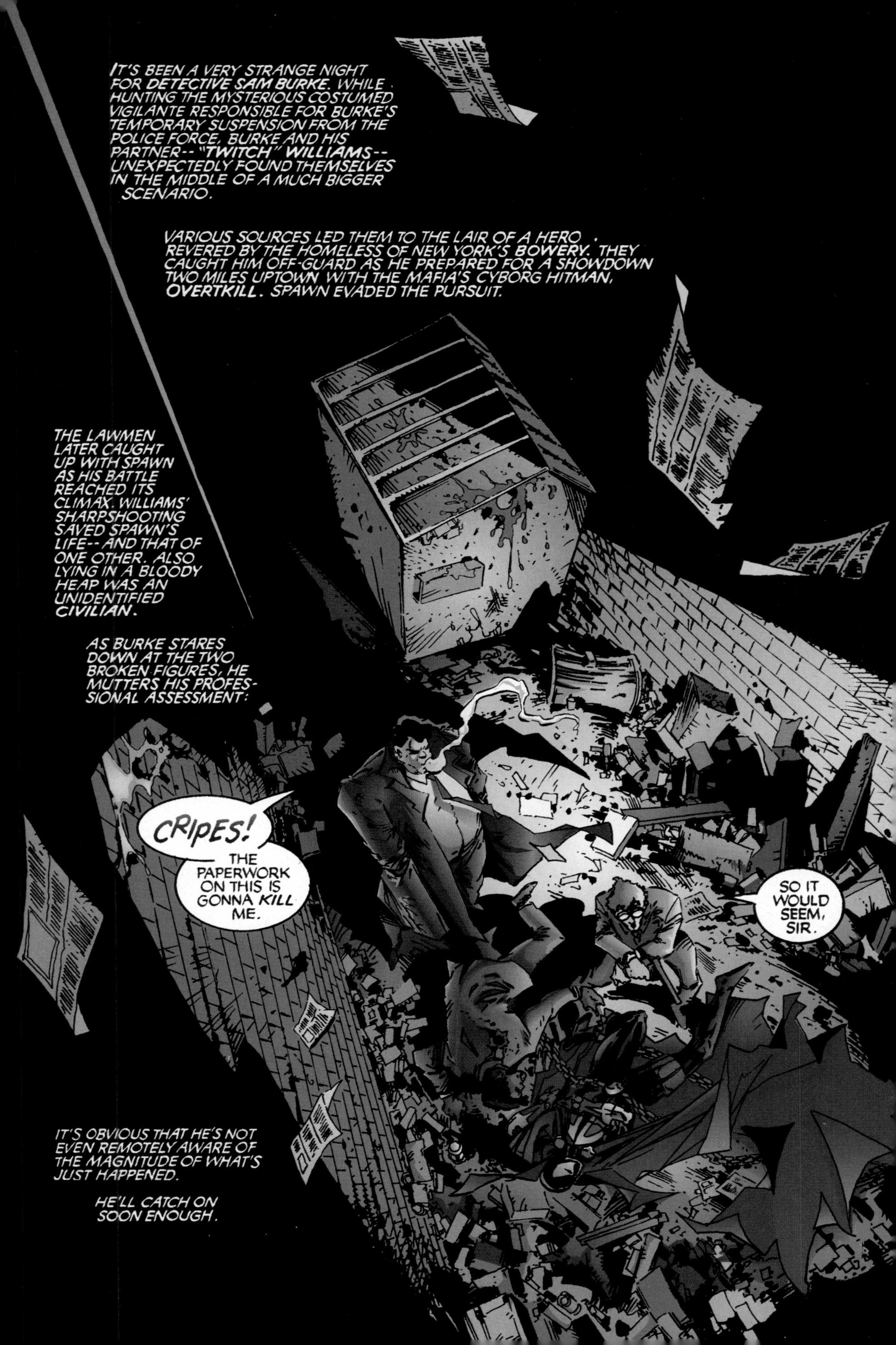
IT'S BEEN A VERY STRANGE NIGHT FOR DETECTIVE SAM BURKE. WHILE HUNTING THE MYSTERIOUS COSTUMED VIGILANTE RESPONSIBLE FOR BURKE'S TEMPORARY SUSPENSION FROM THE POLICE FORCE, BURKE AND HIS PARTNER-- "TWITCH" WILLIAMS-- UNEXPECTEDLY FOUND THEMSELVES IN THE MIDDLE OF A MUCH BIGGER SCENARIO.
VARIOUS SOURCES LED THEM TO THE LAIR OF A HERO REVERED BY THE HOMELESS OF NEW YORK'S BOWERY. THEY CAUGHT HIM OFF-GUARD AS HE PREPARED FOR A SHOWDOWN TWO MILES UPTOWN WITH THE MAFIA'S CYBORG HITMAN, OVERTKILL. SPAWN EVADED THE PURSUIT.
THE LAWMEN LATER CAUGHT UP WITH SPAWN AS HIS BATTLE REACHED ITS CLIMAX. WILLIAMS' SHARPSHOOTING SAVED SPAWN'S LIFE-- AND THAT OF ONE OTHER. ALSO LYING IN A BLOODY HEAP WAS AN UNIDENTIFIED CIVILIAN.
AS BURKE STARES DOWN AT THE TWO BROKEN FIGURES, HE MUTTERS HIS PROFESSIONAL ASSESSMENT:
CRIPES! THE PAPERWORK ON THIS IS GONNA KILL ME.
SO IT WOULD SEEM, SIR.
IT'S OBVIOUS THAT HE'S NOT EVEN REMOTELY AWARE OF THE MAGNITUDE OF WHAT'S JUST HAPPENED.
HE'LL CATCH ON SOON ENOUGH.

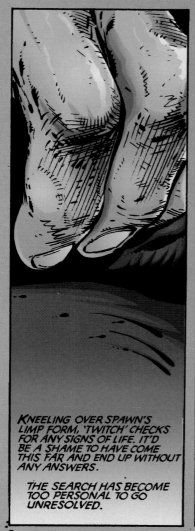

Kneeling over Spawn's limp form, 'Twitch' checks for any signs of life. It'd be a shame to have come this far and end up without any answers.

The search has become too personal to go unresolved.

SO... WHAT'S THE SCOOP?

HE MIGHT BE DEAD.

I'M NOT FINDING A PULSE.

I'LL TRY SOME C.P.R.

THE MASK IS DRAWN BACK, REVEALING WHAT'S LEFT OF THE MAN CALLED AL SIMMONS.

JEEEZUS!!

WHAT THE HELL HAPPENED TO HIM?!

MY GOD.

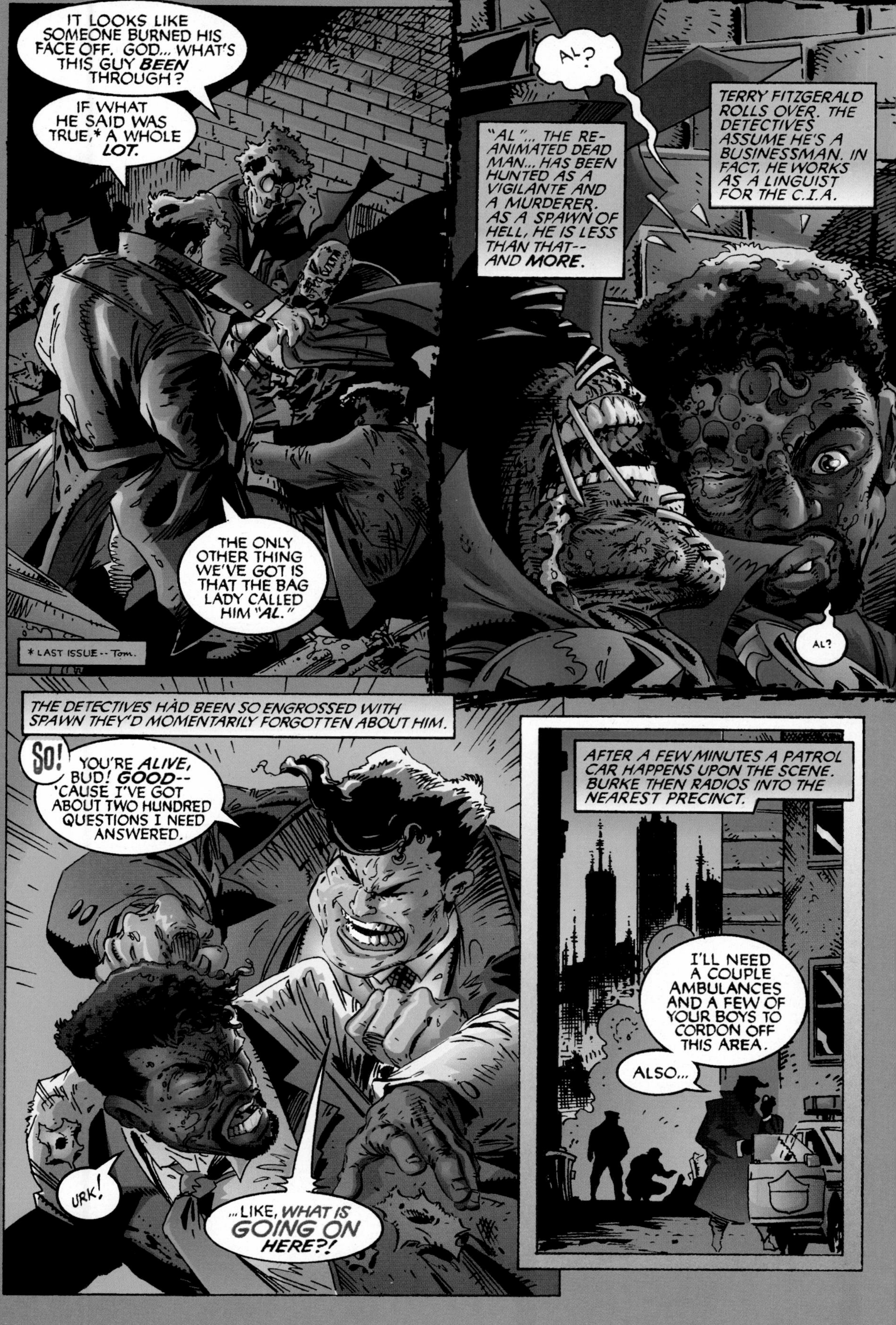
IT LOOKS LIKE SOMEONE BURNED HIS FACE OFF. GOD... WHAT'S THIS GUY BEEN THROUGH?
IF WHAT HE SAID WAS TRUE,* A WHOLE LOT.
THE ONLY OTHER THING WE'VE GOT IS THAT THE BAG LADY CALLED HIM "AL."
* LAST ISSUE -- Tom.
AL?
"AL"... THE RE-ANIMATED DEAD MAN... HAS BEEN HUNTED AS A VIGILANTE AND A MURDERER. AS A SPAWN OF HELL, HE IS LESS THAN THAT-- AND MORE.
TERRY FITZGERALD ROLLS OVER. THE DETECTIVES ASSUME HE'S A BUSINESSMAN. IN FACT, HE WORKS AS A LINGUIST FOR THE C.I.A.
AL?
THE DETECTIVES HAD BEEN SO ENGROSSED WITH SPAWN THEY'D MOMENTARILY FORGOTTEN ABOUT HIM.
SO! YOU'RE ALIVE, BUD! GOOD-- 'CAUSE I'VE GOT ABOUT TWO HUNDRED QUESTIONS I NEED ANSWERED.
URK!
...LIKE, WHAT IS GOING ON HERE?!
AFTER A FEW MINUTES A PATROL CAR HAPPENS UPON THE SCENE. BURKE THEN RADIOS INTO THE NEAREST PRECINCT.
I'LL NEED A COUPLE AMBULANCES AND A FEW OF YOUR BOYS TO CORDON OFF THIS AREA.
ALSO...

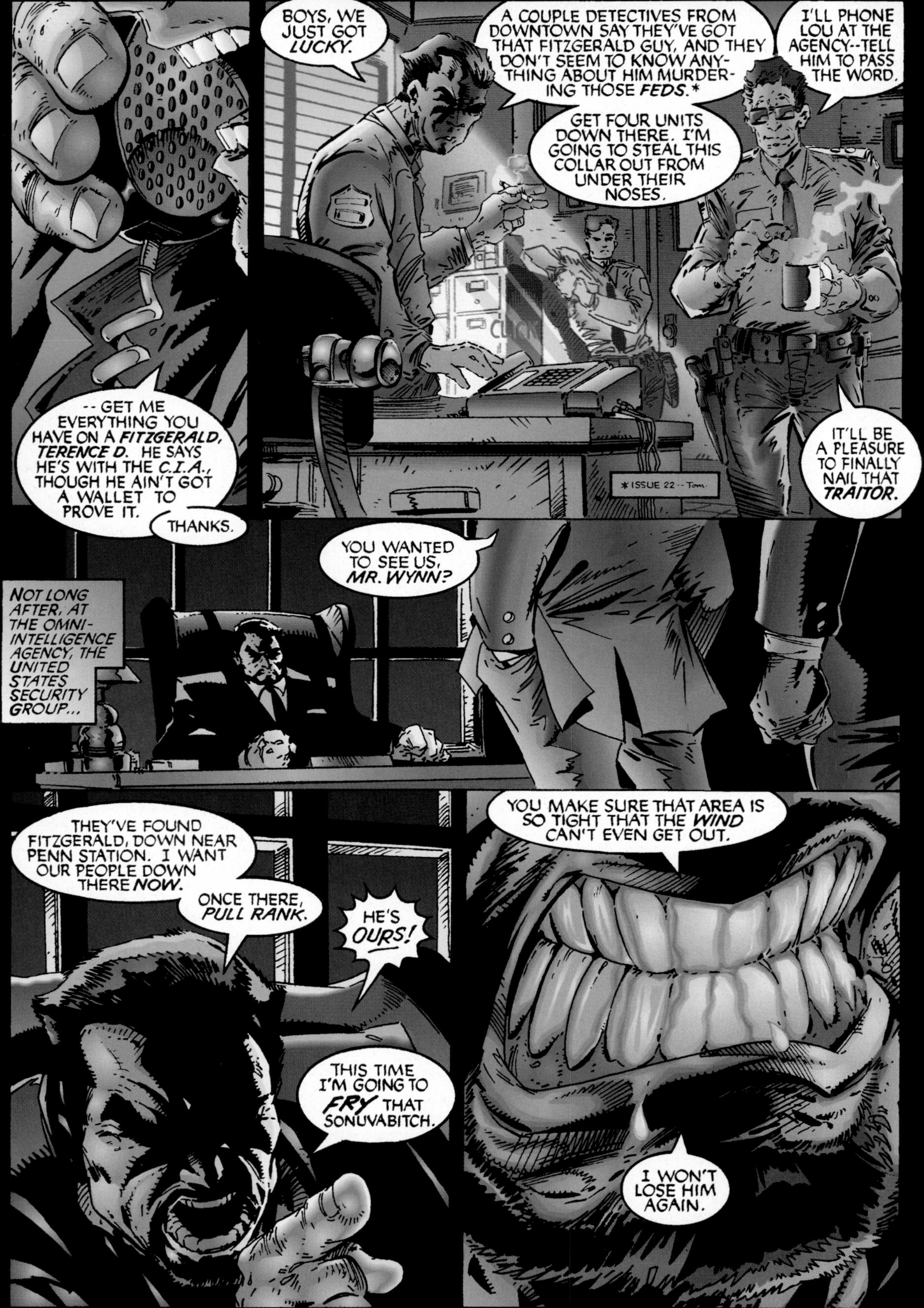
-- GET ME EVERYTHING YOU HAVE ON A FITZGERALD, TERENCE D. HE SAYS HE'S WITH THE C.I.A., THOUGH HE AIN'T GOT A WALLET TO PROVE IT.
THANKS.
BOYS, WE JUST GOT LUCKY.
A COUPLE DETECTIVES FROM DOWNTOWN SAY THEY'VE GOT THAT FITZGERALD GUY, AND THEY DON'T SEEM TO KNOW ANYTHING ABOUT HIM MURDERING THOSE FEDS.*
GET FOUR UNITS DOWN THERE. I'M GOING TO STEAL THIS COLLAR OUT FROM UNDER THEIR NOSES.
I'LL PHONE LOU AT THE AGENCY--TELL HIM TO PASS THE WORD.
IT'LL BE A PLEASURE TO FINALLY NAIL THAT TRAITOR.
CLICK
*ISSUE 22 -- Tom.
NOT LONG AFTER, AT THE OMNI-INTELLIGENCE AGENCY, THE UNITED STATES SECURITY GROUP...
YOU WANTED TO SEE US, MR. WYNN?
THEY'VE FOUND FITZGERALD, DOWN NEAR PENN STATION. I WANT OUR PEOPLE DOWN THERE NOW.
ONCE THERE, PULL RANK.
HE'S OURS!
THIS TIME I'M GOING TO FRY THAT SONUVABITCH.
YOU MAKE SURE THAT AREA IS SO TIGHT THAT THE WIND CAN'T EVEN GET OUT.
I WON'T LOSE HIM AGAIN.

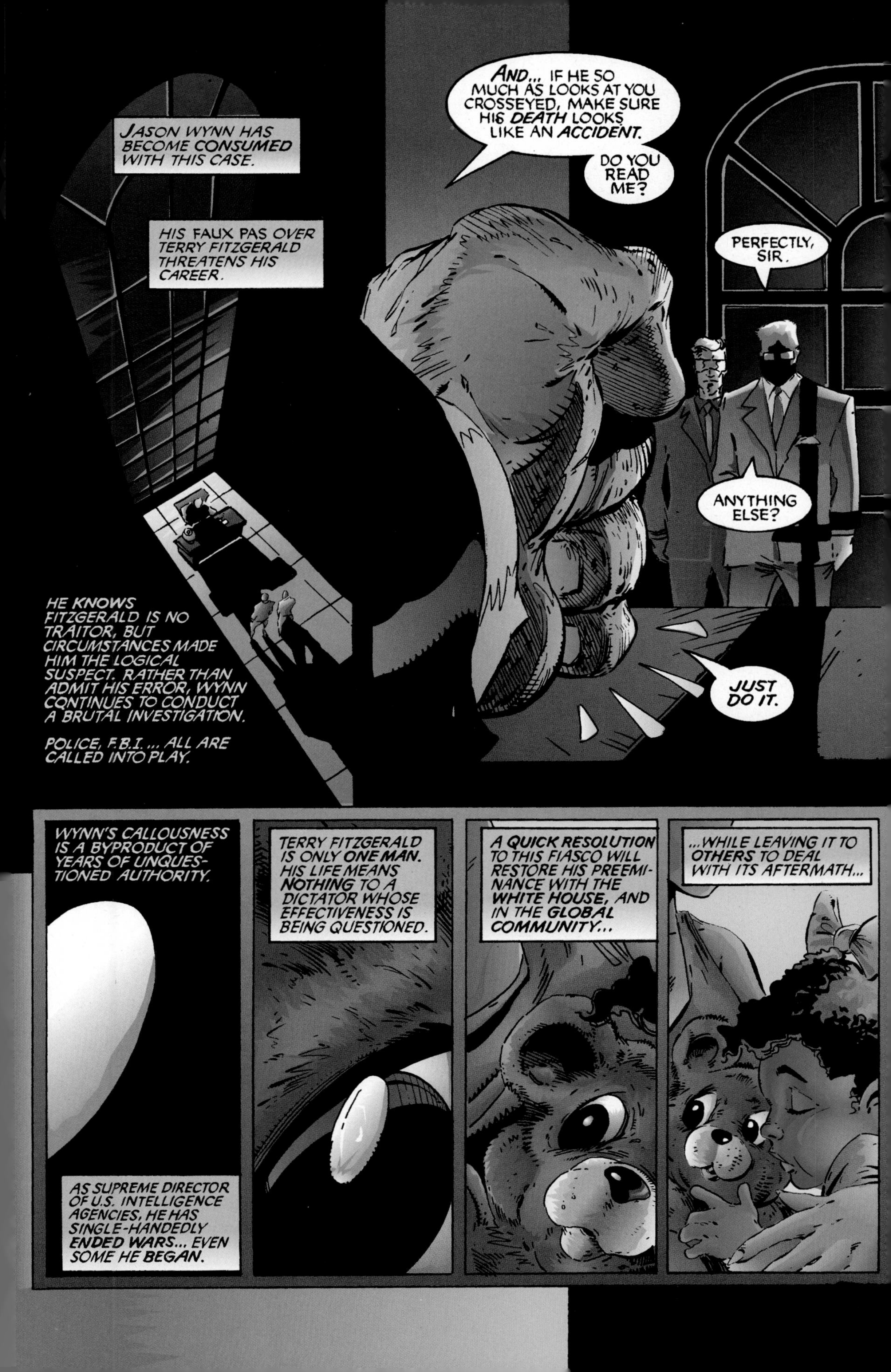
JASON WYNN HAS BECOME CONSUMED WITH THIS CASE.
HIS FAUX PAS OVER TERRY FITZGERALD THREATENS HIS CAREER.
HE KNOWS FITZGERALD IS NO TRAITOR, BUT CIRCUMSTANCES MADE HIM THE LOGICAL SUSPECT. RATHER THAN ADMIT HIS ERROR, WYNN CONTINUES TO CONDUCT A BRUTAL INVESTIGATION.
POLICE, F.B.I. ... ALL ARE CALLED INTO PLAY.
AND... IF HE SO MUCH AS LOOKS AT YOU CROSSEYED, MAKE SURE HIS DEATH LOOKS LIKE AN ACCIDENT.
DO YOU READ ME?
PERFECTLY, SIR.
ANYTHING ELSE?
JUST DO IT.
WYNN'S CALLOUSNESS IS A BYPRODUCT OF YEARS OF UNQUESTIONED AUTHORITY.
AS SUPREME DIRECTOR OF U.S. INTELLIGENCE AGENCIES, HE HAS SINGLE-HANDEDLY ENDED WARS... EVEN SOME HE BEGAN.
TERRY FITZGERALD IS ONLY ONE MAN. HIS LIFE MEANS NOTHING TO A DICTATOR WHOSE EFFECTIVENESS IS BEING QUESTIONED.
A QUICK RESOLUTION TO THIS FIASCO WILL RESTORE HIS PREEMINANCE WITH THE WHITE HOUSE, AND IN THE GLOBAL COMMUNITY...
...WHILE LEAVING IT TO OTHERS TO DEAL WITH ITS AFTERMATH...

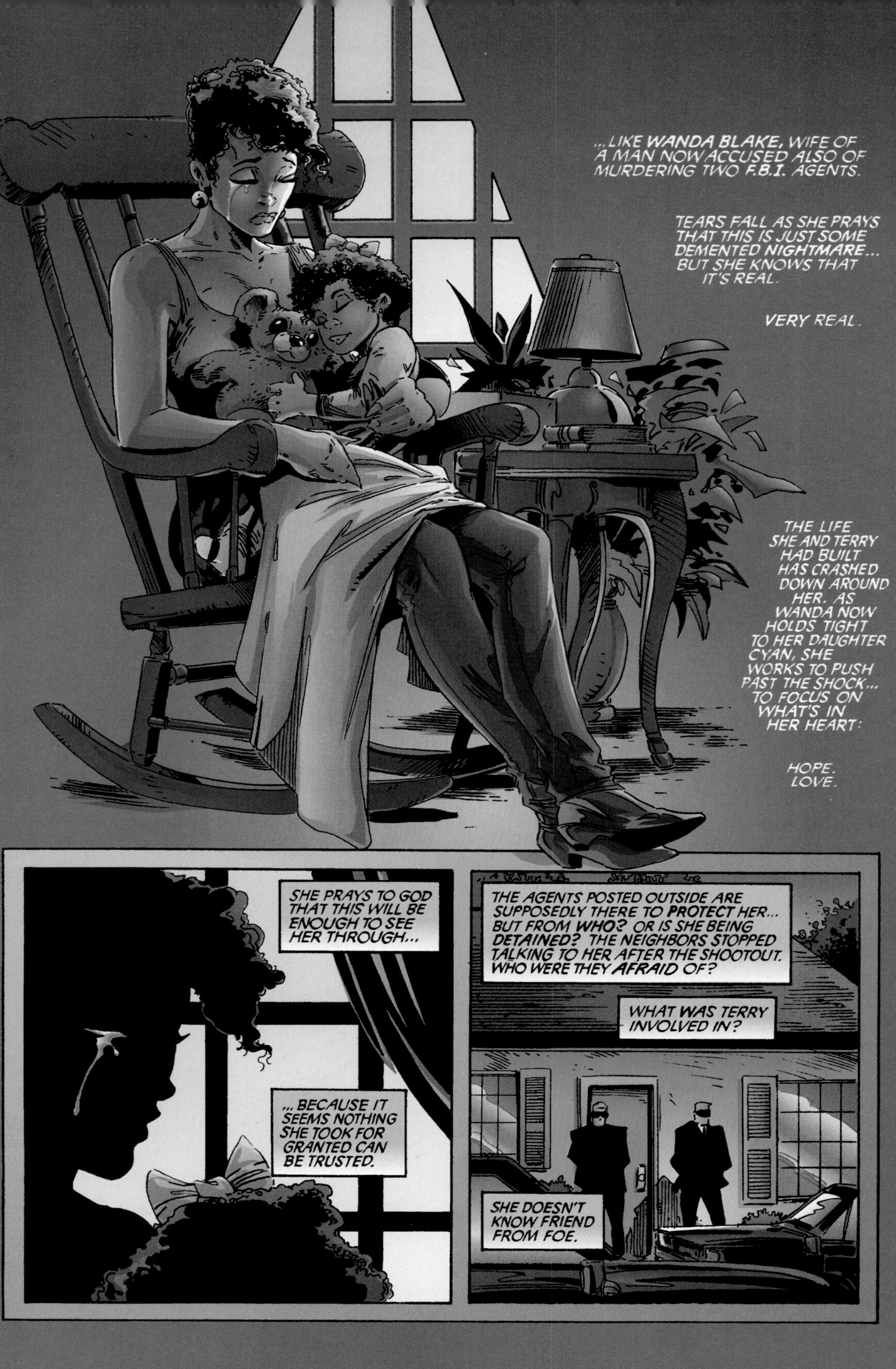
...LIKE WANDA BLAKE, WIFE OF A MAN NOW ACCUSED ALSO OF MURDERING TWO F.B.I. AGENTS.
TEARS FALL AS SHE PRAYS THAT THIS IS JUST SOME DEMENTED NIGHTMARE... BUT SHE KNOWS THAT IT'S REAL.
VERY REAL.
THE LIFE SHE AND TERRY HAD BUILT HAS CRASHED DOWN AROUND HER. AS WANDA NOW HOLDS TIGHT TO HER DAUGHTER CYAN, SHE WORKS TO PUSH PAST THE SHOCK... TO FOCUS ON WHAT'S IN HER HEART:
HOPE. LOVE.
SHE PRAYS TO GOD THAT THIS WILL BE ENOUGH TO SEE HER THROUGH...
...BECAUSE IT SEEMS NOTHING SHE TOOK FOR GRANTED CAN BE TRUSTED.
THE AGENTS POSTED OUTSIDE ARE SUPPOSEDLY THERE TO PROTECT HER... BUT FROM WHO? OR IS SHE BEING DETAINED? THE NEIGHBORS STOPPED TALKING TO HER AFTER THE SHOOTOUT. WHO WERE THEY AFRAID OF?
WHAT WAS TERRY INVOLVED IN?
SHE DOESN'T KNOW FRIEND FROM FOE.

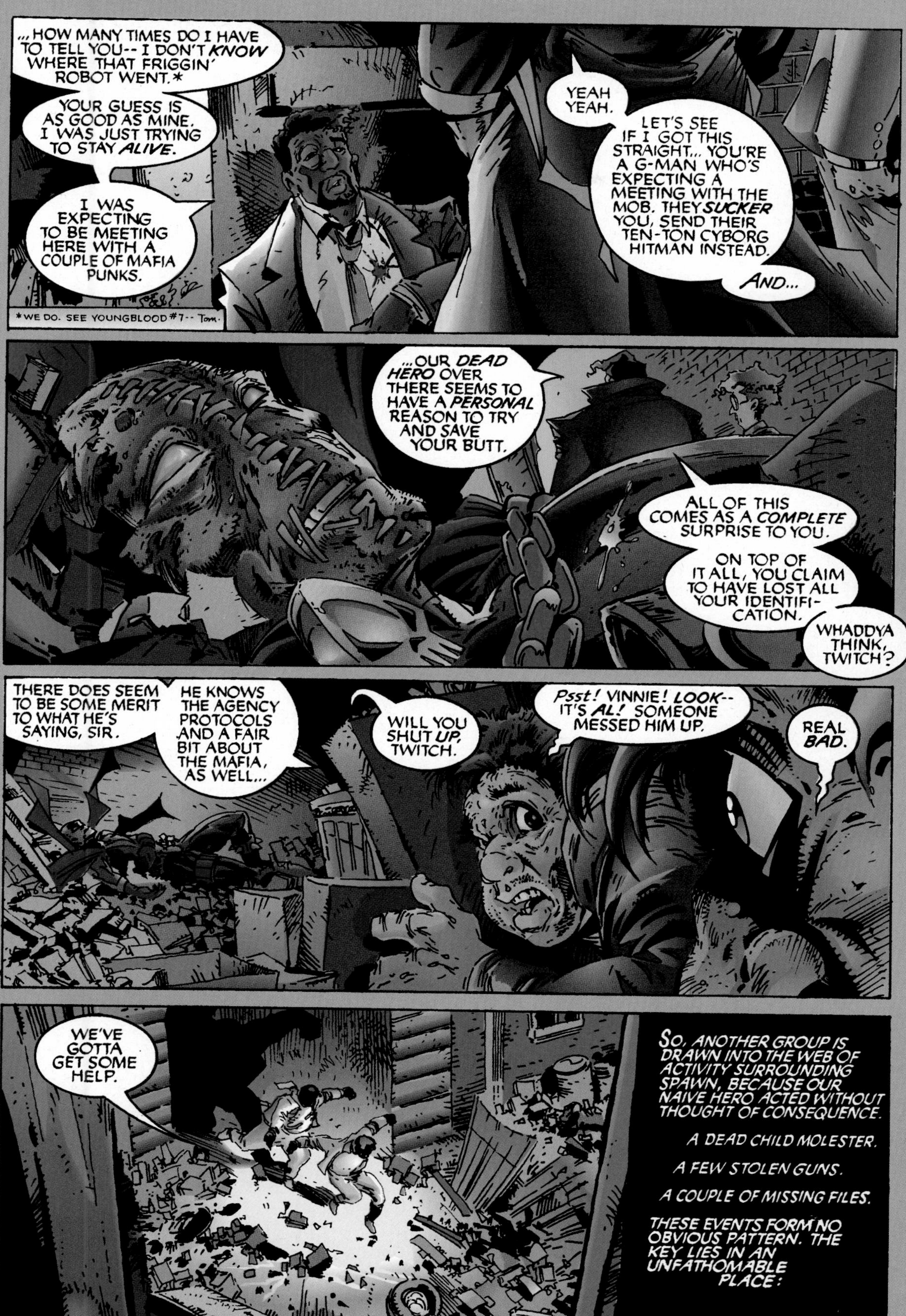
...HOW MANY TIMES DO I HAVE TO TELL YOU-- I DON'T KNOW WHERE THAT FRIGGIN' ROBOT WENT.*
YOUR GUESS IS AS GOOD AS MINE. I WAS JUST TRYING TO STAY ALIVE.
I WAS EXPECTING TO BE MEETING HERE WITH A COUPLE OF MAFIA PUNKS.
YEAH YEAH.
LET'S SEE IF I GOT THIS STRAIGHT... YOU'RE A G-MAN WHO'S EXPECTING A MEETING WITH THE MOB. THEY SUCKER YOU, SEND THEIR TEN-TON CYBORG HITMAN INSTEAD.
AND...
*WE DO. SEE YOUNGBLOOD #7-- Tom.
...OUR DEAD HERO OVER THERE SEEMS TO HAVE A PERSONAL REASON TO TRY AND SAVE YOUR BUTT.
ALL OF THIS COMES AS A COMPLETE SURPRISE TO YOU.
ON TOP OF IT ALL, YOU CLAIM TO HAVE LOST ALL YOUR IDENTIFI-CATION.
WHADDYA THINK, TWITCH?
THERE DOES SEEM TO BE SOME MERIT TO WHAT HE'S SAYING, SIR.
HE KNOWS THE AGENCY PROTOCOLS AND A FAIR BIT ABOUT THE MAFIA, AS WELL...
WILL YOU SHUT UP, TWITCH.
Psst! VINNIE! LOOK-- IT'S AL! SOMEONE MESSED HIM UP.
REAL BAD.
WE'VE GOTTA GET SOME HELP.
SO, ANOTHER GROUP IS DRAWN INTO THE WEB OF ACTIVITY SURROUNDING SPAWN, BECAUSE OUR NAIVE HERO ACTED WITHOUT THOUGHT OF CONSEQUENCE.
A DEAD CHILD MOLESTER.
A FEW STOLEN GUNS.
A COUPLE OF MISSING FILES.
THESE EVENTS FORM NO OBVIOUS PATTERN. THE KEY LIES IN AN UNFATHOMABLE PLACE:

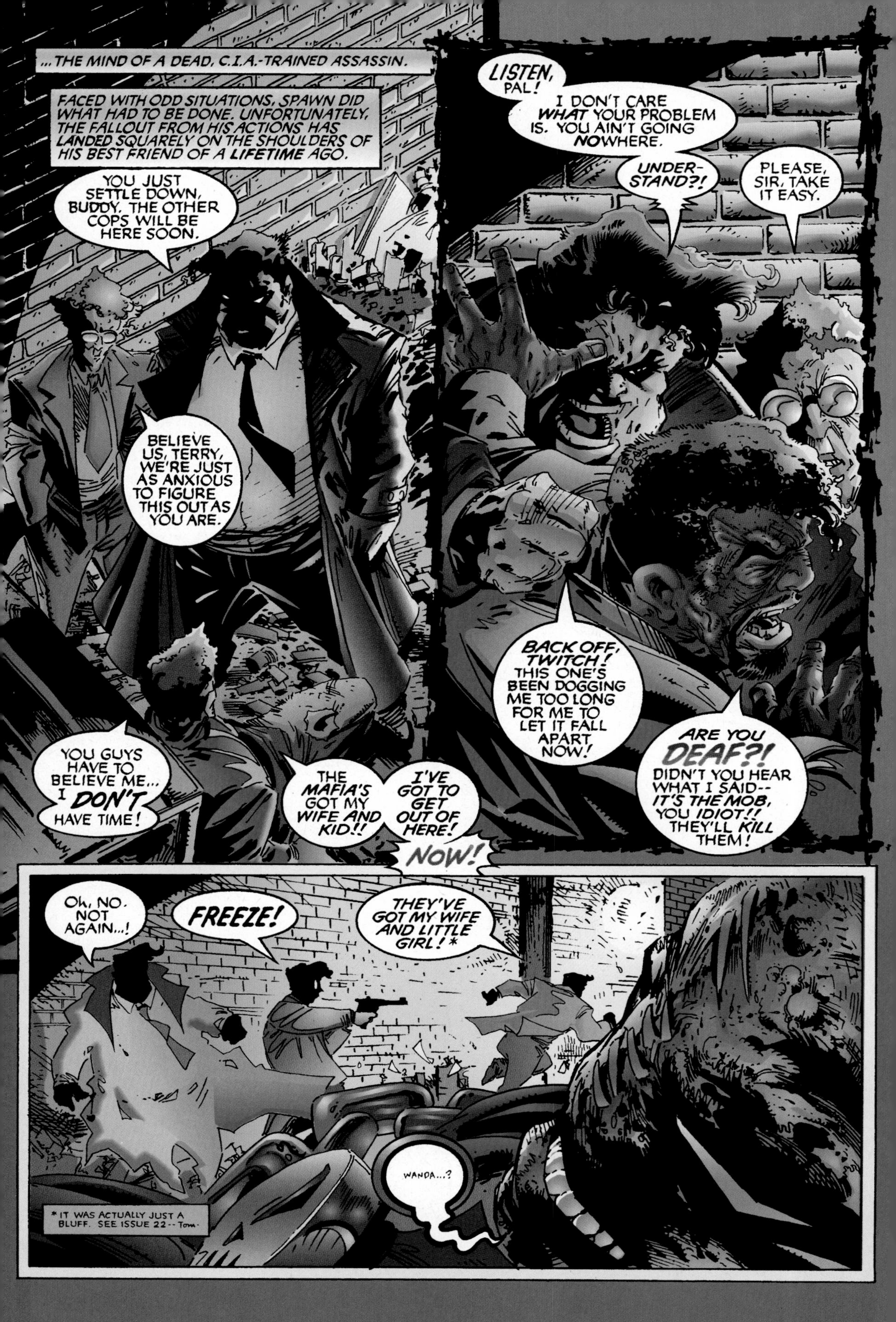
...THE MIND OF A DEAD, C.I.A.-TRAINED ASSASSIN.
FACED WITH ODD SITUATIONS, SPAWN DID WHAT HAD TO BE DONE. UNFORTUNATELY, THE FALLOUT FROM HIS ACTIONS HAS LANDED SQUARELY ON THE SHOULDERS OF HIS BEST FRIEND OF A LIFETIME AGO.
YOU JUST SETTLE DOWN, BUDDY. THE OTHER COPS WILL BE HERE SOON.
BELIEVE US, TERRY, WE'RE JUST AS ANXIOUS TO FIGURE THIS OUT AS YOU ARE.
YOU GUYS HAVE TO BELIEVE ME... I DON'T HAVE TIME!
THE MAFIA'S GOT MY WIFE AND KID!!
I'VE GOT TO GET OUT OF HERE!
NOW!
LISTEN, PAL!
I DON'T CARE WHAT YOUR PROBLEM IS. YOU AIN'T GOING NOWHERE.
UNDER-STAND?!
PLEASE, SIR, TAKE IT EASY.
BACK OFF, TWITCH! THIS ONE'S BEEN DOGGING ME TOO LONG FOR ME TO LET IT FALL APART NOW!
ARE YOU DEAF?! DIDN'T YOU HEAR WHAT I SAID-- IT'S THE MOB, YOU IDIOT!! THEY'LL KILL THEM!
Oh, NO. NOT AGAIN...!
FREEZE!
THEY'VE GOT MY WIFE AND LITTLE GIRL! *
WANDA...?
* IT WAS ACTUALLY JUST A BLUFF. SEE ISSUE 22 -- Tom

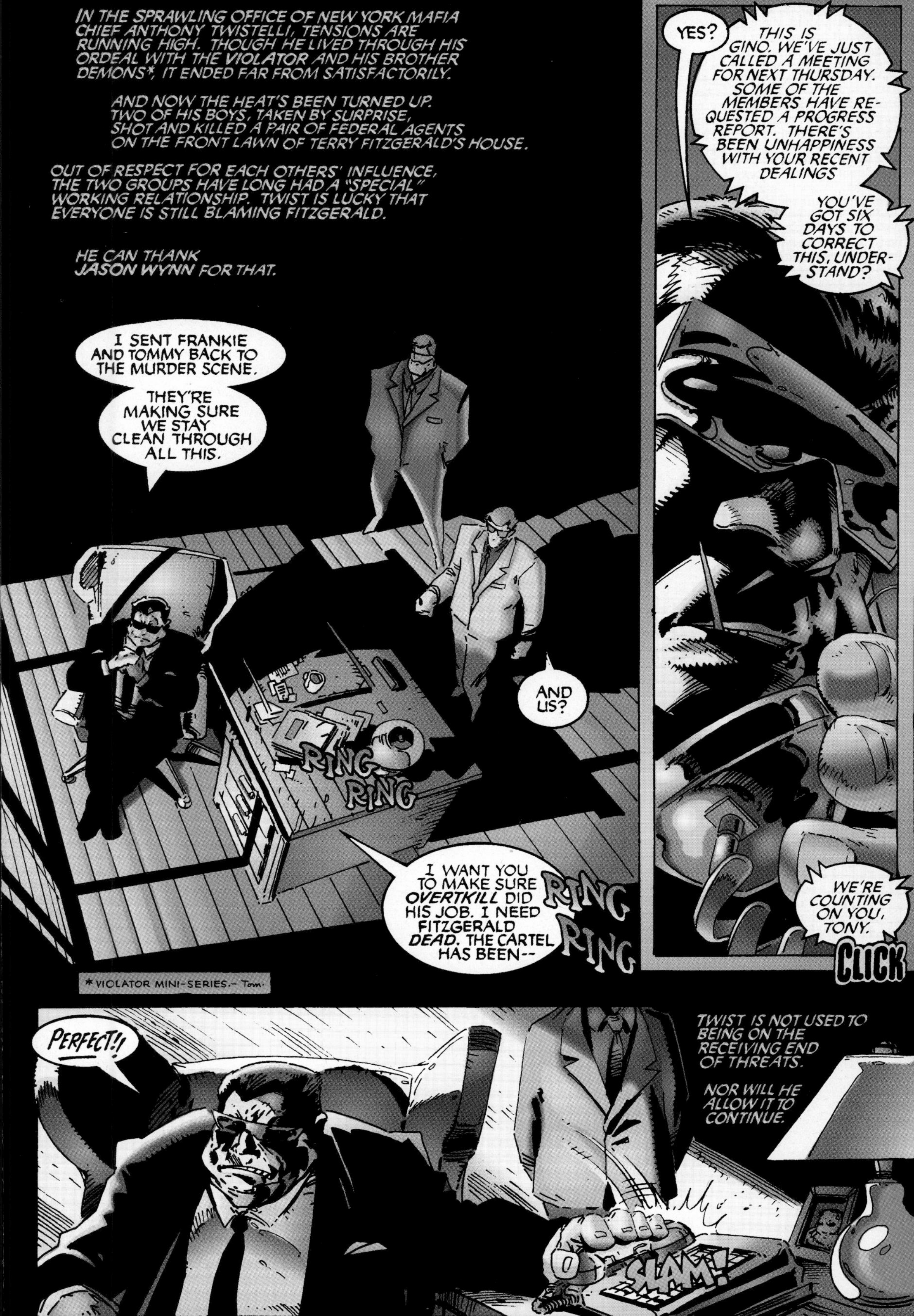
IN THE SPRAWLING OFFICE OF NEW YORK MAFIA CHIEF ANTHONY TWISTELLI, TENSIONS ARE RUNNING HIGH. THOUGH HE LIVED THROUGH HIS ORDEAL WITH THE VIOLATOR AND HIS BROTHER DEMONS*, IT ENDED FAR FROM SATISFACTORILY.
AND NOW THE HEAT'S BEEN TURNED UP. TWO OF HIS BOYS, TAKEN BY SURPRISE, SHOT AND KILLED A PAIR OF FEDERAL AGENTS ON THE FRONT LAWN OF TERRY FITZGERALD'S HOUSE.
OUT OF RESPECT FOR EACH OTHERS' INFLUENCE, THE TWO GROUPS HAVE LONG HAD A "SPECIAL" WORKING RELATIONSHIP. TWIST IS LUCKY THAT EVERYONE IS STILL BLAMING FITZGERALD.
HE CAN THANK JASON WYNN FOR THAT.
I SENT FRANKIE AND TOMMY BACK TO THE MURDER SCENE.
THEY'RE MAKING SURE WE STAY CLEAN THROUGH ALL THIS.
AND US?
RING RING
I WANT YOU TO MAKE SURE OVERTKILL DID HIS JOB. I NEED FITZGERALD DEAD. THE CARTEL HAS BEEN--
RING RING
YES?
THIS IS GINO. WE'VE JUST CALLED A MEETING FOR NEXT THURSDAY. SOME OF THE MEMBERS HAVE REQUESTED A PROGRESS REPORT. THERE'S BEEN UNHAPPINESS WITH YOUR RECENT DEALINGS
YOU'VE GOT SIX DAYS TO CORRECT THIS, UNDERSTAND?
WE'RE COUNTING ON YOU, TONY.
CLICK
*VIOLATOR MINI-SERIES.- Tom.
PERFECT!!
TWIST IS NOT USED TO BEING ON THE RECEIVING END OF THREATS.
NOR WILL HE ALLOW IT TO CONTINUE.
SLAM!

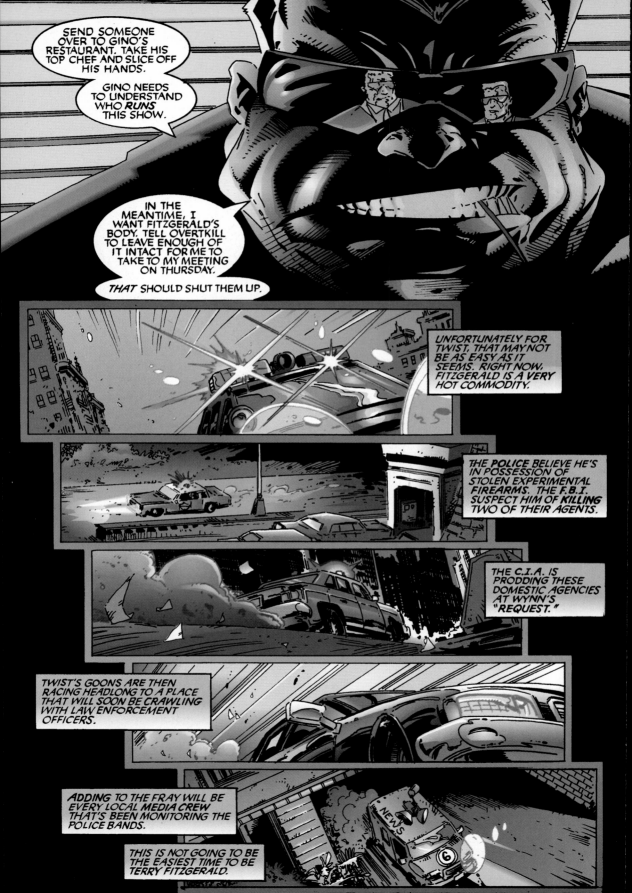

SEND SOMEONE OVER TO GINO'S RESTAURANT. TAKE HIS TOP CHEF AND SLICE OFF HIS HANDS.

GINO NEEDS TO UNDERSTAND WHO *RUNS* THIS SHOW.

IN THE MEANTIME, I WANT FITZGERALD'S BODY. TELL OVERTKILL TO LEAVE ENOUGH OF IT INTACT FOR ME TO TAKE TO MY MEETING ON THURSDAY.

THAT SHOULD SHUT THEM UP.

UNFORTUNATELY FOR TWIST, THAT MAY NOT BE AS EASY AS IT SEEMS. RIGHT NOW, FITZGERALD IS A VERY HOT COMMODITY.

THE *POLICE* BELIEVE HE'S IN POSSESSION OF STOLEN EXPERIMENTAL FIREARMS. THE F.B.I. SUSPECT HIM OF *KILLING* TWO OF THEIR AGENTS.

THE C.I.A. IS PRODDING THESE DOMESTIC AGENCIES AT WYNN'S "REQUEST."

TWIST'S GOONS ARE THEN RACING HEADLONG TO A PLACE THAT WILL SOON BE CRAWLING WITH LAW ENFORCEMENT OFFICERS.

ADDING TO THE FRAY WILL BE EVERY LOCAL MEDIA CREW THAT'S BEEN MONITORING THE POLICE BANDS.

THIS IS NOT GOING TO BE THE EASIEST TIME TO BE TERRY FITZGERALD.

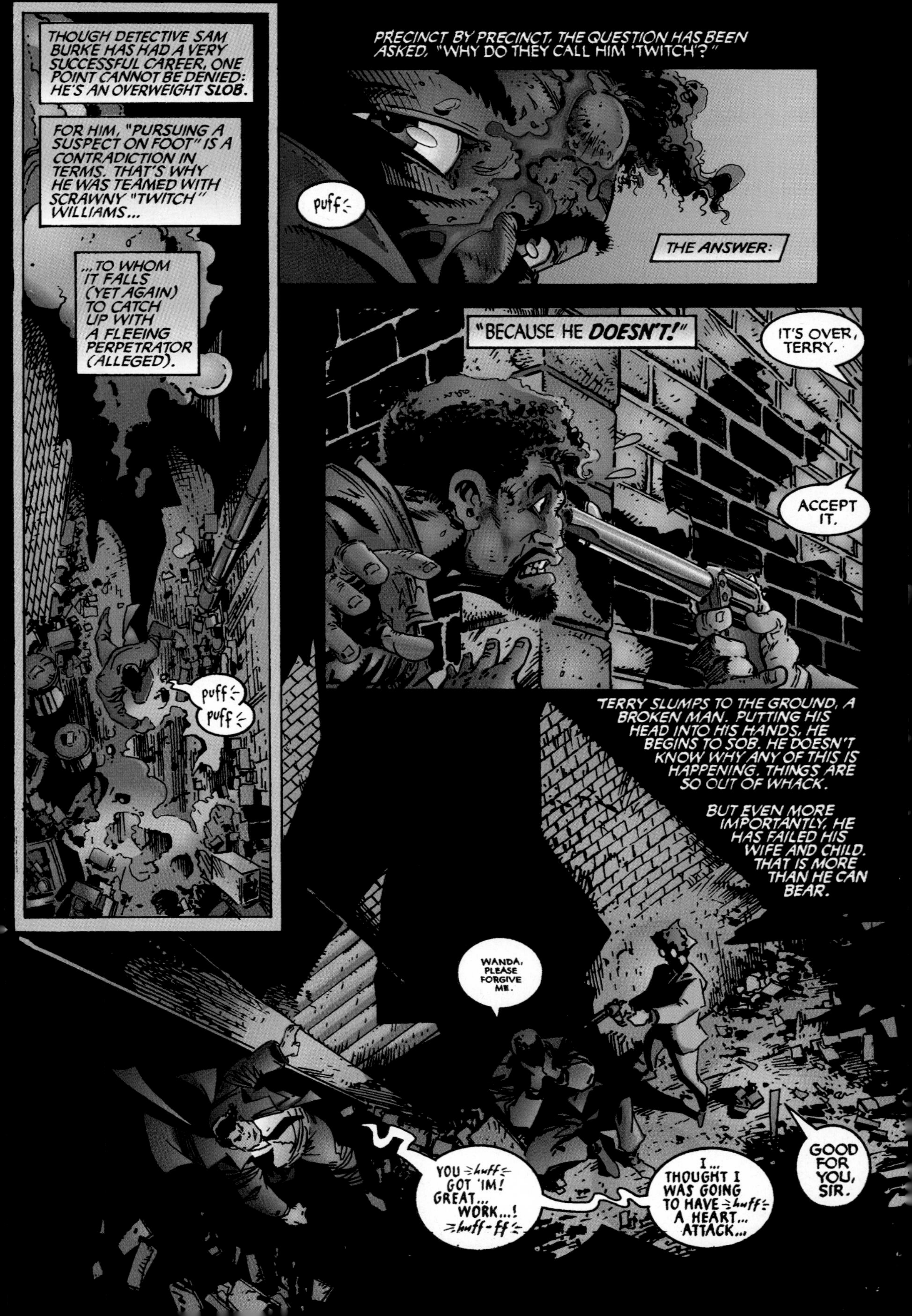
THOUGH DETECTIVE SAM BURKE HAS HAD A VERY SUCCESSFUL CAREER, ONE POINT CANNOT BE DENIED: HE'S AN OVERWEIGHT SLOB.
FOR HIM, "PURSUING A SUSPECT ON FOOT" IS A CONTRADICTION IN TERMS. THAT'S WHY HE WAS TEAMED WITH SCRAWNY "TWITCH" WILLIAMS...
...TO WHOM IT FALLS (YET AGAIN) TO CATCH UP WITH A FLEEING PERPETRATOR (ALLEGED).
puff
puff
PRECINCT BY PRECINCT, THE QUESTION HAS BEEN ASKED, "WHY DO THEY CALL HIM 'TWITCH'?"
puff
THE ANSWER:
"BECAUSE HE DOESN'T!"
IT'S OVER, TERRY.
ACCEPT IT.
TERRY SLUMPS TO THE GROUND, A BROKEN MAN. PUTTING HIS HEAD INTO HIS HANDS, HE BEGINS TO SOB. HE DOESN'T KNOW WHY ANY OF THIS IS HAPPENING. THINGS ARE SO OUT OF WHACK.
BUT EVEN MORE IMPORTANTLY, HE HAS FAILED HIS WIFE AND CHILD. THAT IS MORE THAN HE CAN BEAR.
WANDA, PLEASE FORGIVE ME.
YOU huff GOT 'IM! GREAT... WORK...! huff-ff
I... THOUGHT I WAS GOING TO HAVE huff A HEART... ATTACK...
GOOD FOR YOU, SIR.

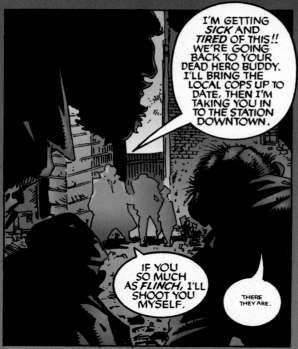

I'M GETTING *SICK* AND *TIRED* OF THIS!! WE'RE GOING BACK TO YOUR *DEAD HERO* BUDDY. I'LL BRING THE LOCAL COPS UP TO DATE, THEN I'M TAKING YOU IN TO THE STATION DOWNTOWN.

IF YOU SO MUCH AS *FLINCH*, I'LL SHOOT YOU MYSELF.

THERE THEY ARE.

HEY!

KUNK!

GET OUT OF HERE! GET OUT OF OUR ALLEY! *OUT OF OUR ALLEY!*

THEY STAND POISED IN THE MOONLIGHT, READY TO TAKE BACK WHAT IS THEIRS-- READY TO DEFEND THEIR FALLEN KING: *SPAWN.*

CANS. BOTTLES. WOOD. WHATEVER. THEY PELT THE TWO DETECTIVES RELENTLESSLY. TERRY SEES ANOTHER OPPOR- TUNITY TO FLEE.

NOW DISTANCED FROM THE POLICE, HE'S SPOTTED BY THE FIRST GROUP ON THE SCENE -- *THE C.I.A.*

SAY GOODNIGHT, TRAITOR.

The proverbial 'pedal' is put to the 'metal.'

SIR, WE NEED TO FALL BACK!

I KNOW! I KNOW!

YOU GRAB FITZY! I'LL COVER YOU!

EVERYONE'S GOING *CRAZY* TONIGHT!

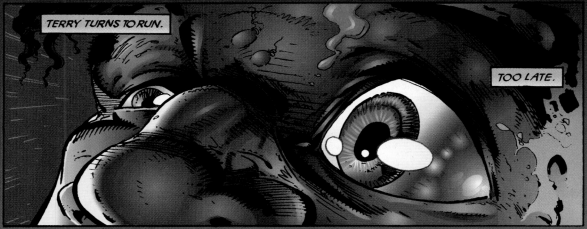

TERRY TURNS TO RUN.

TOO LATE.

HE STANDS FROZEN, STARING AT THE HEADLIGHTS LIKE SOME WILD ANIMAL ON THE HIGHWAY.

HE KNOWS HIS LUCK HAS FINALLY RUN OUT.

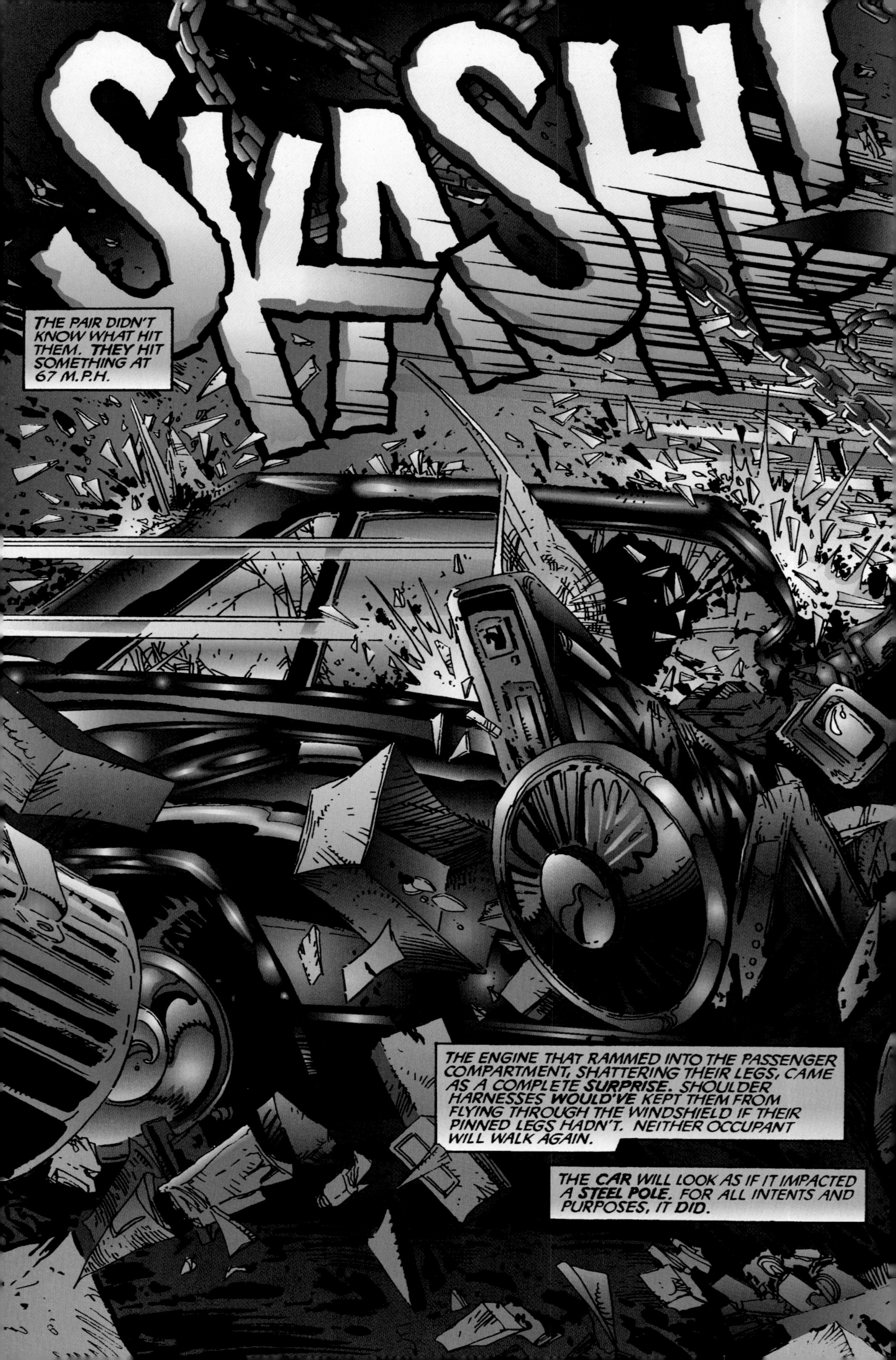
SMASH!
THE PAIR DIDN'T KNOW WHAT HIT THEM. THEY HIT SOMETHING AT 67 M.P.H.
THE ENGINE THAT RAMMED INTO THE PASSENGER COMPARTMENT, SHATTERING THEIR LEGS, CAME AS A COMPLETE SURPRISE. SHOULDER HARNESSES WOULD'VE KEPT THEM FROM FLYING THROUGH THE WINDSHIELD IF THEIR PINNED LEGS HADN'T. NEITHER OCCUPANT WILL WALK AGAIN.
THE CAR WILL LOOK AS IF IT IMPACTED A STEEL POLE. FOR ALL INTENTS AND PURPOSES, IT DID.

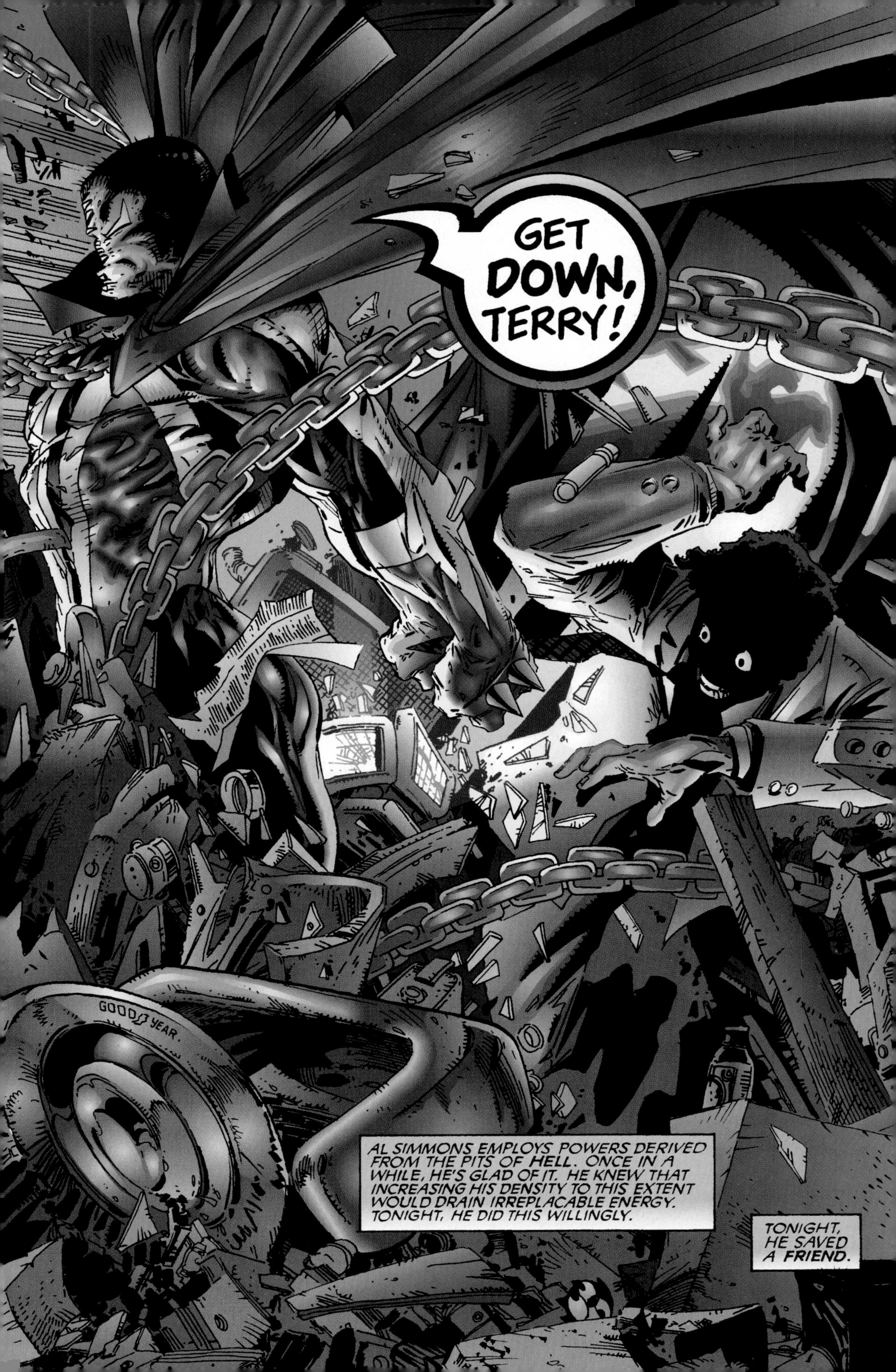
GET DOWN, TERRY!
AL SIMMONS EMPLOYS POWERS DERIVED FROM THE PITS OF HELL. ONCE IN A WHILE, HE'S GLAD OF IT. HE KNEW THAT INCREASING HIS DENSITY TO THIS EXTENT WOULD DRAIN IRREPLACABLE ENERGY. TONIGHT, HE DID THIS WILLINGLY.
TONIGHT, HE SAVED A FRIEND.
GOODYEAR

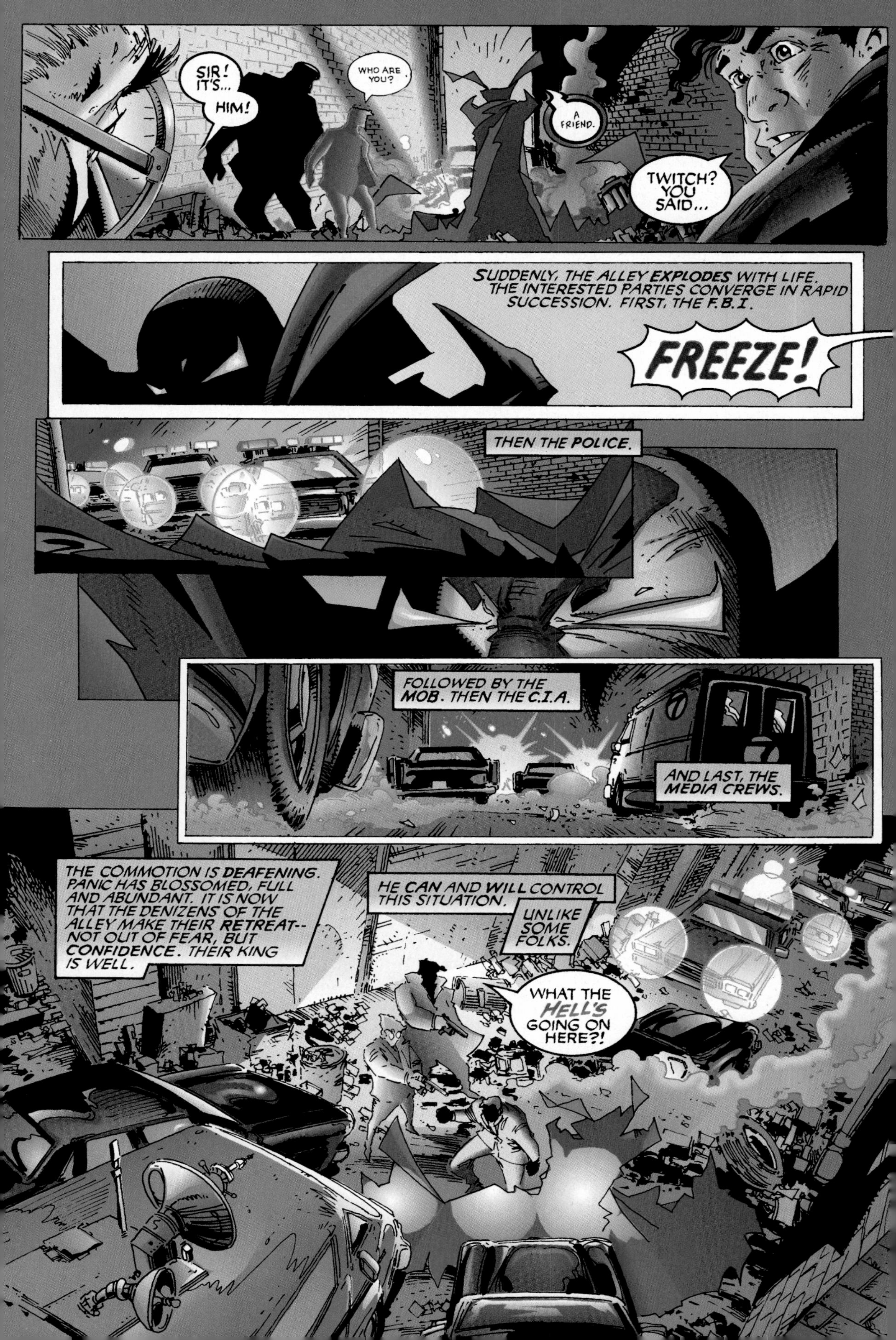
SIR! IT'S... HIM!
WHO ARE YOU?
A FRIEND.
TWITCH? YOU SAID...
SUDDENLY, THE ALLEY EXPLODES WITH LIFE. THE INTERESTED PARTIES CONVERGE IN RAPID SUCCESSION. FIRST, THE F.B.I.
FREEZE!
THEN THE POLICE.
FOLLOWED BY THE MOB. THEN THE C.I.A.
AND LAST, THE MEDIA CREWS.
THE COMMOTION IS DEAFENING. PANIC HAS BLOSSOMED, FULL AND ABUNDANT. IT IS NOW THAT THE DENIZENS OF THE ALLEY MAKE THEIR RETREAT-- NOT OUT OF FEAR, BUT CONFIDENCE. THEIR KING IS WELL.
HE CAN AND WILL CONTROL THIS SITUATION.
UNLIKE SOME FOLKS.
WHAT THE HELL'S GOING ON HERE?!

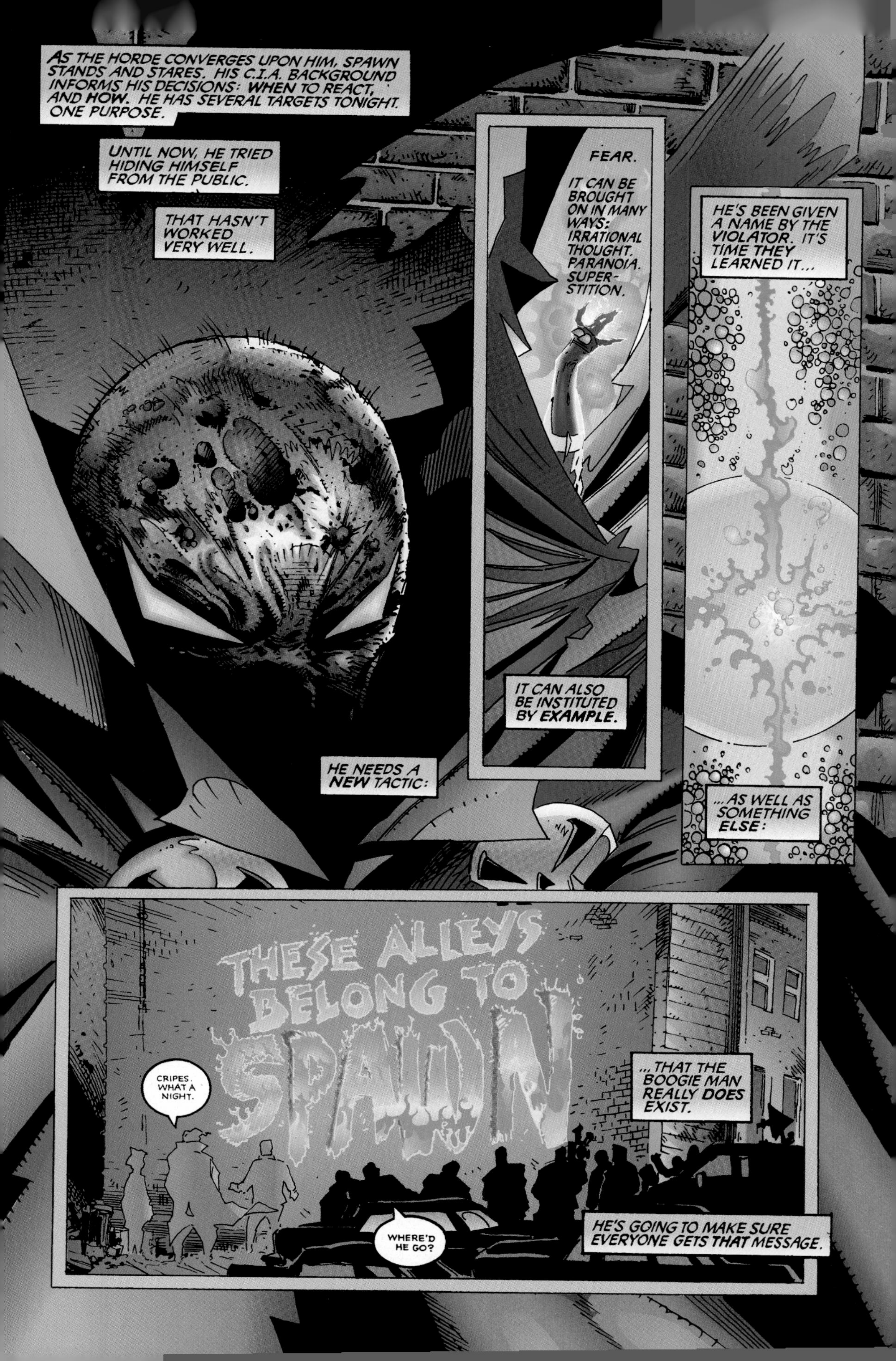

AS THE HORDE CONVERGES UPON HIM, SPAWN STANDS AND STARES. HIS C.I.A. BACKGROUND INFORMS HIS DECISIONS: WHEN TO REACT, AND HOW. HE HAS SEVERAL TARGETS TONIGHT. ONE PURPOSE.
UNTIL NOW, HE TRIED HIDING HIMSELF FROM THE PUBLIC.
THAT HASN'T WORKED VERY WELL.
HE NEEDS A NEW TACTIC:
FEAR.
IT CAN BE BROUGHT ON IN MANY WAYS: IRRATIONAL THOUGHT. PARANOIA. SUPER-STITION.
IT CAN ALSO BE INSTITUTED BY EXAMPLE.
HE'S BEEN GIVEN A NAME BY THE VIOLATOR. IT'S TIME THEY LEARNED IT...
...AS WELL AS SOMETHING ELSE:
THESE ALLEYS BELONG TO SPAWN
CRIPES. WHAT A NIGHT.
...THAT THE BOOGIE MAN REALLY DOES EXIST.
WHERE'D HE GO?
HE'S GOING TO MAKE SURE EVERYONE GETS THAT MESSAGE.

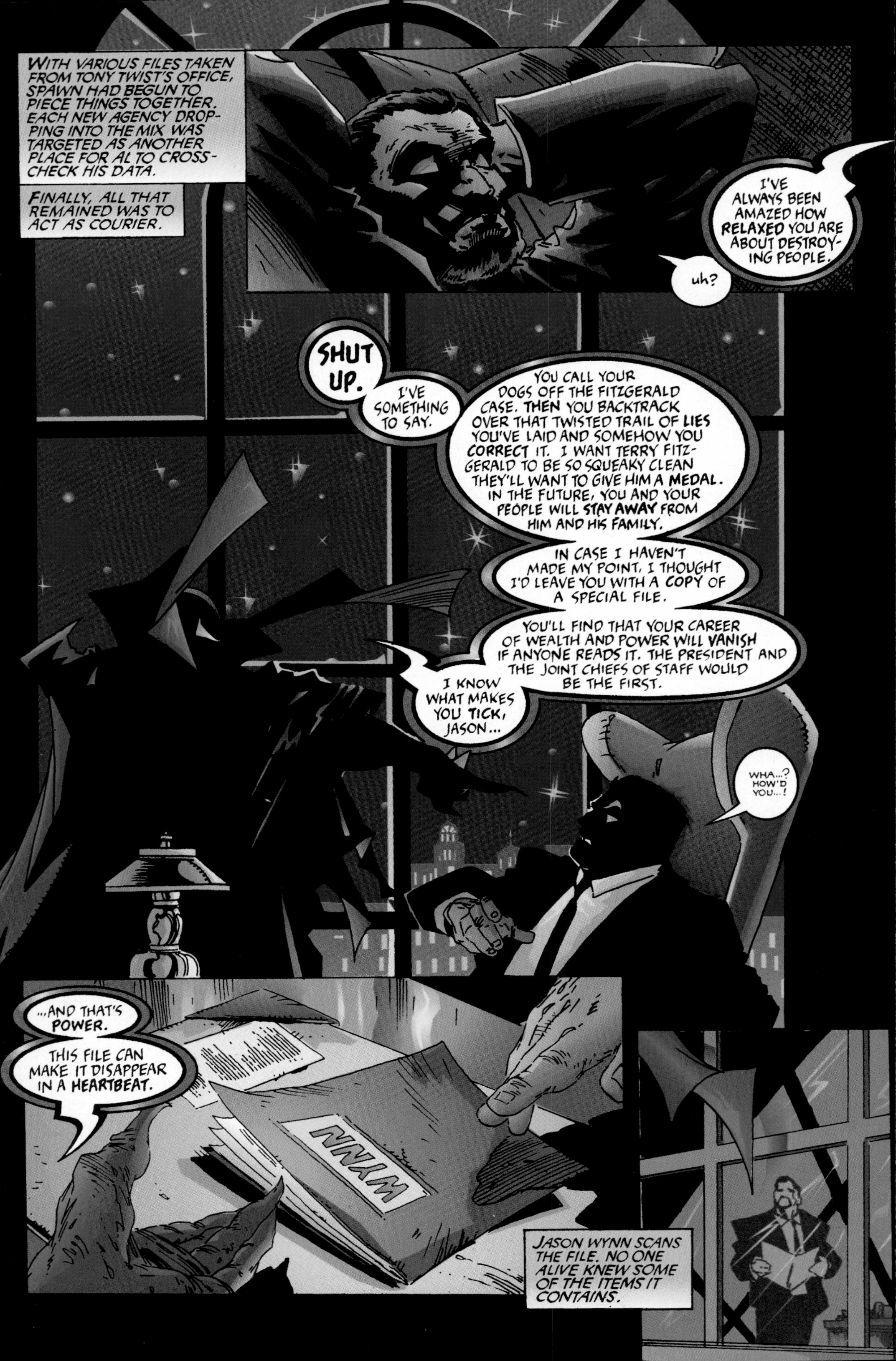
WITH VARIOUS FILES TAKEN FROM TONY TWIST'S OFFICE, SPAWN HAD BEGUN TO PIECE THINGS TOGETHER. EACH NEW AGENCY DROPPING INTO THE MIX WAS TARGETED AS ANOTHER PLACE FOR AL TO CROSS-CHECK HIS DATA.
FINALLY, ALL THAT REMAINED WAS TO ACT AS COURIER.
I'VE ALWAYS BEEN AMAZED HOW RELAXED YOU ARE ABOUT DESTROYING PEOPLE.
uh?
SHUT UP.
I'VE SOMETHING TO SAY.
YOU CALL YOUR DOGS OFF THE FITZGERALD CASE. THEN YOU BACKTRACK OVER THAT TWISTED TRAIL OF LIES YOU'VE LAID AND SOMEHOW YOU CORRECT IT. I WANT TERRY FITZGERALD TO BE SO SQUEAKY CLEAN THEY'LL WANT TO GIVE HIM A MEDAL. IN THE FUTURE, YOU AND YOUR PEOPLE WILL STAY AWAY FROM HIM AND HIS FAMILY.
IN CASE I HAVEN'T MADE MY POINT, I THOUGHT I'D LEAVE YOU WITH A COPY OF A SPECIAL FILE.
YOU'LL FIND THAT YOUR CAREER OF WEALTH AND POWER WILL VANISH IF ANYONE READS IT. THE PRESIDENT AND THE JOINT CHIEFS OF STAFF WOULD BE THE FIRST.
I KNOW WHAT MAKES YOU TICK, JASON...
WHA...? HOW'D YOU...!
...AND THAT'S POWER.
THIS FILE CAN MAKE IT DISAPPEAR IN A HEARTBEAT.
WYNN
JASON WYNN SCANS THE FILE. NO ONE ALIVE KNEW SOME OF THE ITEMS IT CONTAINS.

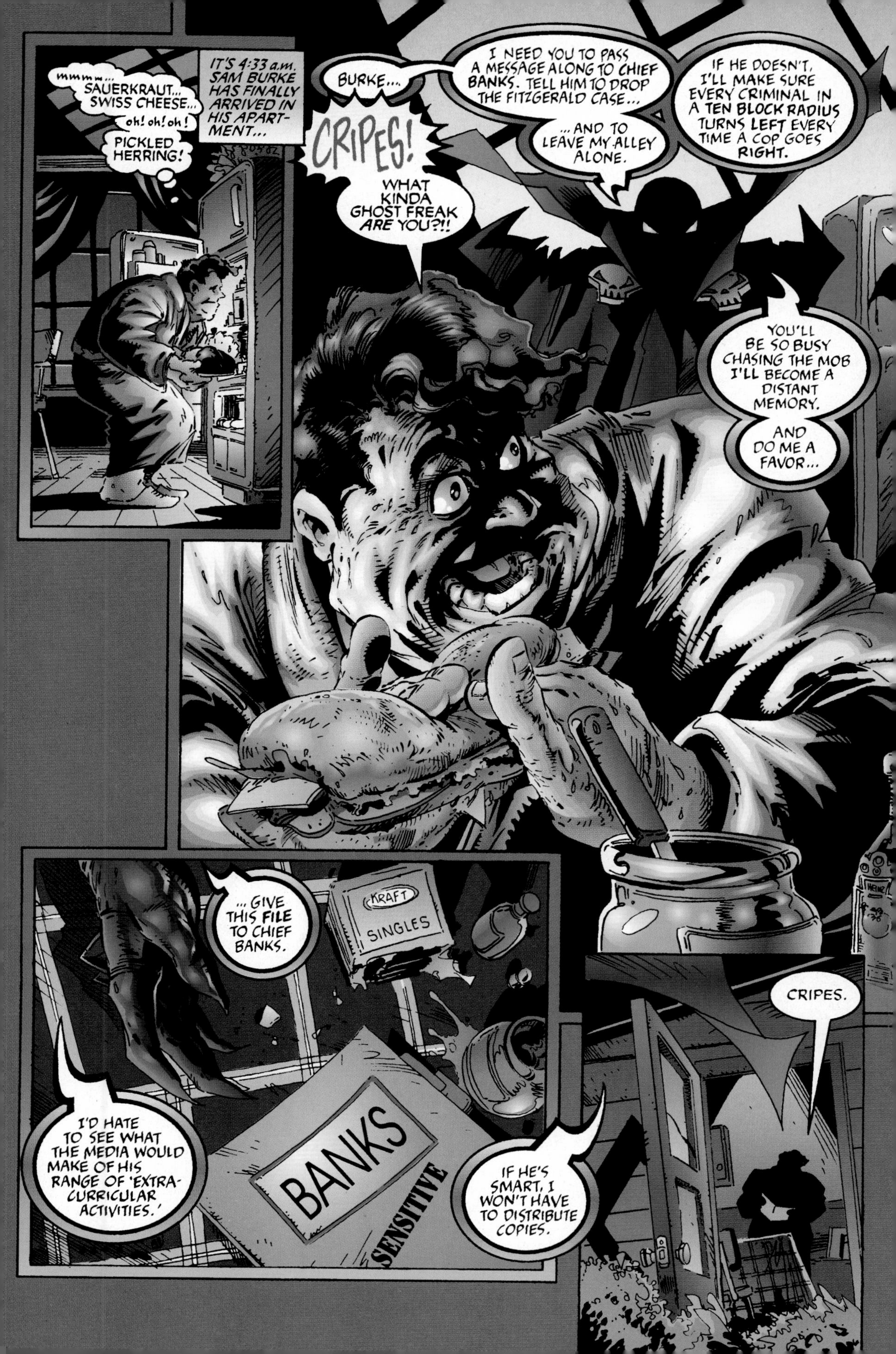
mmmm... SAUERKRAUT... SWISS CHEESE... oh! oh! oh! PICKLED HERRING!
IT'S 4:33 a.m. SAM BURKE HAS FINALLY ARRIVED IN HIS APARTMENT...
BURKE...
I NEED YOU TO PASS A MESSAGE ALONG TO CHIEF BANKS. TELL HIM TO DROP THE FITZGERALD CASE...
...AND TO LEAVE MY ALLEY ALONE.
IF HE DOESN'T, I'LL MAKE SURE EVERY CRIMINAL IN A TEN BLOCK RADIUS TURNS LEFT EVERY TIME A COP GOES RIGHT.
CRIPES!
WHAT KINDA GHOST FREAK ARE YOU?!!
YOU'LL BE SO BUSY CHASING THE MOB I'LL BECOME A DISTANT MEMORY.
AND DO ME A FAVOR...
...GIVE THIS FILE TO CHIEF BANKS.
KRAFT SINGLES
I'D HATE TO SEE WHAT THE MEDIA WOULD MAKE OF HIS RANGE OF 'EXTRA-CURRICULAR ACTIVITIES.'
BANKS
SENSITIVE
IF HE'S SMART, I WON'T HAVE TO DISTRIBUTE COPIES.
CRIPES.

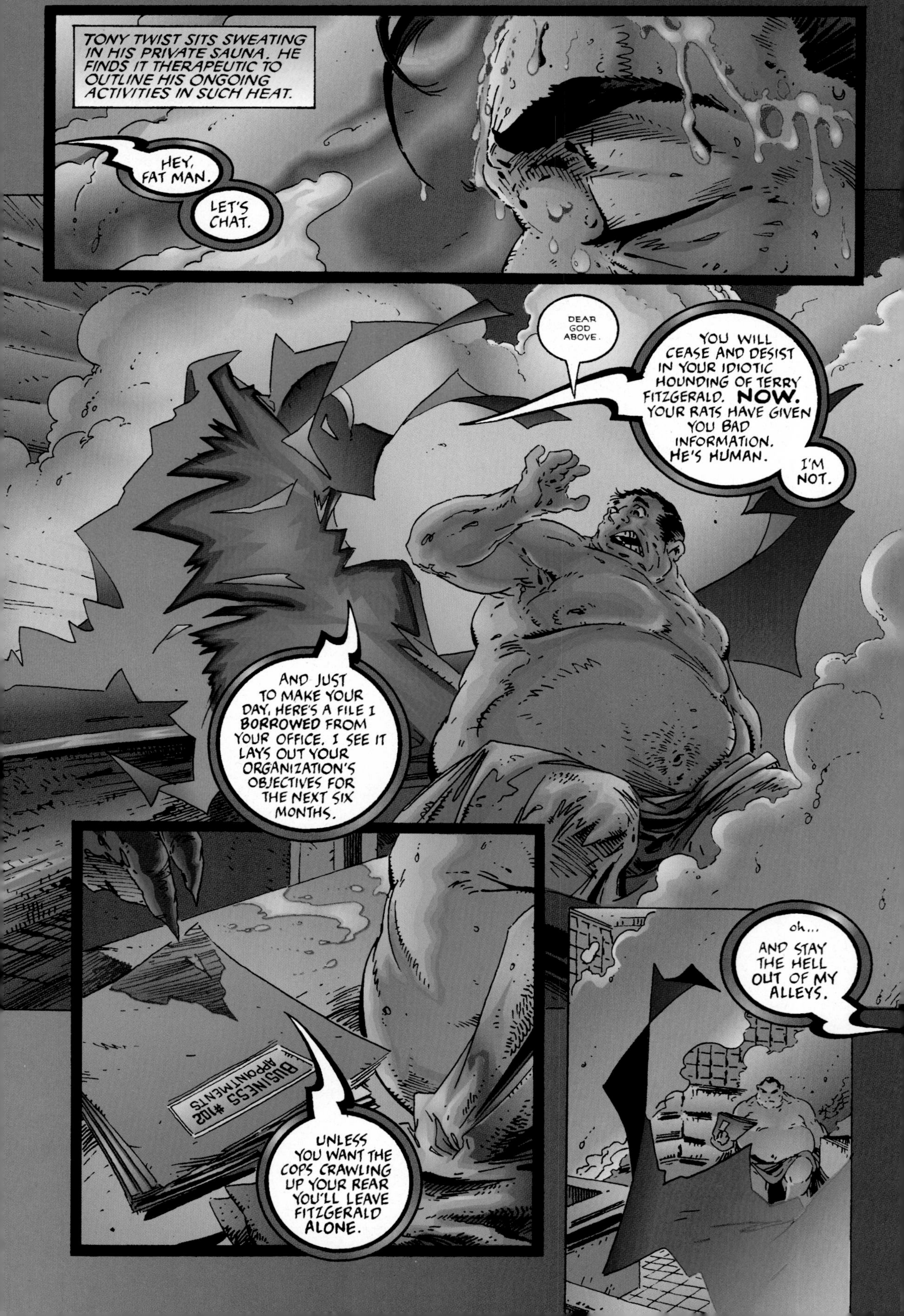
TONY TWIST SITS SWEATING IN HIS PRIVATE SAUNA. HE FINDS IT THERAPEUTIC TO OUTLINE HIS ONGOING ACTIVITIES IN SUCH HEAT.
HEY, FAT MAN.
LET'S CHAT.
DEAR GOD ABOVE.
YOU WILL CEASE AND DESIST IN YOUR IDIOTIC HOUNDING OF TERRY FITZGERALD. NOW. YOUR RATS HAVE GIVEN YOU BAD INFORMATION. HE'S HUMAN.
I'M NOT.
AND JUST TO MAKE YOUR DAY, HERE'S A FILE I BORROWED FROM YOUR OFFICE. I SEE IT LAYS OUT YOUR ORGANIZATION'S OBJECTIVES FOR THE NEXT SIX MONTHS.
BUSINESS APPOINTMENTS 2001#
UNLESS YOU WANT THE COPS CRAWLING UP YOUR REAR YOU'LL LEAVE FITZGERALD ALONE.
oh...
AND STAY THE HELL OUT OF MY ALLEYS.

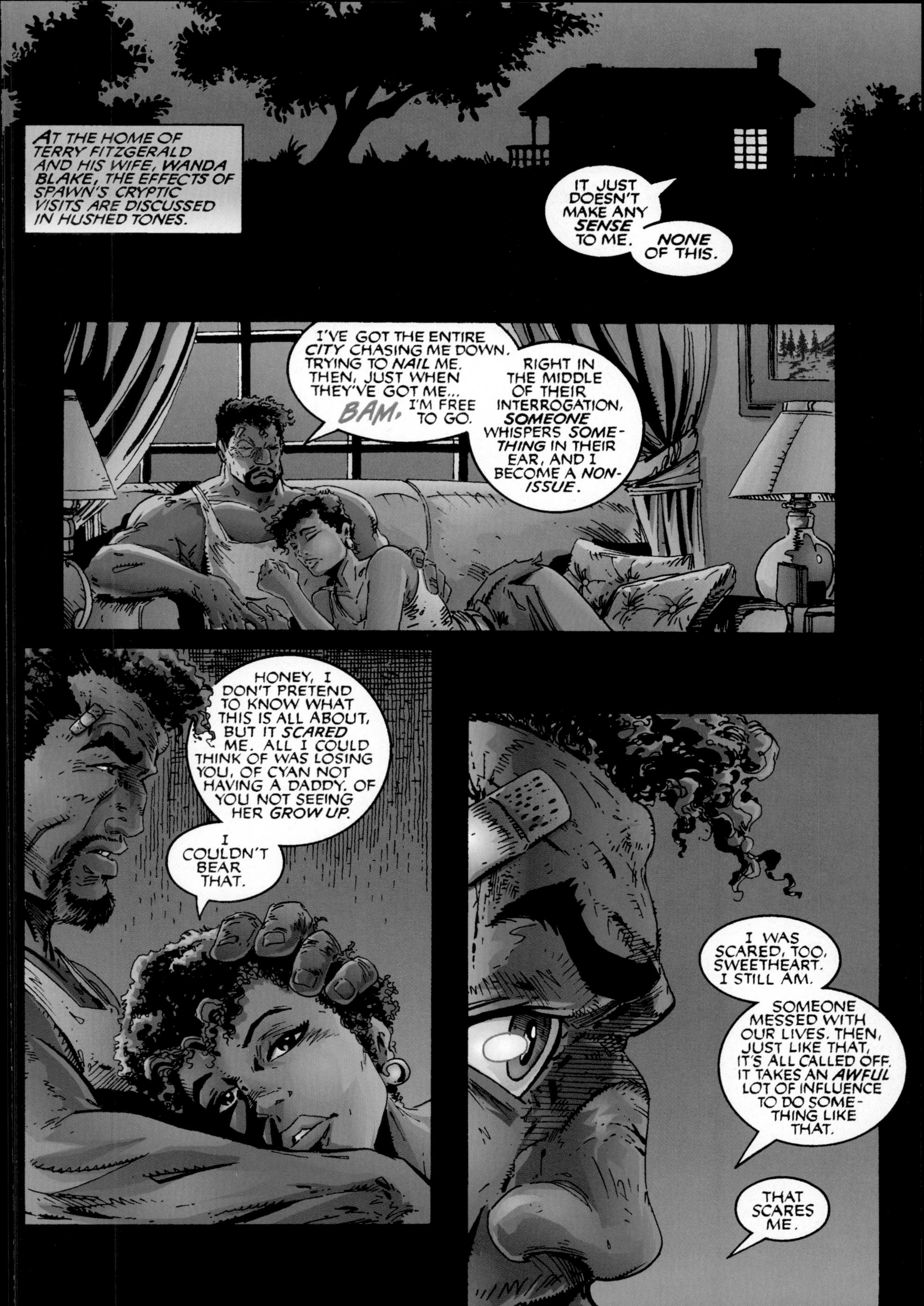
AT THE HOME OF TERRY FITZGERALD AND HIS WIFE, WANDA BLAKE, THE EFFECTS OF SPAWN'S CRYPTIC VISITS ARE DISCUSSED IN HUSHED TONES.
IT JUST DOESN'T MAKE ANY SENSE TO ME. NONE OF THIS.
I'VE GOT THE ENTIRE CITY CHASING ME DOWN, TRYING TO NAIL ME. THEN, JUST WHEN THEY'VE GOT ME... BAM, I'M FREE TO GO.
RIGHT IN THE MIDDLE OF THEIR INTERROGATION, SOMEONE WHISPERS SOME-THING IN THEIR EAR, AND I BECOME A NON-ISSUE.
HONEY, I DON'T PRETEND TO KNOW WHAT THIS IS ALL ABOUT, BUT IT SCARED ME. ALL I COULD THINK OF WAS LOSING YOU, OF CYAN NOT HAVING A DADDY, OF YOU NOT SEEING HER GROW UP.
I COULDN'T BEAR THAT.
I WAS SCARED, TOO, SWEETHEART. I STILL AM.
SOMEONE MESSED WITH OUR LIVES. THEN, JUST LIKE THAT, IT'S ALL CALLED OFF. IT TAKES AN AWFUL LOT OF INFLUENCE TO DO SOME-THING LIKE THAT.
THAT SCARES ME.

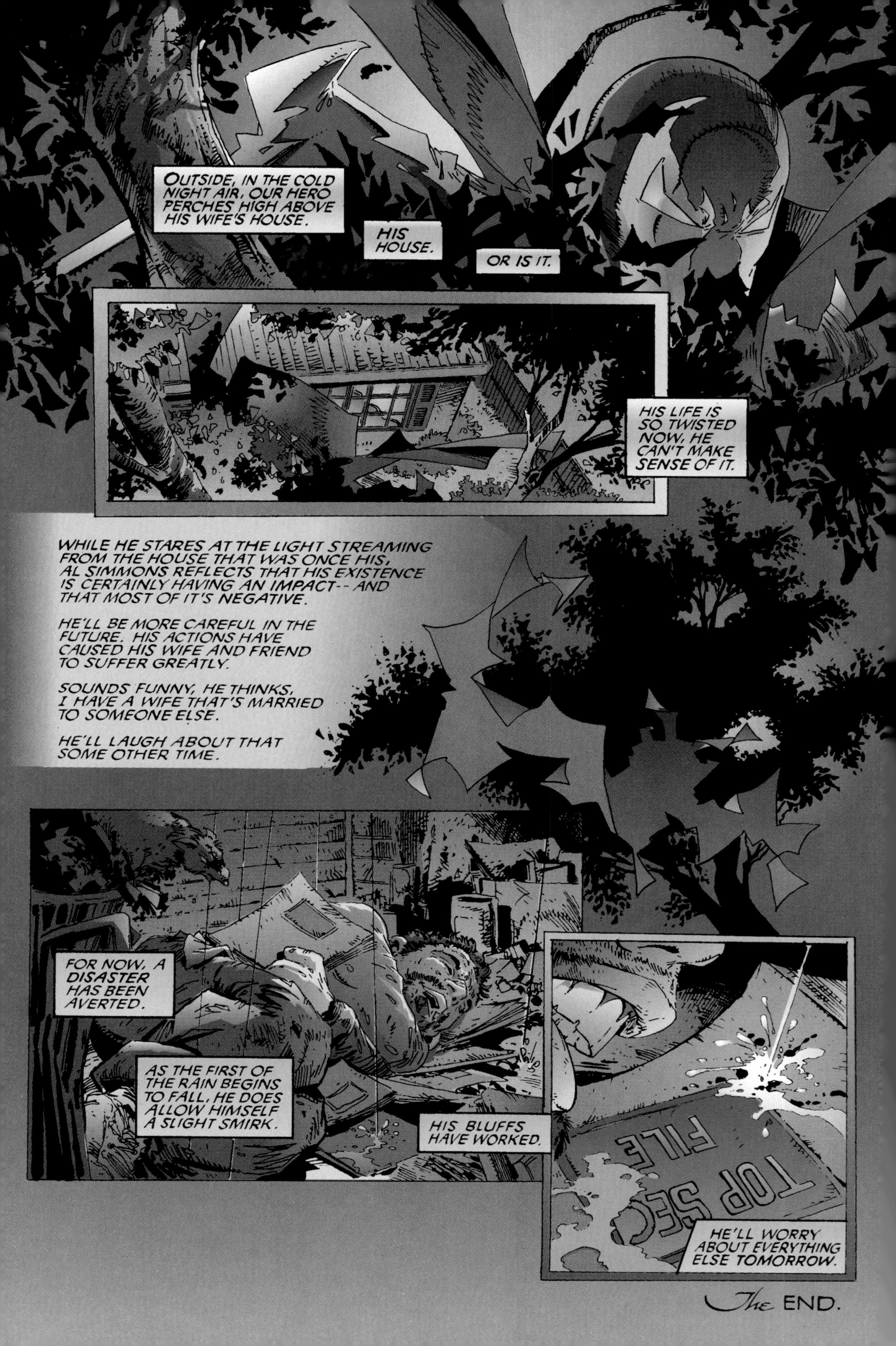
OUTSIDE, IN THE COLD NIGHT AIR, OUR HERO PERCHES HIGH ABOVE HIS WIFE'S HOUSE.
HIS HOUSE.
OR IS IT.
HIS LIFE IS SO TWISTED NOW, HE CAN'T MAKE SENSE OF IT.
WHILE HE STARES AT THE LIGHT STREAMING FROM THE HOUSE THAT WAS ONCE HIS, AL SIMMONS REFLECTS THAT HIS EXISTENCE IS CERTAINLY HAVING AN IMPACT-- AND THAT MOST OF IT'S NEGATIVE.
HE'LL BE MORE CAREFUL IN THE FUTURE. HIS ACTIONS HAVE CAUSED HIS WIFE AND FRIEND TO SUFFER GREATLY.
SOUNDS FUNNY, HE THINKS, I HAVE A WIFE THAT'S MARRIED TO SOMEONE ELSE.
HE'LL LAUGH ABOUT THAT SOME OTHER TIME.
FOR NOW, A DISASTER HAS BEEN AVERTED.
AS THE FIRST OF THE RAIN BEGINS TO FALL, HE DOES ALLOW HIMSELF A SLIGHT SMIRK.
HIS BLUFFS HAVE WORKED.
TOP SEC
FILE
HE'LL WORRY ABOUT EVERYTHING ELSE TOMORROW.
The END.

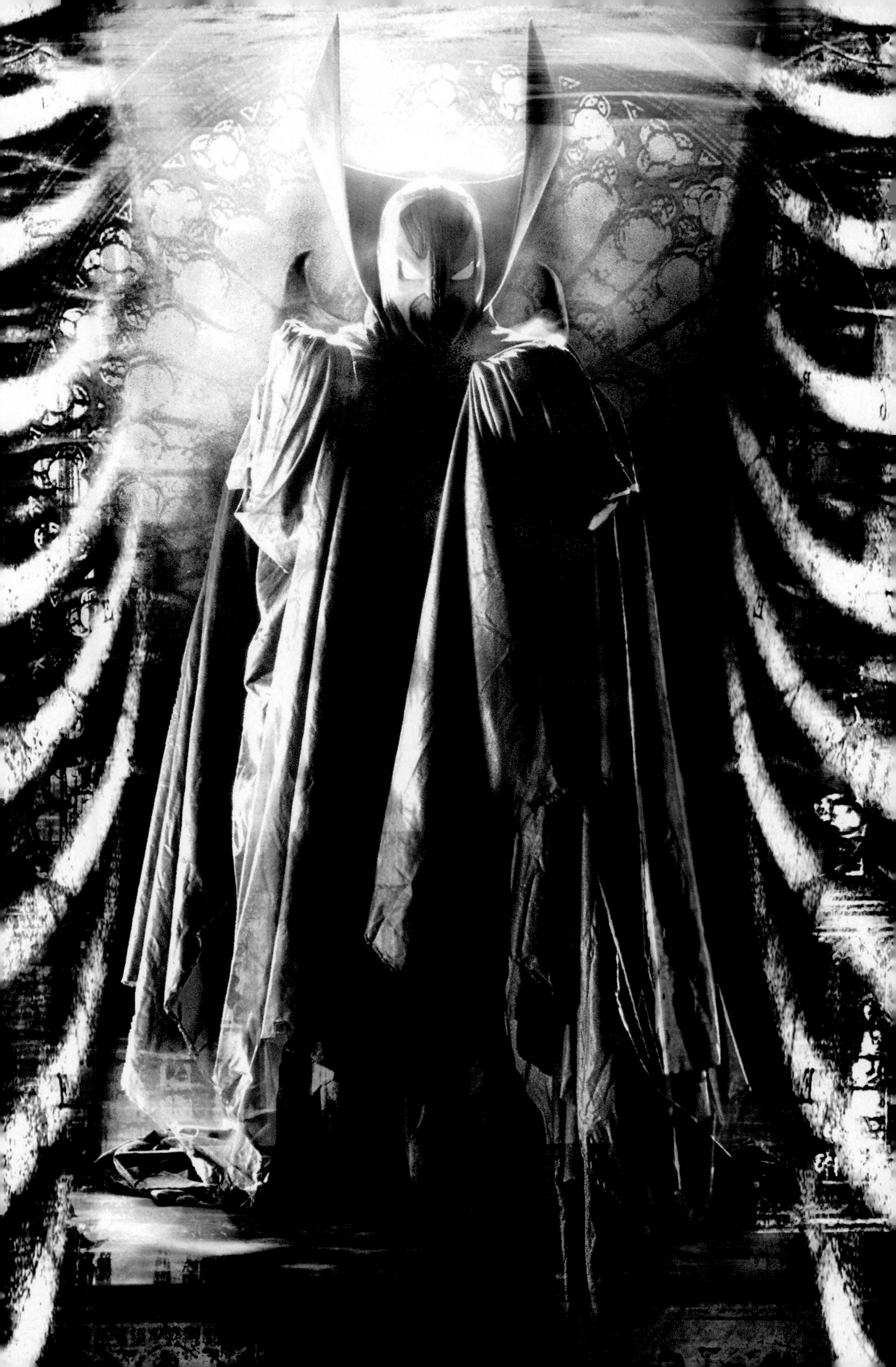

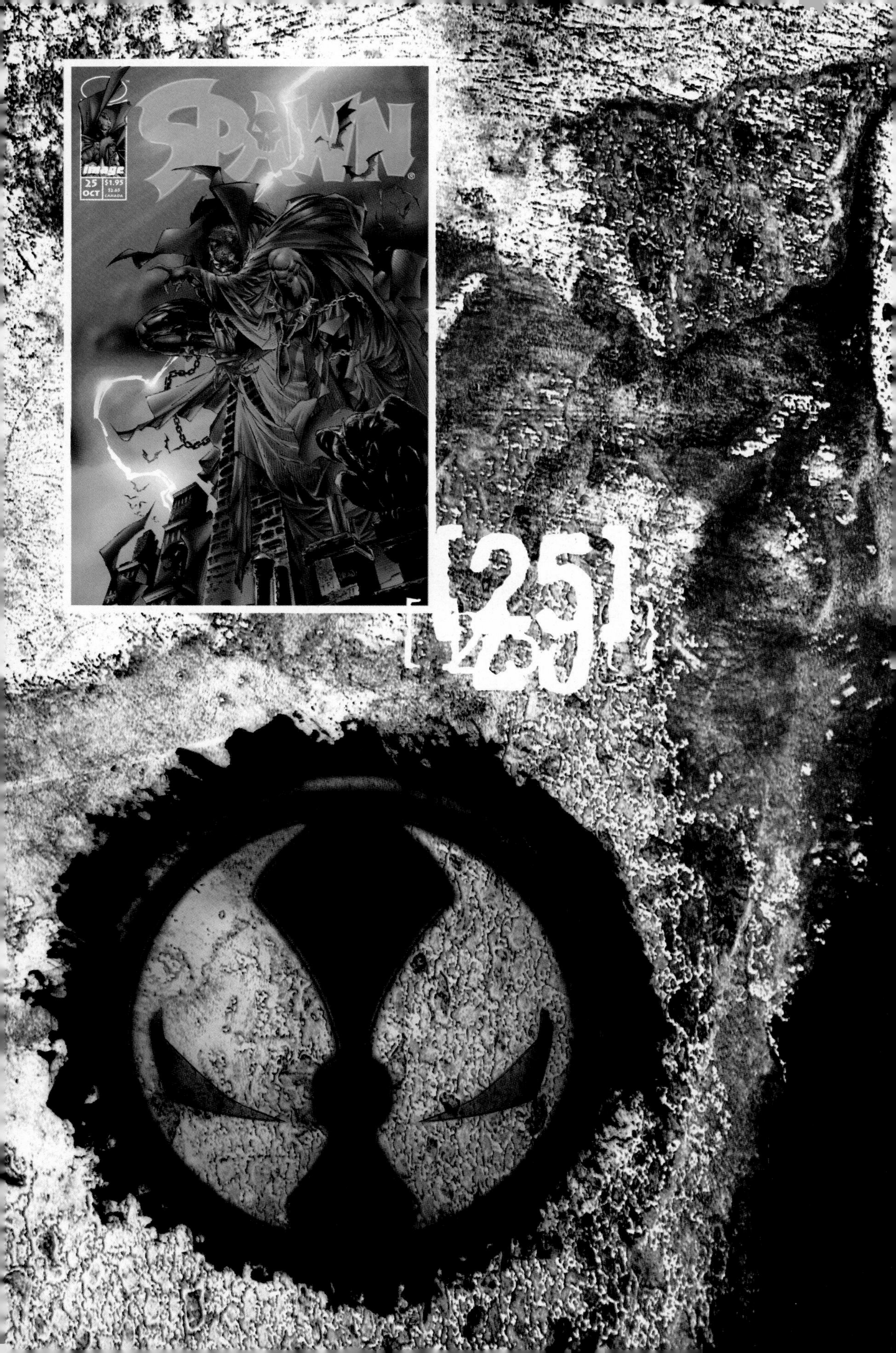
SPAWN
image
25
OCT
$1.95
$2.65
CANADA

[25]

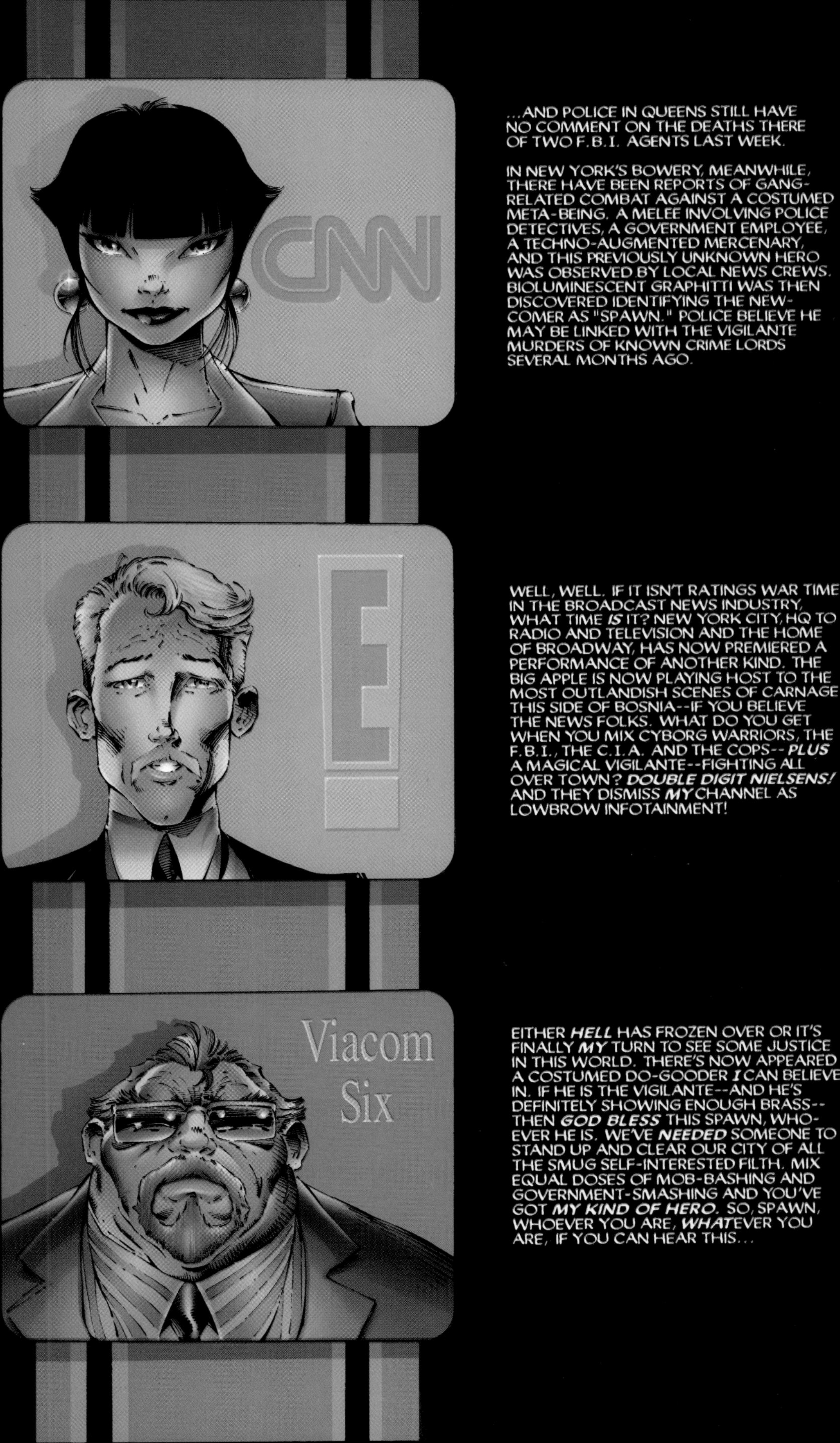
CNN
...AND POLICE IN QUEENS STILL HAVE NO COMMENT ON THE DEATHS THERE OF TWO F.B.I. AGENTS LAST WEEK.
IN NEW YORK'S BOWERY, MEANWHILE, THERE HAVE BEEN REPORTS OF GANG-RELATED COMBAT AGAINST A COSTUMED META-BEING. A MELEE INVOLVING POLICE DETECTIVES, A GOVERNMENT EMPLOYEE, A TECHNO-AUGMENTED MERCENARY, AND THIS PREVIOUSLY UNKNOWN HERO WAS OBSERVED BY LOCAL NEWS CREWS. BIOLUMINESCENT GRAPHITTI WAS THEN DISCOVERED IDENTIFYING THE NEW-COMER AS "SPAWN." POLICE BELIEVE HE MAY BE LINKED WITH THE VIGILANTE MURDERS OF KNOWN CRIME LORDS SEVERAL MONTHS AGO.
E!
WELL, WELL. IF IT ISN'T RATINGS WAR TIME IN THE BROADCAST NEWS INDUSTRY, WHAT TIME ***IS*** IT? NEW YORK CITY, HQ TO RADIO AND TELEVISION AND THE HOME OF BROADWAY, HAS NOW PREMIERED A PERFORMANCE OF ANOTHER KIND. THE BIG APPLE IS NOW PLAYING HOST TO THE MOST OUTLANDISH SCENES OF CARNAGE THIS SIDE OF BOSNIA--IF YOU BELIEVE THE NEWS FOLKS. WHAT DO YOU GET WHEN YOU MIX CYBORG WARRIORS, THE F.B.I., THE C.I.A. AND THE COPS-- ***PLUS*** A MAGICAL VIGILANTE--FIGHTING ALL OVER TOWN? ***DOUBLE DIGIT NIELSENS!*** AND THEY DISMISS ***MY*** CHANNEL AS LOWBROW INFOTAINMENT!
Viacom Six
EITHER ***HELL*** HAS FROZEN OVER OR IT'S FINALLY ***MY*** TURN TO SEE SOME JUSTICE IN THIS WORLD. THERE'S NOW APPEARED A COSTUMED DO-GOODER ***I*** CAN BELIEVE IN. IF HE IS THE VIGILANTE--AND HE'S DEFINITELY SHOWING ENOUGH BRASS-- THEN ***GOD BLESS*** THIS SPAWN, WHO-EVER HE IS. WE'VE ***NEEDED*** SOMEONE TO STAND UP AND CLEAR OUR CITY OF ALL THE SMUG SELF-INTERESTED FILTH. MIX EQUAL DOSES OF MOB-BASHING AND GOVERNMENT-SMASHING AND YOU'VE GOT ***MY KIND OF HERO.*** SO, SPAWN, WHOEVER YOU ARE, ***WHAT***EVER YOU ARE, IF YOU CAN HEAR THIS...

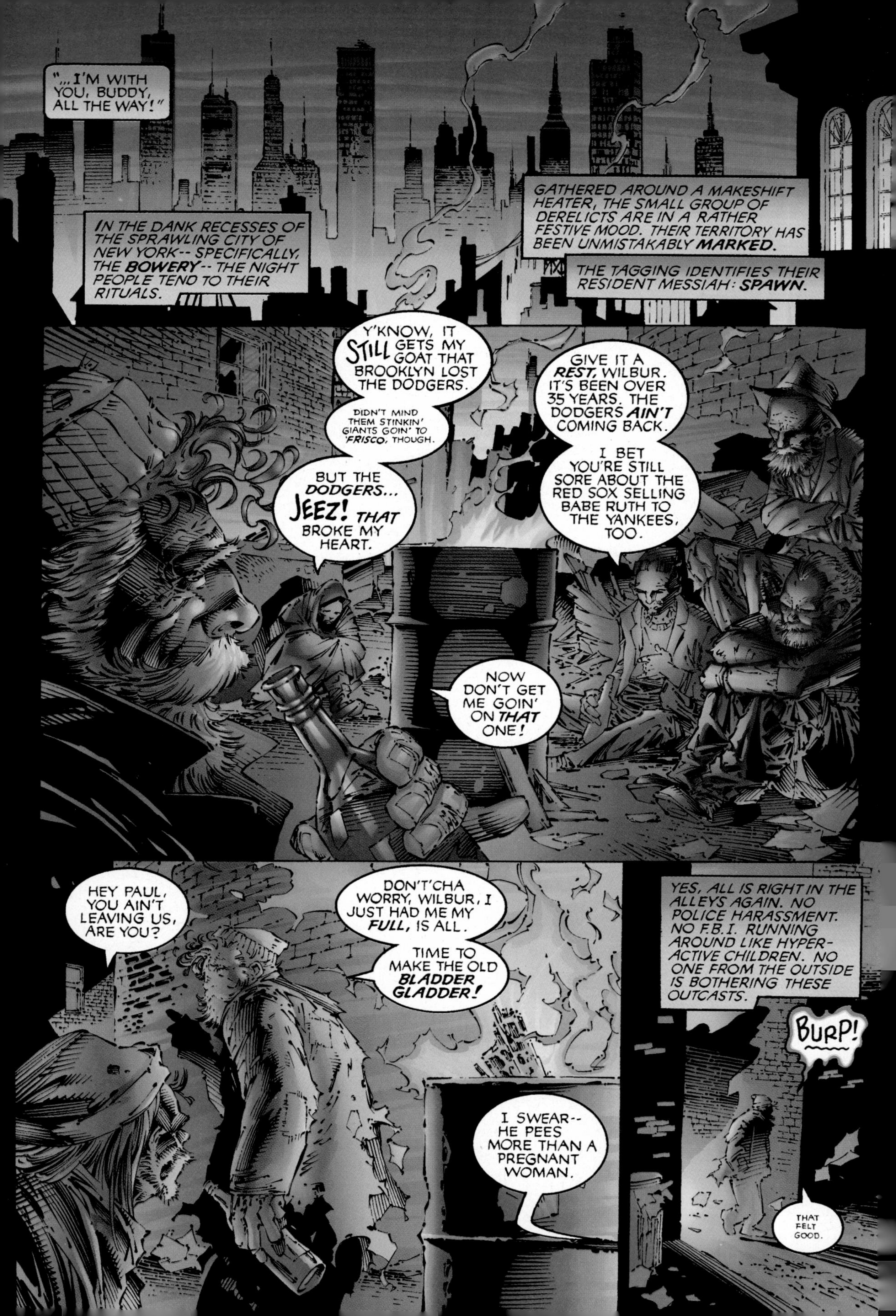
"...I'M WITH YOU, BUDDY, ALL THE WAY!"
IN THE DANK RECESSES OF THE SPRAWLING CITY OF NEW YORK-- SPECIFICALLY, THE BOWERY-- THE NIGHT PEOPLE TEND TO THEIR RITUALS.
GATHERED AROUND A MAKESHIFT HEATER, THE SMALL GROUP OF DERELICTS ARE IN A RATHER FESTIVE MOOD. THEIR TERRITORY HAS BEEN UNMISTAKABLY MARKED.
THE TAGGING IDENTIFIES THEIR RESIDENT MESSIAH: SPAWN.
Y'KNOW, IT STILL GETS MY GOAT THAT BROOKLYN LOST THE DODGERS.
DIDN'T MIND THEM STINKIN' GIANTS GOIN' TO 'FRISCO, THOUGH.
BUT THE DODGERS... JEEZ! THAT BROKE MY HEART.
GIVE IT A REST, WILBUR. IT'S BEEN OVER 35 YEARS. THE DODGERS AIN'T COMING BACK.
I BET YOU'RE STILL SORE ABOUT THE RED SOX SELLING BABE RUTH TO THE YANKEES, TOO.
NOW DON'T GET ME GOIN' ON THAT ONE!
HEY PAUL, YOU AIN'T LEAVING US, ARE YOU?
DON'T'CHA WORRY, WILBUR, I JUST HAD ME MY FULL, IS ALL.
TIME TO MAKE THE OLD BLADDER GLADDER!
I SWEAR-- HE PEES MORE THAN A PREGNANT WOMAN.
YES, ALL IS RIGHT IN THE ALLEYS AGAIN. NO POLICE HARASSMENT. NO F.B.I. RUNNING AROUND LIKE HYPER-ACTIVE CHILDREN. NO ONE FROM THE OUTSIDE IS BOTHERING THESE OUTCASTS.
BURP!
THAT FELT GOOD.

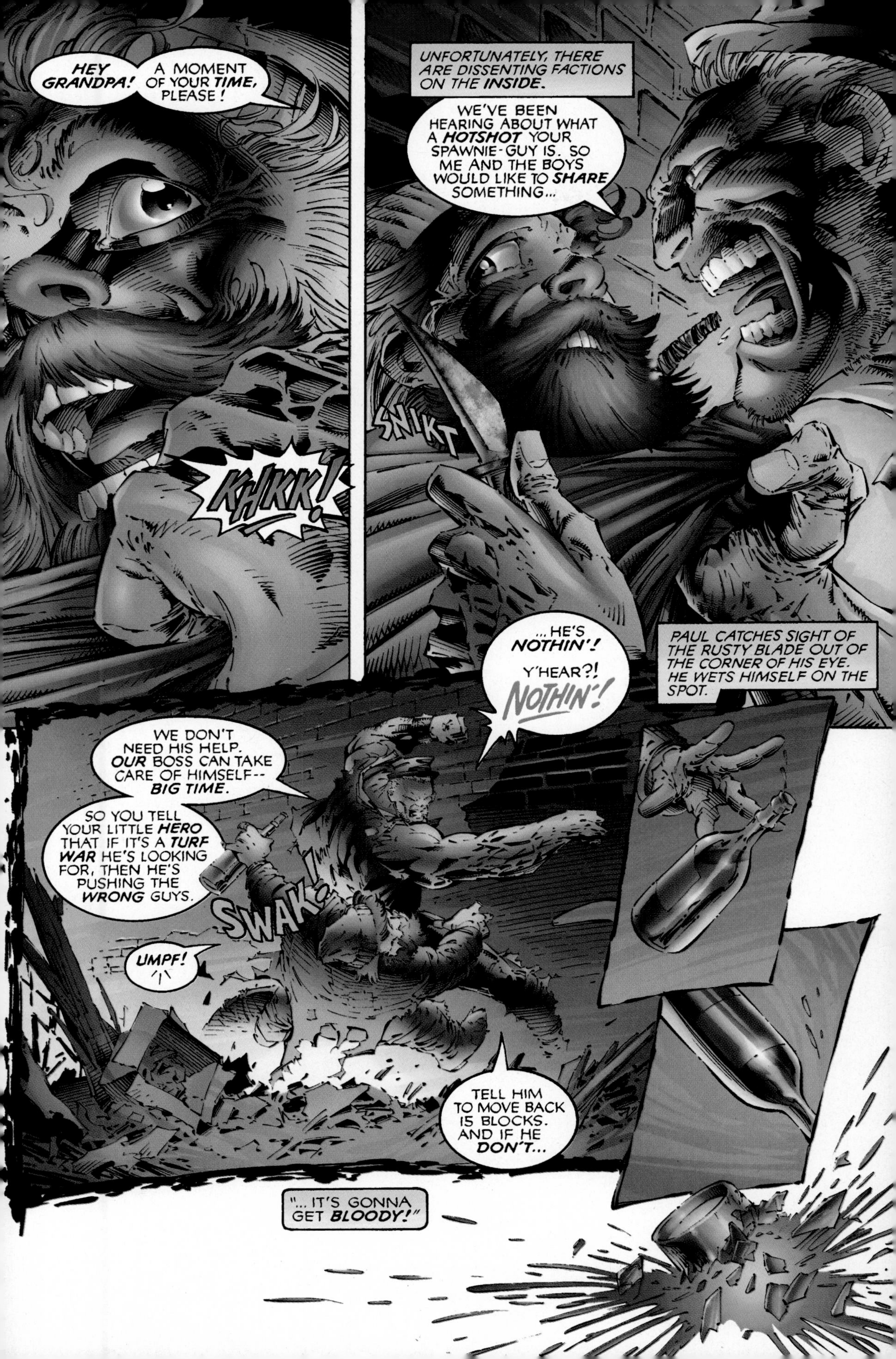
HEY GRANDPA!
A MOMENT OF YOUR TIME, PLEASE!
KHKK!
UNFORTUNATELY, THERE ARE DISSENTING FACTIONS ON THE INSIDE.
WE'VE BEEN HEARING ABOUT WHAT A HOTSHOT YOUR SPAWNIE-GUY IS. SO ME AND THE BOYS WOULD LIKE TO SHARE SOMETHING...
SNIKT
...HE'S NOTHIN'! Y'HEAR?! NOTHIN'!
PAUL CATCHES SIGHT OF THE RUSTY BLADE OUT OF THE CORNER OF HIS EYE. HE WETS HIMSELF ON THE SPOT.
WE DON'T NEED HIS HELP. OUR BOSS CAN TAKE CARE OF HIMSELF-- BIG TIME.
SO YOU TELL YOUR LITTLE HERO THAT IF IT'S A TURF WAR HE'S LOOKING FOR, THEN HE'S PUSHING THE WRONG GUYS.
SWAK!
UMPF!
TELL HIM TO MOVE BACK 15 BLOCKS. AND IF HE DON'T...
"...IT'S GONNA GET BLOODY!"

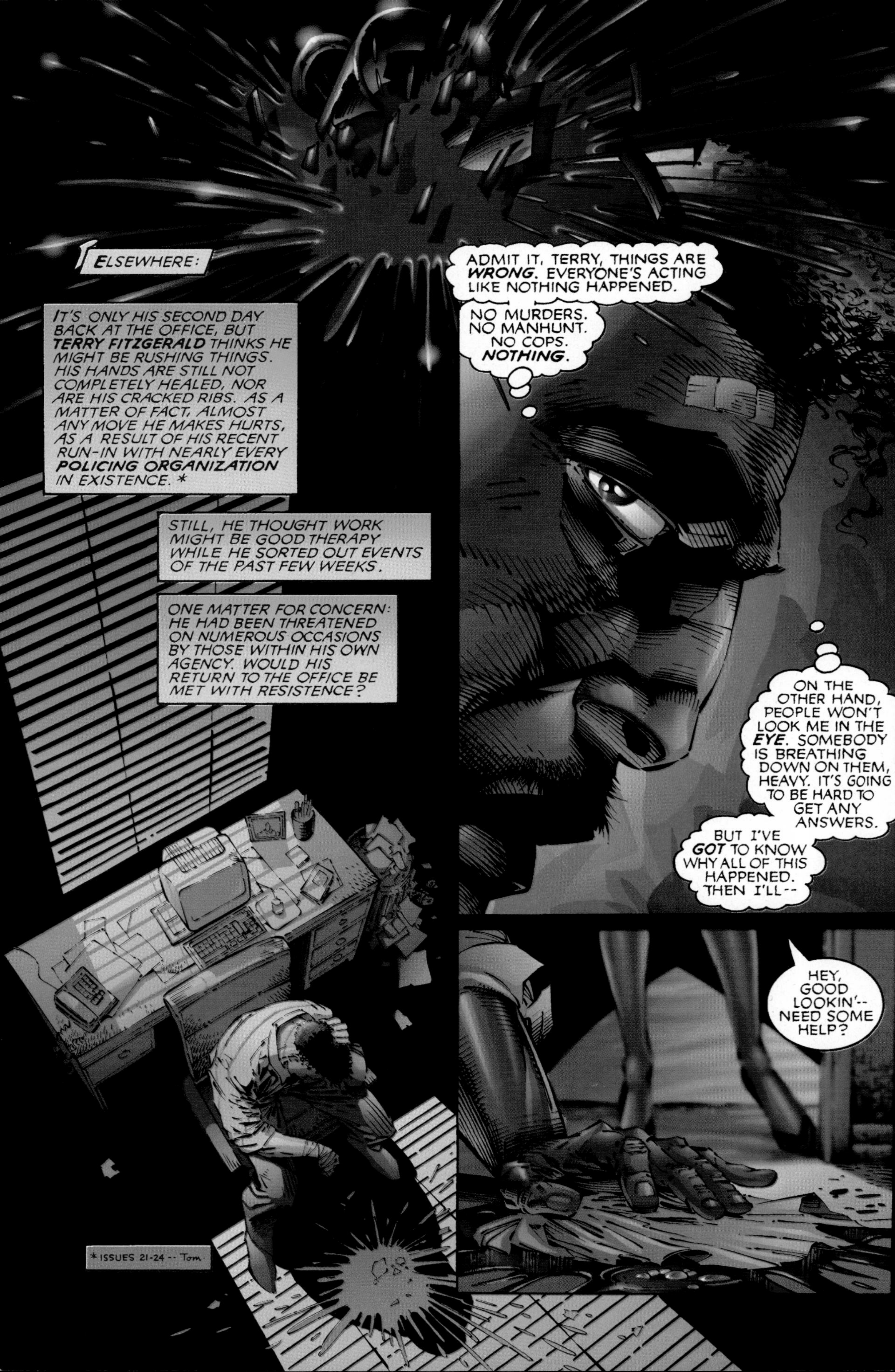
ELSEWHERE:
IT'S ONLY HIS SECOND DAY BACK AT THE OFFICE, BUT TERRY FITZGERALD THINKS HE MIGHT BE RUSHING THINGS. HIS HANDS ARE STILL NOT COMPLETELY HEALED, NOR ARE HIS CRACKED RIBS. AS A MATTER OF FACT, ALMOST ANY MOVE HE MAKES HURTS, AS A RESULT OF HIS RECENT RUN-IN WITH NEARLY EVERY POLICING ORGANIZATION IN EXISTENCE. *
STILL, HE THOUGHT WORK MIGHT BE GOOD THERAPY WHILE HE SORTED OUT EVENTS OF THE PAST FEW WEEKS.
ONE MATTER FOR CONCERN: HE HAD BEEN THREATENED ON NUMEROUS OCCASIONS BY THOSE WITHIN HIS OWN AGENCY. WOULD HIS RETURN TO THE OFFICE BE MET WITH RESISTENCE?
* ISSUES 21-24 -- Tom.
ADMIT IT, TERRY, THINGS ARE WRONG. EVERYONE'S ACTING LIKE NOTHING HAPPENED.
NO MURDERS. NO MANHUNT. NO COPS. NOTHING.
ON THE OTHER HAND, PEOPLE WON'T LOOK ME IN THE EYE. SOMEBODY IS BREATHING DOWN ON THEM, HEAVY. IT'S GOING TO BE HARD TO GET ANY ANSWERS.
BUT I'VE GOT TO KNOW WHY ALL OF THIS HAPPENED. THEN I'LL--
HEY, GOOD LOOKIN'-- NEED SOME HELP?

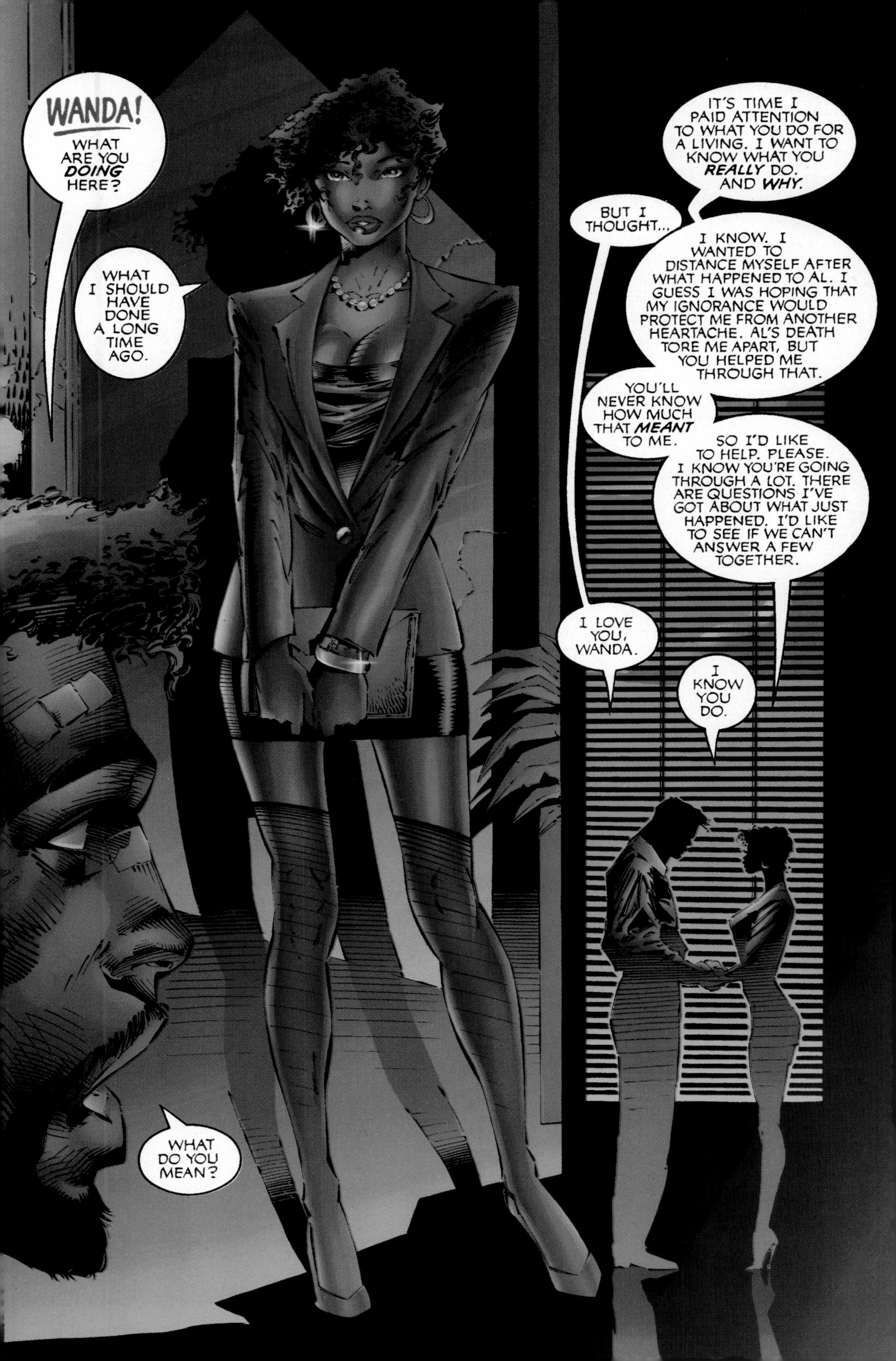
WANDA! WHAT ARE YOU DOING HERE?
WHAT I SHOULD HAVE DONE A LONG TIME AGO.
WHAT DO YOU MEAN?
IT'S TIME I PAID ATTENTION TO WHAT YOU DO FOR A LIVING. I WANT TO KNOW WHAT YOU REALLY DO. AND WHY.
BUT I THOUGHT...
I KNOW. I WANTED TO DISTANCE MYSELF AFTER WHAT HAPPENED TO AL. I GUESS I WAS HOPING THAT MY IGNORANCE WOULD PROTECT ME FROM ANOTHER HEARTACHE. AL'S DEATH TORE ME APART, BUT YOU HELPED ME THROUGH THAT.
YOU'LL NEVER KNOW HOW MUCH THAT MEANT TO ME.
SO I'D LIKE TO HELP. PLEASE. I KNOW YOU'RE GOING THROUGH A LOT. THERE ARE QUESTIONS I'VE GOT ABOUT WHAT JUST HAPPENED. I'D LIKE TO SEE IF WE CAN'T ANSWER A FEW TOGETHER.
I LOVE YOU, WANDA.
I KNOW YOU DO.

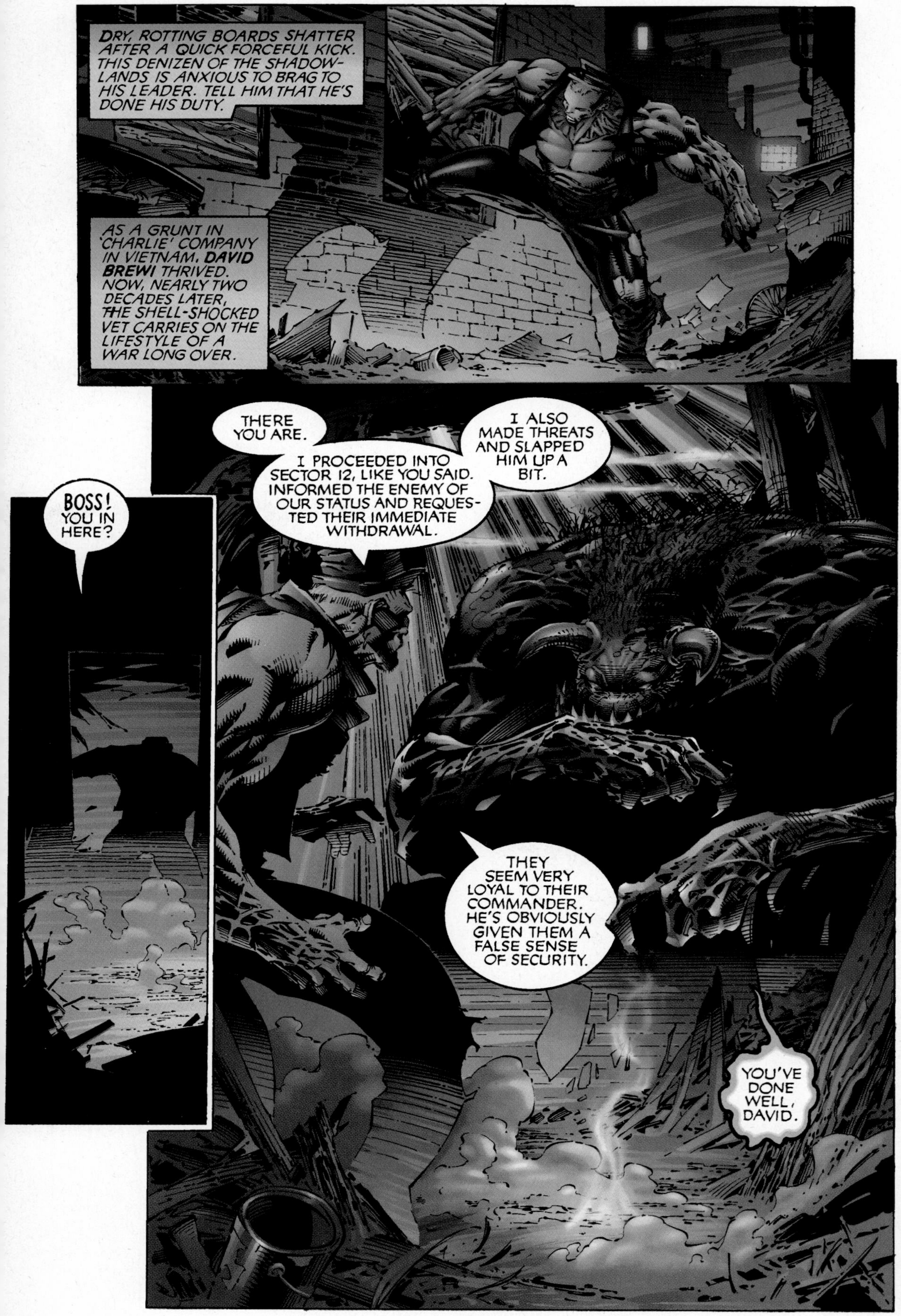
DRY, ROTTING BOARDS SHATTER AFTER A QUICK FORCEFUL KICK. THIS DENIZEN OF THE SHADOW-LANDS IS ANXIOUS TO BRAG TO HIS LEADER. TELL HIM THAT HE'S DONE HIS DUTY.
AS A GRUNT IN 'CHARLIE' COMPANY IN VIETNAM, DAVID BREWI THRIVED. NOW, NEARLY TWO DECADES LATER, THE SHELL-SHOCKED VET CARRIES ON THE LIFESTYLE OF A WAR LONG OVER.
BOSS! YOU IN HERE?
THERE YOU ARE.
I PROCEEDED INTO SECTOR 12, LIKE YOU SAID. INFORMED THE ENEMY OF OUR STATUS AND REQUESTED THEIR IMMEDIATE WITHDRAWAL.
I ALSO MADE THREATS AND SLAPPED HIM UP A BIT.
THEY SEEM VERY LOYAL TO THEIR COMMANDER. HE'S OBVIOUSLY GIVEN THEM A FALSE SENSE OF SECURITY.
YOU'VE DONE WELL, DAVID.

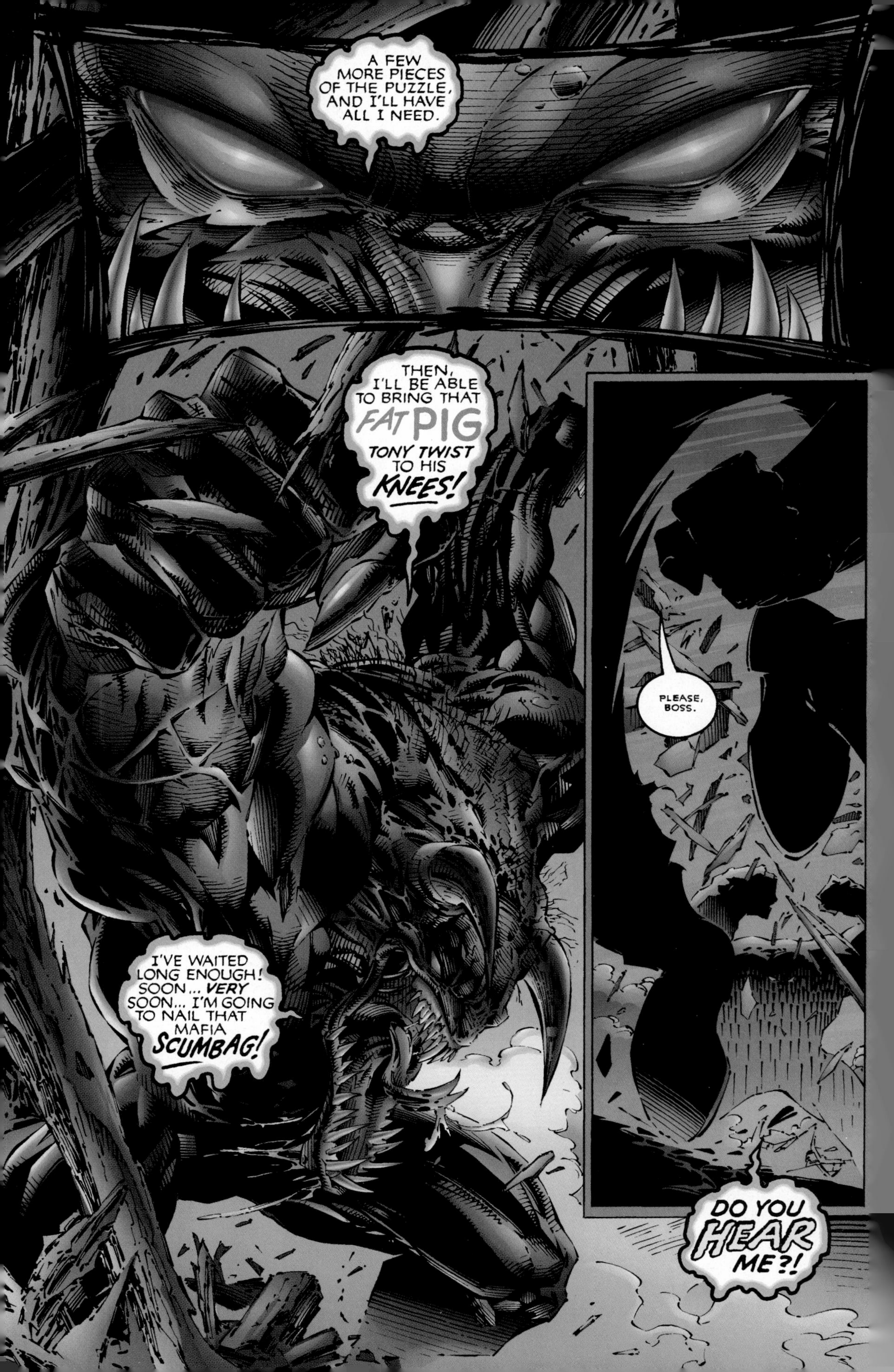
A FEW MORE PIECES OF THE PUZZLE, AND I'LL HAVE ALL I NEED.
THEN, I'LL BE ABLE TO BRING THAT FAT PIG TONY TWIST TO HIS KNEES!
PLEASE, BOSS.
I'VE WAITED LONG ENOUGH! SOON... VERY SOON... I'M GOING TO NAIL THAT MAFIA SCUMBAG!
DO YOU HEAR ME?!

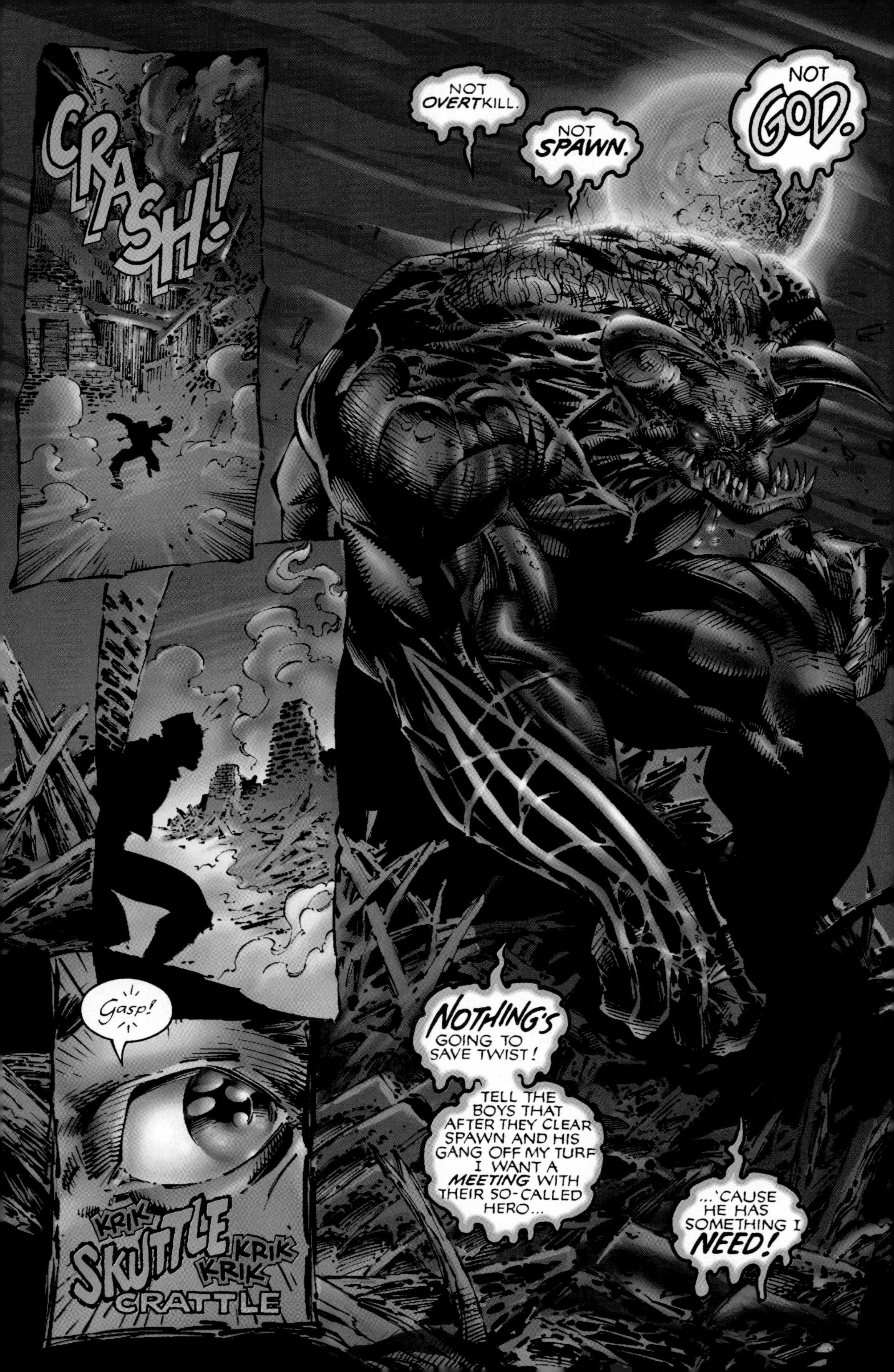
CRASH!
NOT OVERTKILL.
NOT SPAWN.
NOT GOD.
Gasp!
KRIK
SKUTTLE
KRIK
KRIK
CRATTLE
NOTHING's GOING TO SAVE TWIST!
TELL THE BOYS THAT AFTER THEY CLEAR SPAWN AND HIS GANG OFF MY TURF I WANT A MEETING WITH THEIR SO-CALLED HERO...
...'CAUSE HE HAS SOMETHING I NEED!

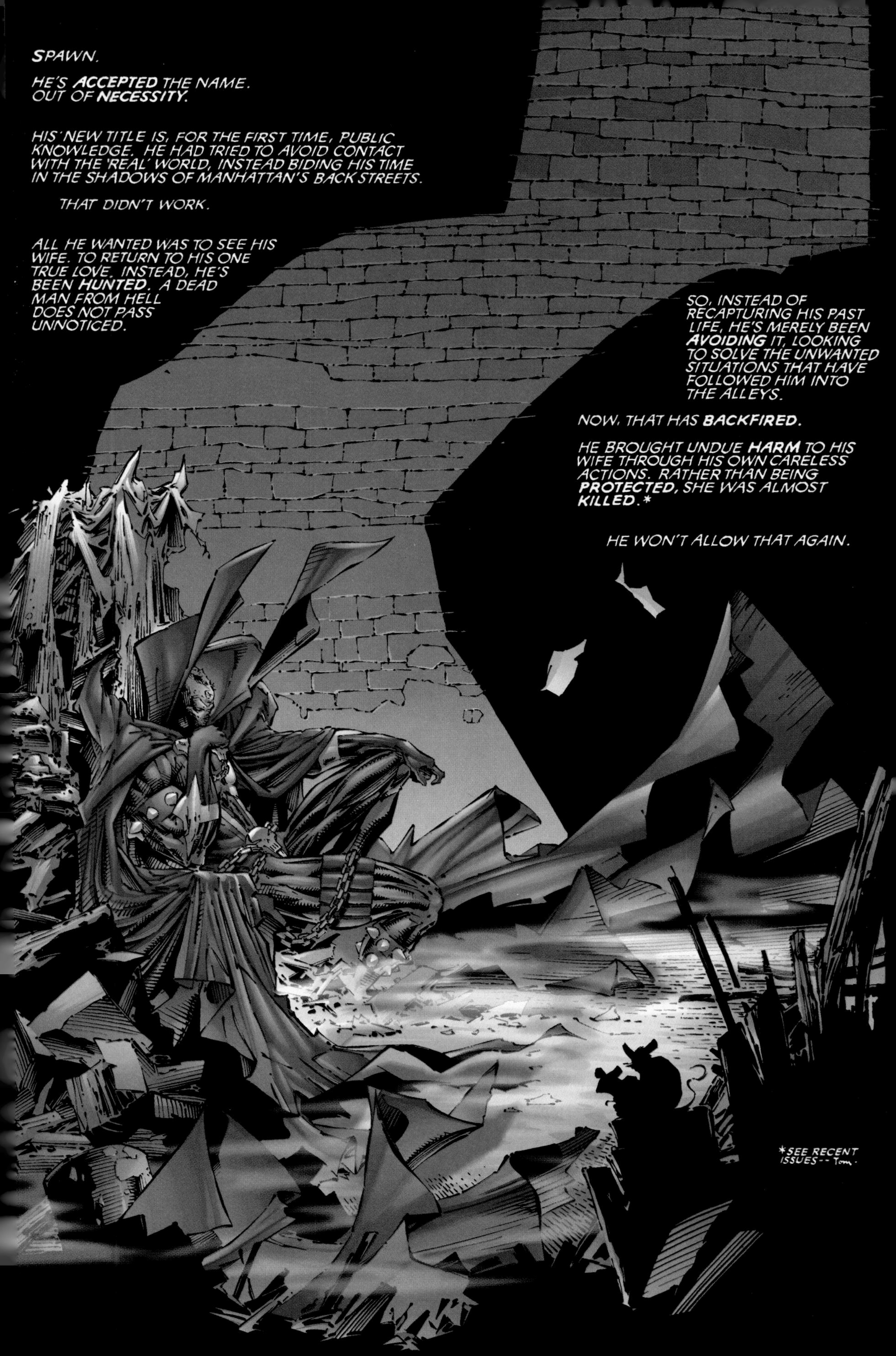
SPAWN.
HE'S ACCEPTED THE NAME. OUT OF NECESSITY.
HIS NEW TITLE IS, FOR THE FIRST TIME, PUBLIC KNOWLEDGE. HE HAD TRIED TO AVOID CONTACT WITH THE 'REAL' WORLD, INSTEAD BIDING HIS TIME IN THE SHADOWS OF MANHATTAN'S BACK STREETS.
THAT DIDN'T WORK.
ALL HE WANTED WAS TO SEE HIS WIFE. TO RETURN TO HIS ONE TRUE LOVE. INSTEAD, HE'S BEEN HUNTED. A DEAD MAN FROM HELL DOES NOT PASS UNNOTICED.
SO, INSTEAD OF RECAPTURING HIS PAST LIFE, HE'S MERELY BEEN AVOIDING IT, LOOKING TO SOLVE THE UNWANTED SITUATIONS THAT HAVE FOLLOWED HIM INTO THE ALLEYS.
NOW, THAT HAS BACKFIRED.
HE BROUGHT UNDUE HARM TO HIS WIFE THROUGH HIS OWN CARELESS ACTIONS. RATHER THAN BEING PROTECTED, SHE WAS ALMOST KILLED.*
HE WON'T ALLOW THAT AGAIN.
*SEE RECENT ISSUES-- Tom.

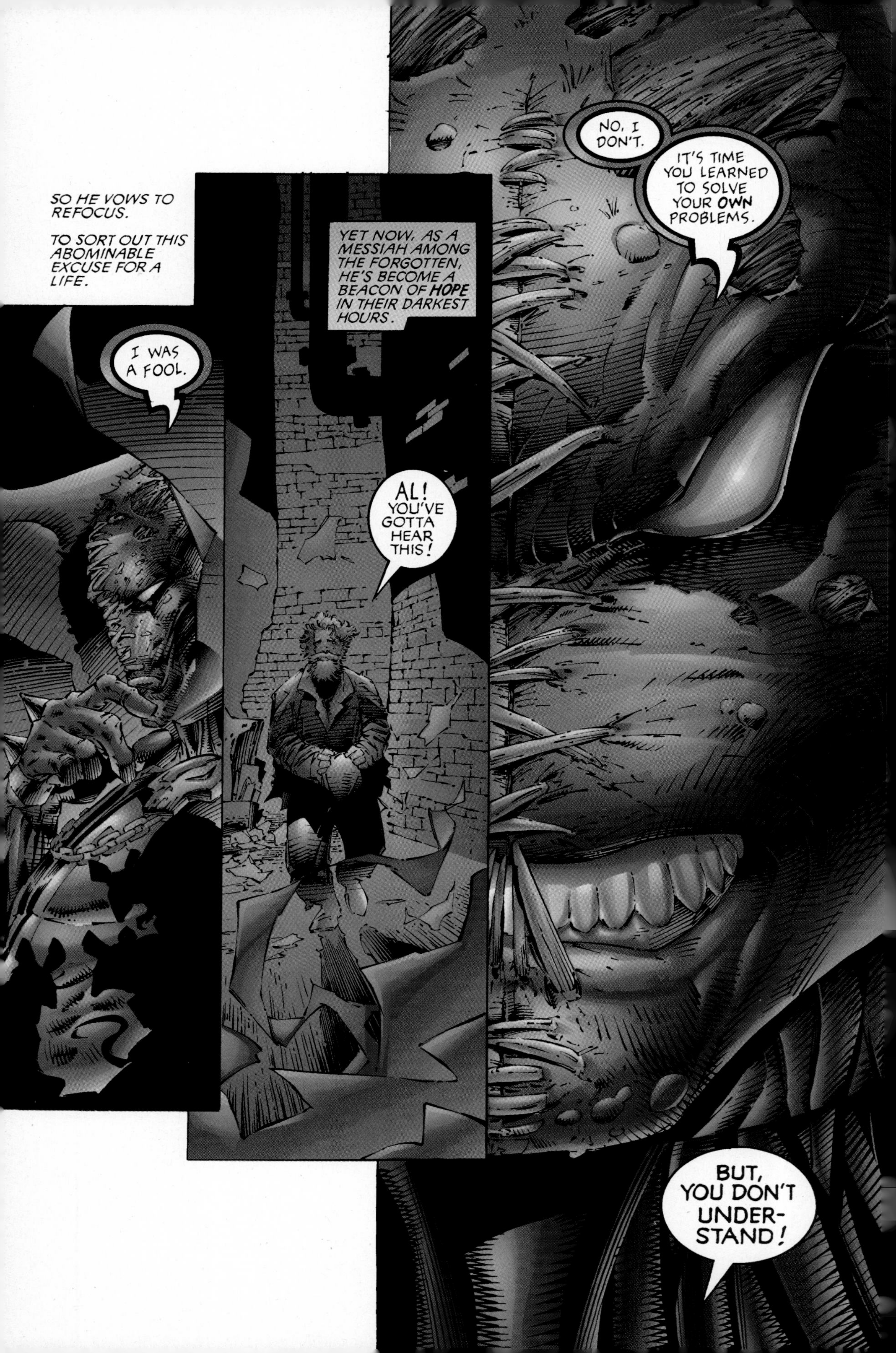
SO HE VOWS TO REFOCUS.
TO SORT OUT THIS ABOMINABLE EXCUSE FOR A LIFE.
I WAS A FOOL.
YET NOW, AS A MESSIAH AMONG THE FORGOTTEN, HE'S BECOME A BEACON OF HOPE IN THEIR DARKEST HOURS.
AL! YOU'VE GOTTA HEAR THIS!
NO, I DON'T.
IT'S TIME YOU LEARNED TO SOLVE YOUR OWN PROBLEMS.
BUT, YOU DON'T UNDER-STAND!

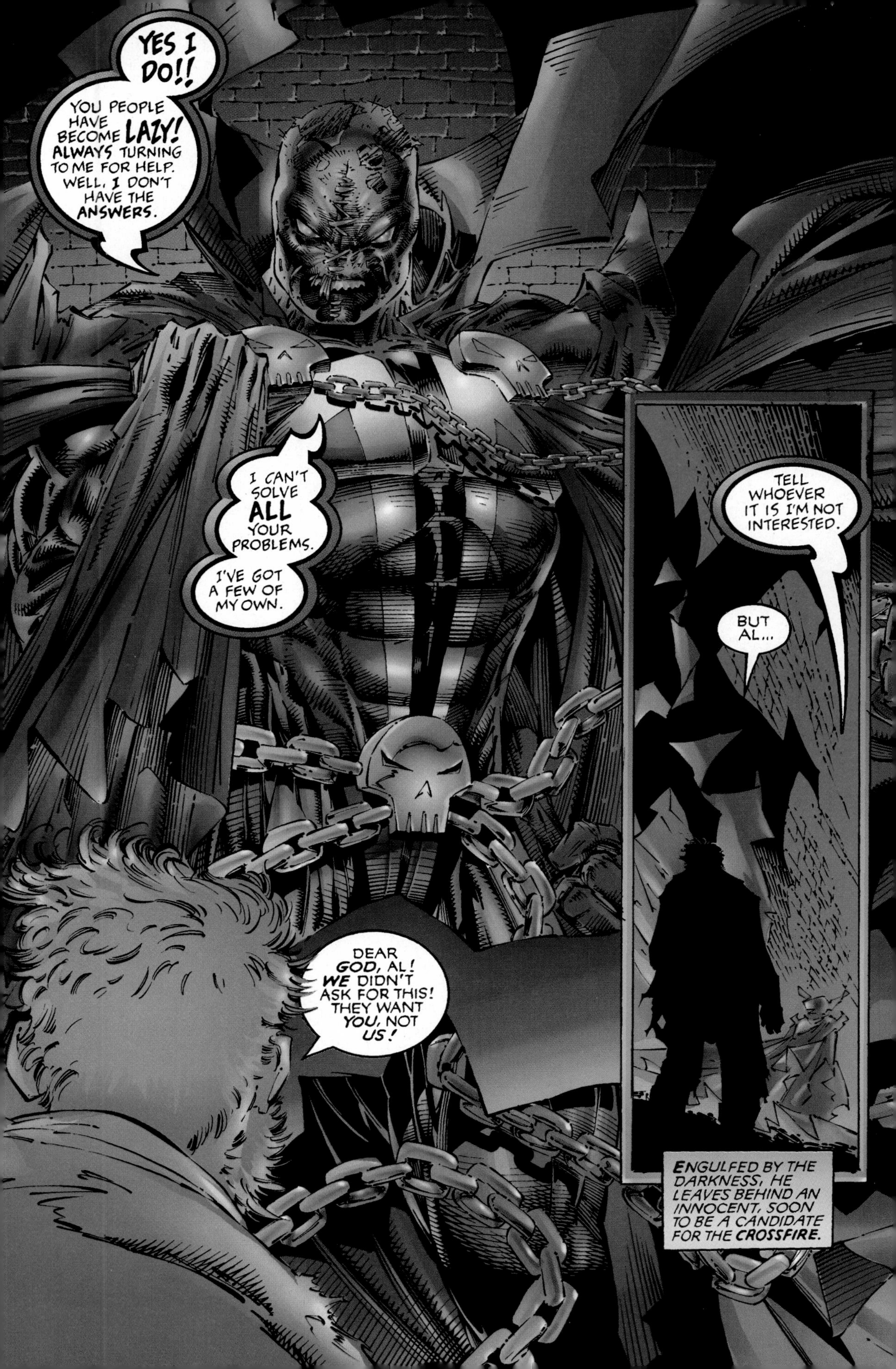
YES I DO!!
YOU PEOPLE HAVE BECOME LAZY! ALWAYS TURNING TO ME FOR HELP. WELL, I DON'T HAVE THE ANSWERS.
I CAN'T SOLVE ALL YOUR PROBLEMS.
I'VE GOT A FEW OF MY OWN.
DEAR GOD, AL! WE DIDN'T ASK FOR THIS! THEY WANT YOU, NOT US!
TELL WHOEVER IT IS I'M NOT INTERESTED.
BUT AL...
ENGULFED BY THE DARKNESS, HE LEAVES BEHIND AN INNOCENT, SOON TO BE A CANDIDATE FOR THE CROSSFIRE.

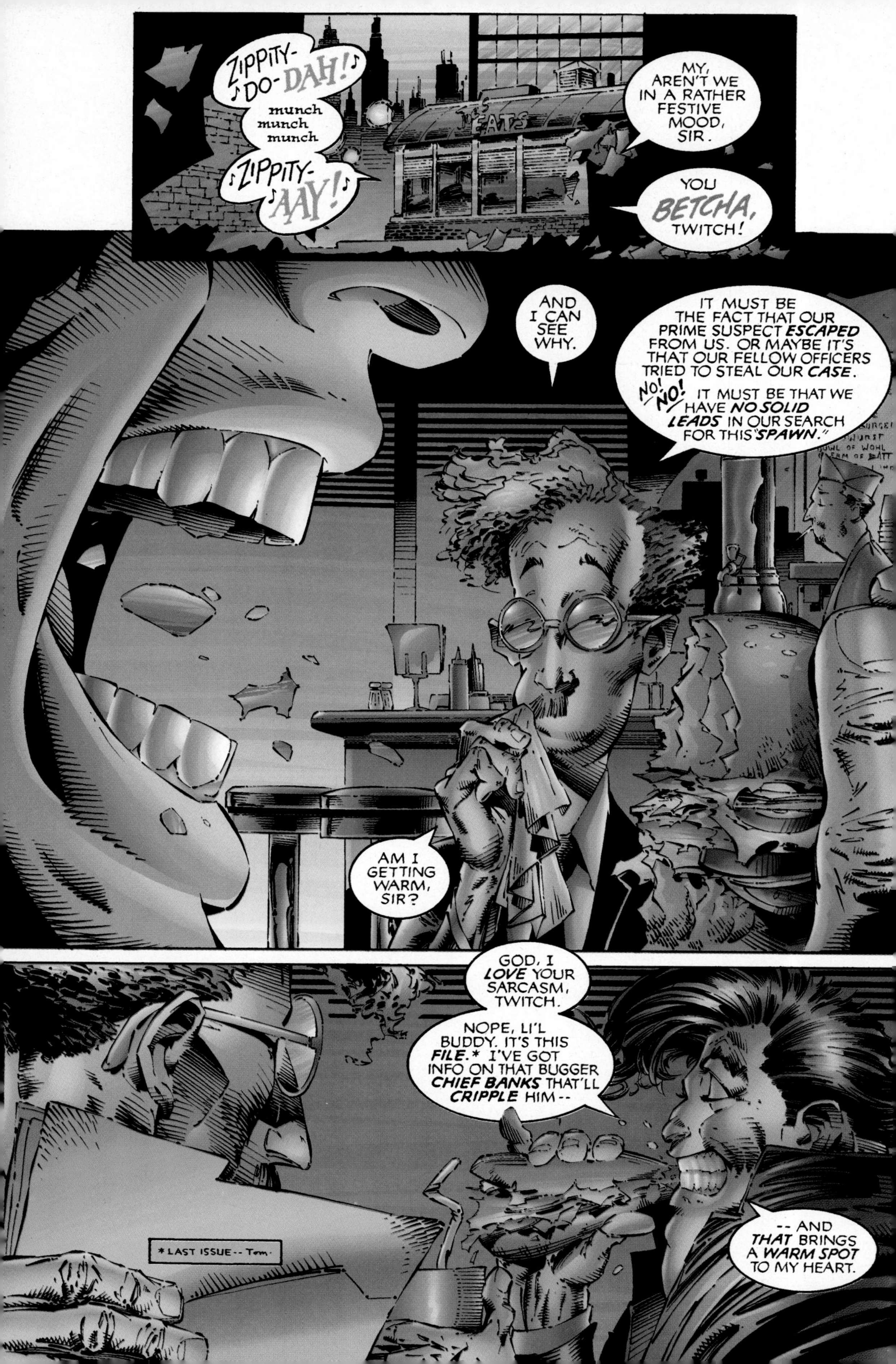
ZIPPITY-DO-DAH!
munch munch munch
ZIPPITY-AAY!
MY, AREN'T WE IN A RATHER FESTIVE MOOD, SIR.
YOU BETCHA, TWITCH!
EATS
AND I CAN SEE WHY.
IT MUST BE THE FACT THAT OUR PRIME SUSPECT ESCAPED FROM US. OR MAYBE IT'S THAT OUR FELLOW OFFICERS TRIED TO STEAL OUR CASE. NO! NO! IT MUST BE THAT WE HAVE NO SOLID LEADS IN OUR SEARCH FOR THIS "SPAWN."
AM I GETTING WARM, SIR?
GOD, I LOVE YOUR SARCASM, TWITCH.
NOPE, LI'L BUDDY. IT'S THIS FILE.* I'VE GOT INFO ON THAT BUGGER CHIEF BANKS THAT'LL CRIPPLE HIM --
-- AND THAT BRINGS A WARM SPOT TO MY HEART.
* LAST ISSUE -- Tom.

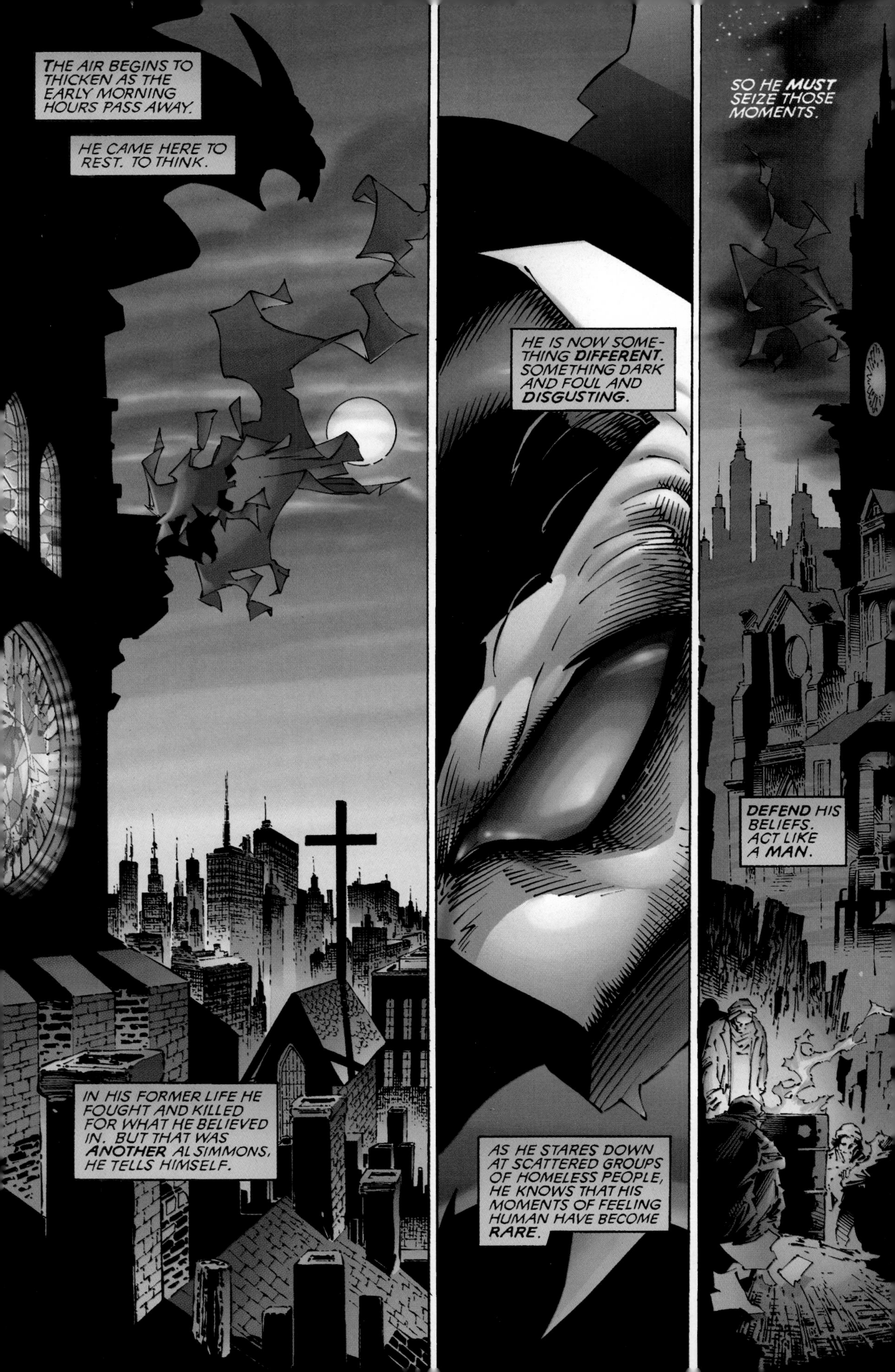
THE AIR BEGINS TO THICKEN AS THE EARLY MORNING HOURS PASS AWAY.
HE CAME HERE TO REST. TO THINK.
IN HIS FORMER LIFE HE FOUGHT AND KILLED FOR WHAT HE BELIEVED IN. BUT THAT WAS ANOTHER AL SIMMONS, HE TELLS HIMSELF.
HE IS NOW SOMETHING DIFFERENT. SOMETHING DARK AND FOUL AND DISGUSTING.
AS HE STARES DOWN AT SCATTERED GROUPS OF HOMELESS PEOPLE, HE KNOWS THAT HIS MOMENTS OF FEELING HUMAN HAVE BECOME RARE.
SO HE MUST SEIZE THOSE MOMENTS.
DEFEND HIS BELIEFS. ACT LIKE A MAN.

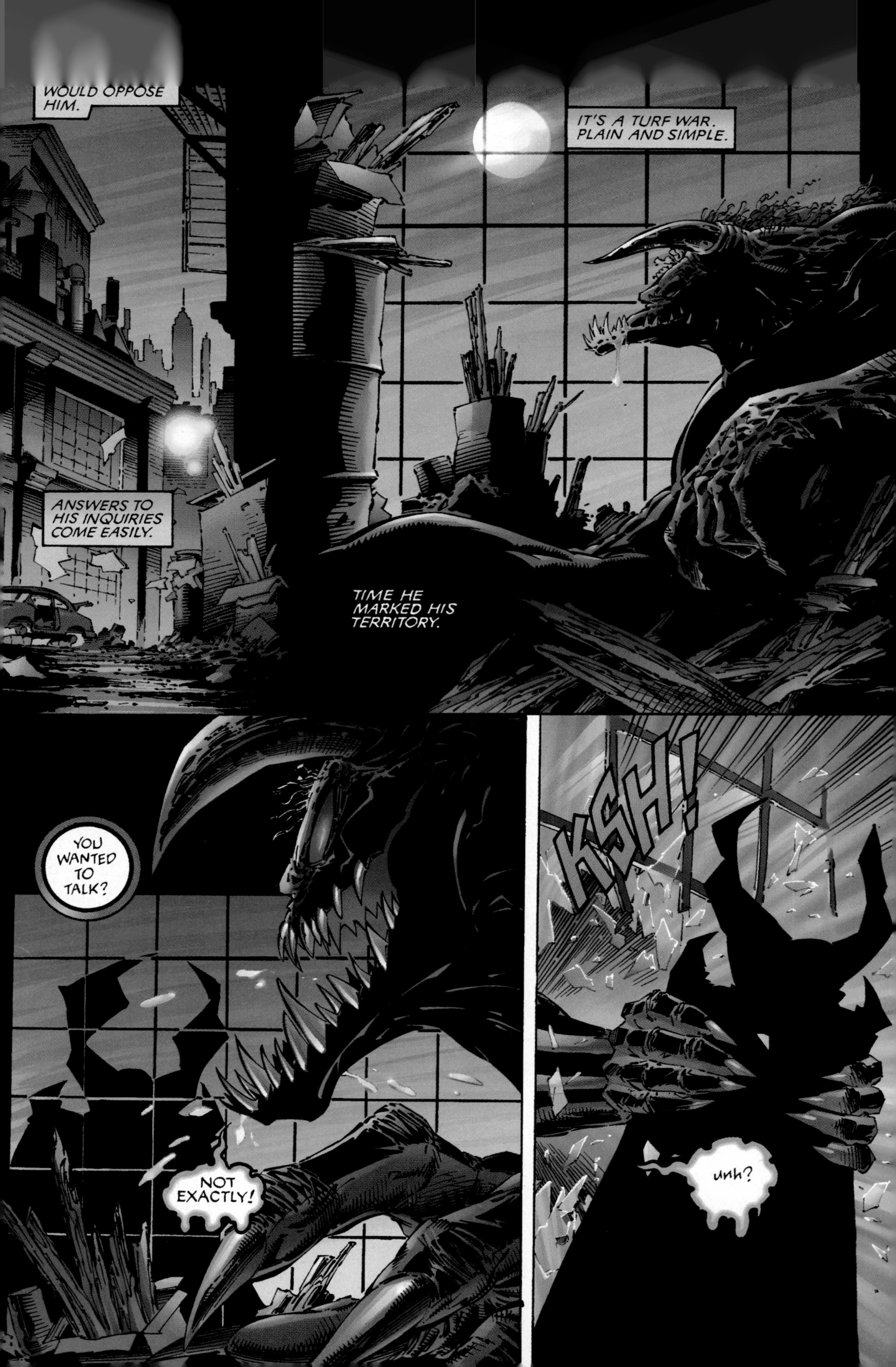
WOULD OPPOSE HIM.
IT'S A TURF WAR. PLAIN AND SIMPLE.
ANSWERS TO HIS INQUIRIES COME EASILY.
TIME HE MARKED HIS TERRITORY.
YOU WANTED TO TALK?
NOT EXACTLY!
KSH!
unh?

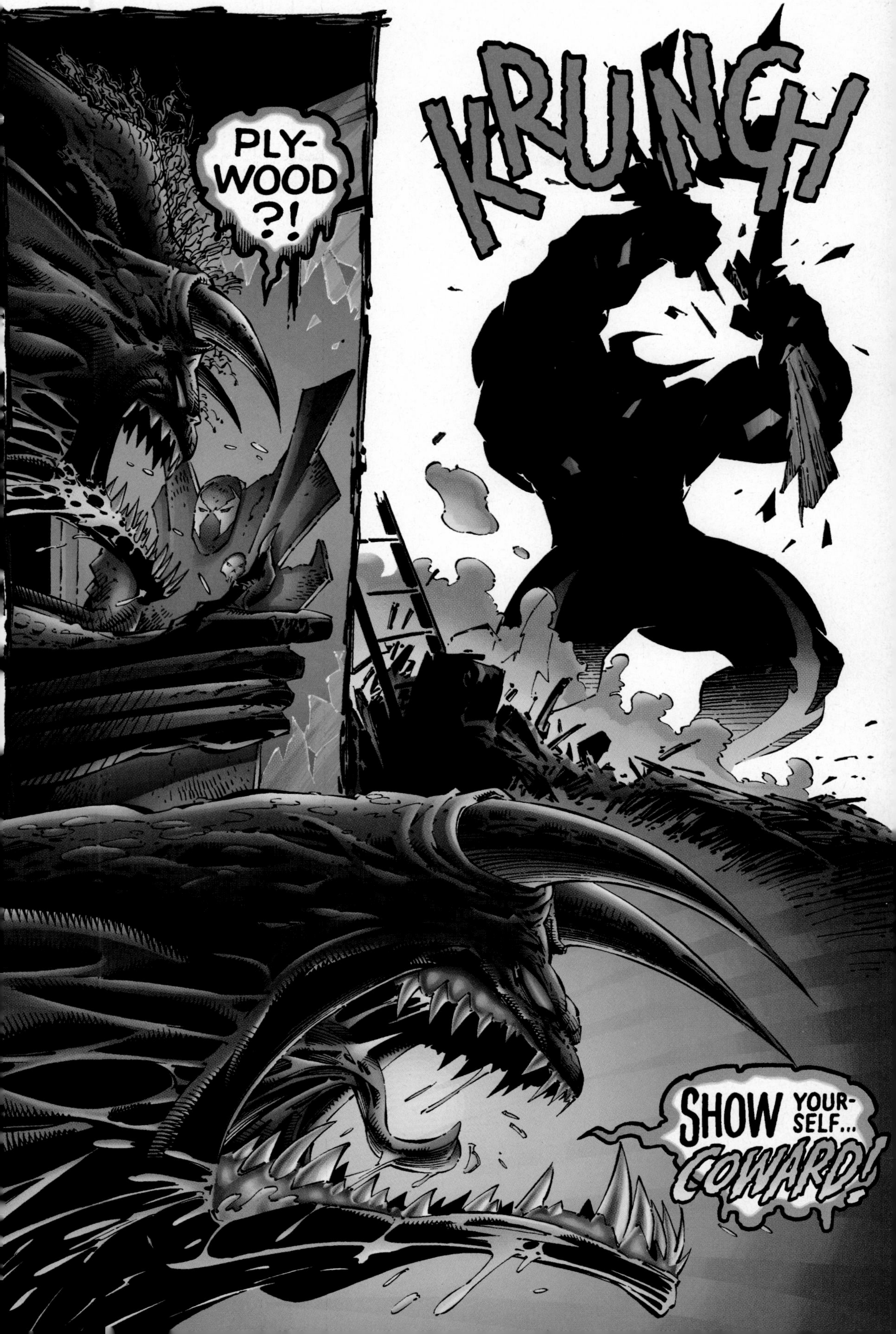
PLY-
WOOD
?!
KRUNCH
SHOW YOURSELF...
COWARD!

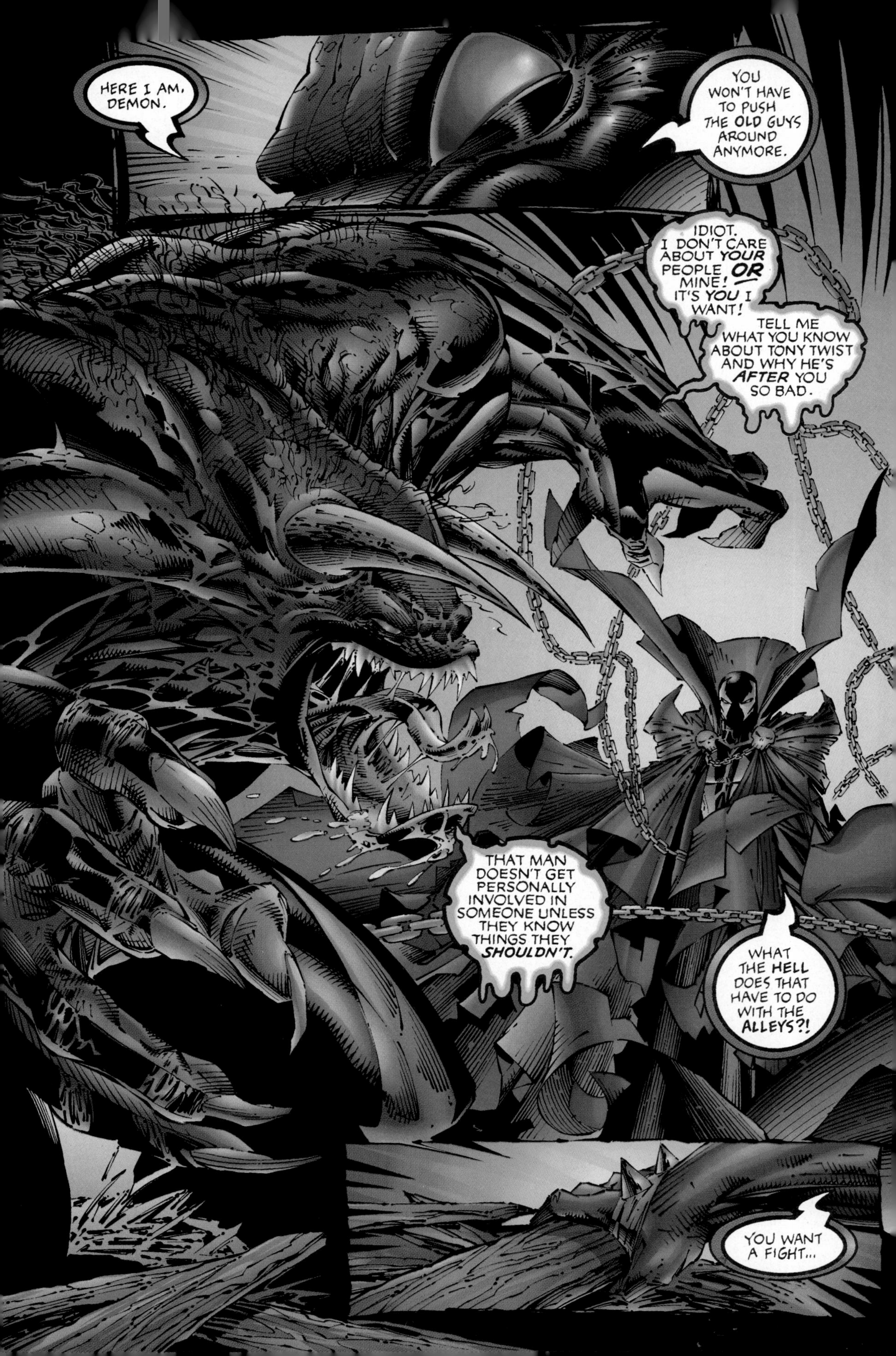
HERE I AM, DEMON.
YOU WON'T HAVE TO PUSH THE OLD GUYS AROUND ANYMORE.
IDIOT. I DON'T CARE ABOUT YOUR PEOPLE OR MINE! IT'S YOU I WANT!
TELL ME WHAT YOU KNOW ABOUT TONY TWIST AND WHY HE'S AFTER YOU SO BAD.
THAT MAN DOESN'T GET PERSONALLY INVOLVED IN SOMEONE UNLESS THEY KNOW THINGS THEY SHOULDN'T.
WHAT THE HELL DOES THAT HAVE TO DO WITH THE ALLEYS?!
YOU WANT A FIGHT...

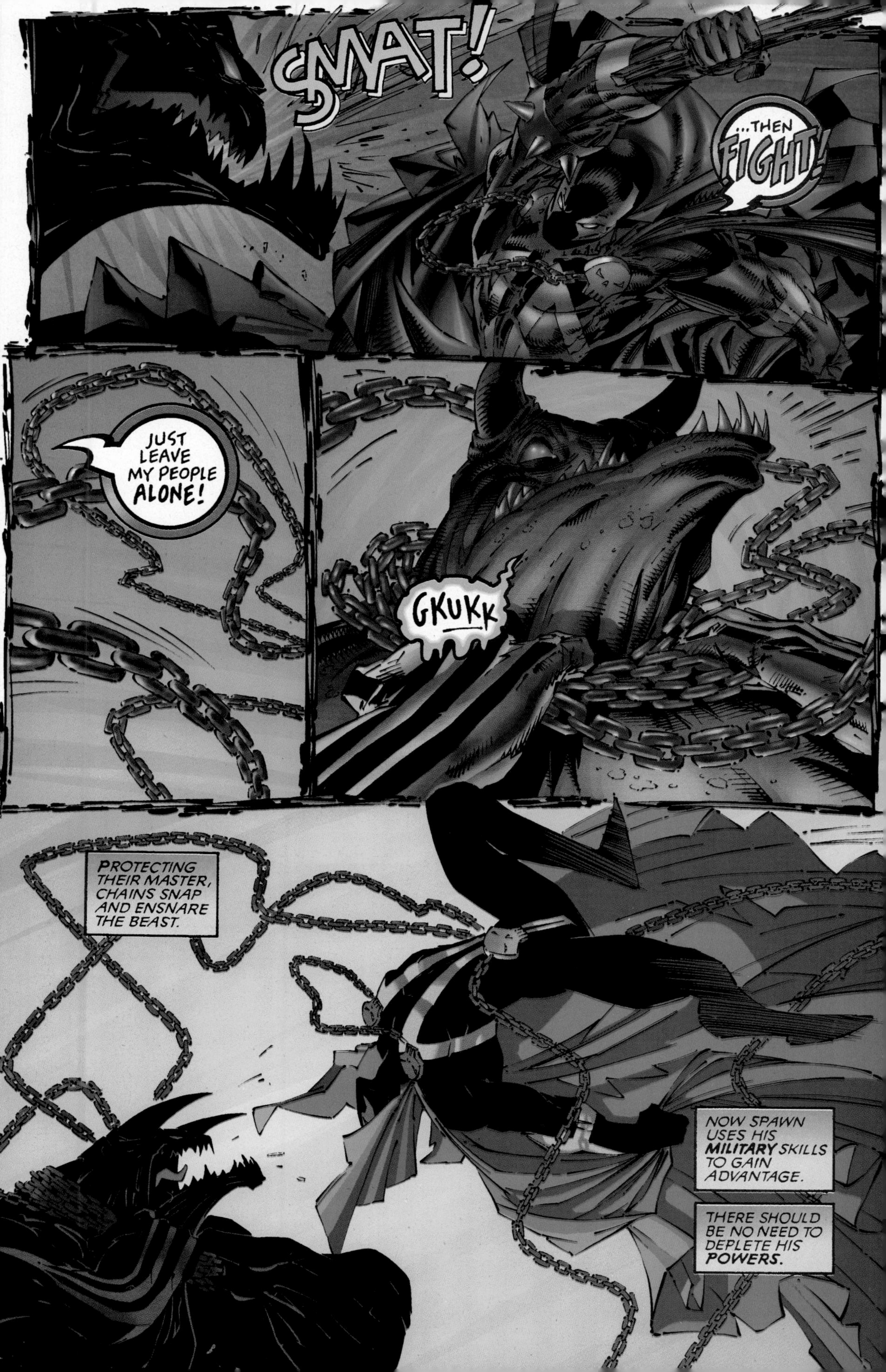
SMAT!
...THEN FIGHT!
JUST LEAVE MY PEOPLE ALONE!
GKUKK
PROTECTING THEIR MASTER, CHAINS SNAP AND ENSNARE THE BEAST.
NOW SPAWN USES HIS MILITARY SKILLS TO GAIN ADVANTAGE.
THERE SHOULD BE NO NEED TO DEPLETE HIS POWERS.

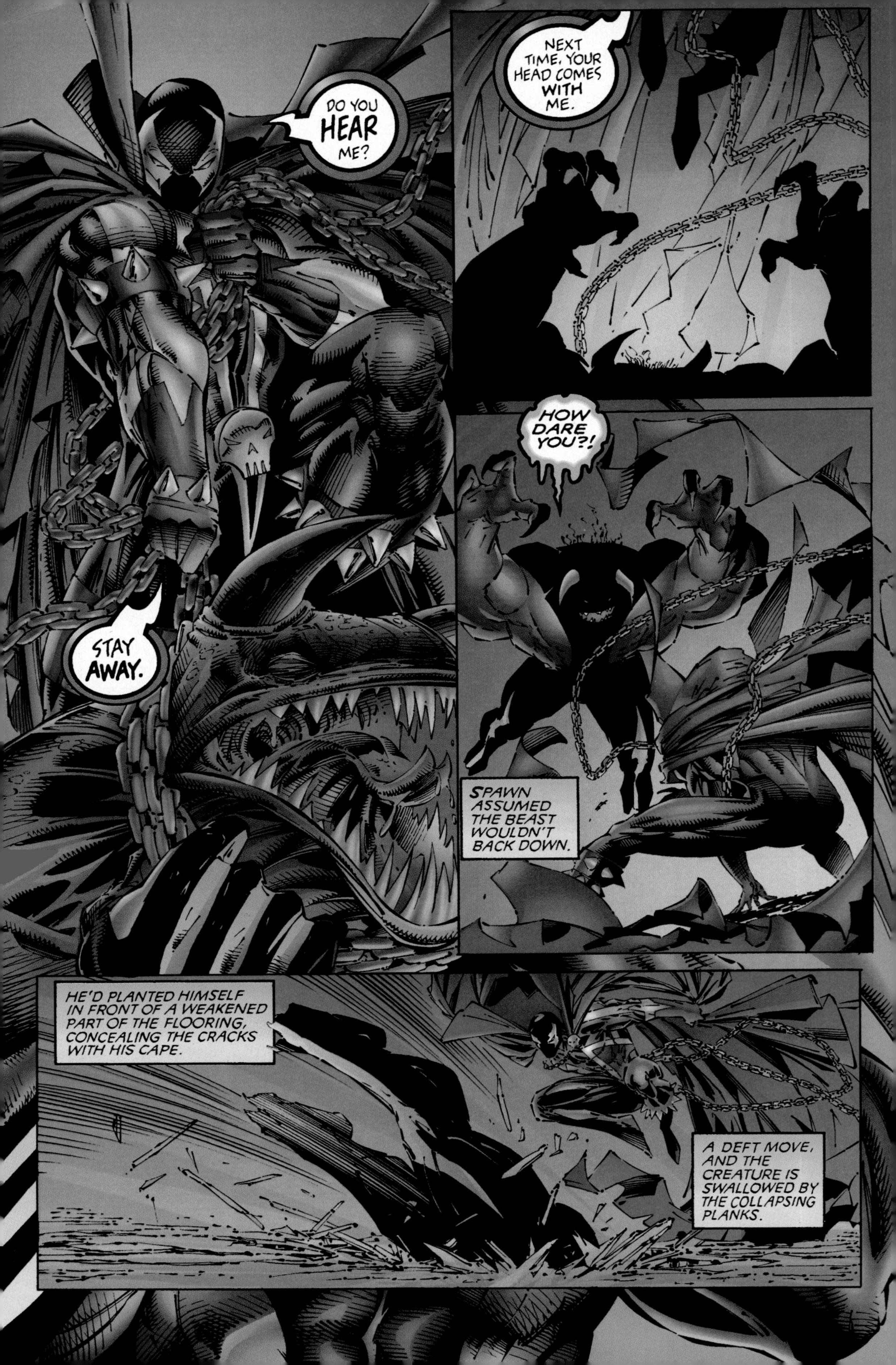
DO YOU HEAR ME?
STAY AWAY.
NEXT TIME, YOUR HEAD COMES WITH ME.
HOW DARE YOU?!
SPAWN ASSUMED THE BEAST WOULDN'T BACK DOWN.
HE'D PLANTED HIMSELF IN FRONT OF A WEAKENED PART OF THE FLOORING, CONCEALING THE CRACKS WITH HIS CAPE.
A DEFT MOVE, AND THE CREATURE IS SWALLOWED BY THE COLLAPSING PLANKS.

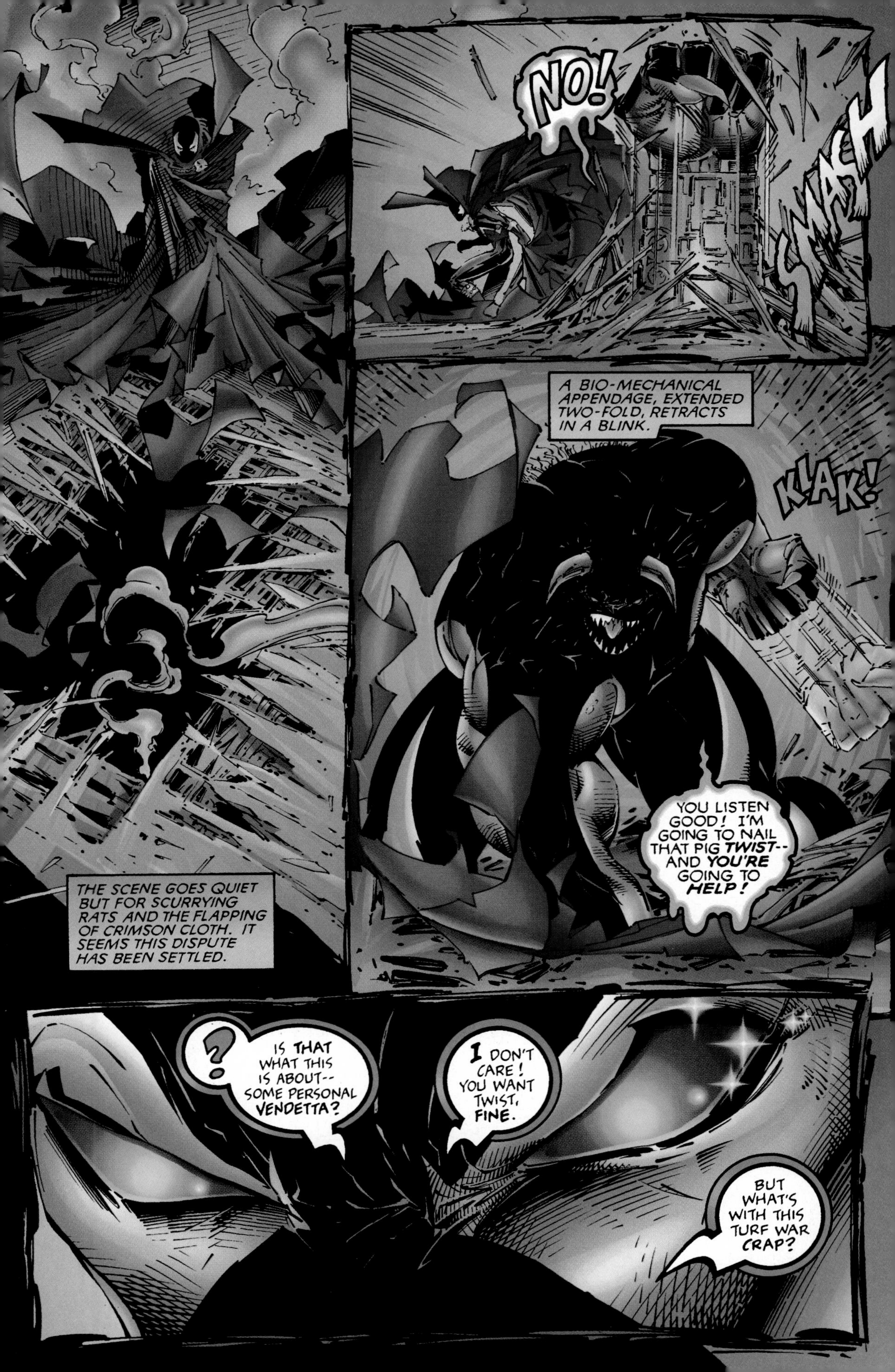
NO!
SMASH
A BIO-MECHANICAL APPENDAGE, EXTENDED TWO-FOLD, RETRACTS IN A BLINK.
KLAK!
YOU LISTEN GOOD! I'M GOING TO NAIL THAT PIG TWIST-- AND YOU'RE GOING TO HELP!
THE SCENE GOES QUIET BUT FOR SCURRYING RATS AND THE FLAPPING OF CRIMSON CLOTH. IT SEEMS THIS DISPUTE HAS BEEN SETTLED.
? IS THAT WHAT THIS IS ABOUT-- SOME PERSONAL VENDETTA?
I DON'T CARE! YOU WANT TWIST, FINE.
BUT WHAT'S WITH THIS TURF WAR CRAP?

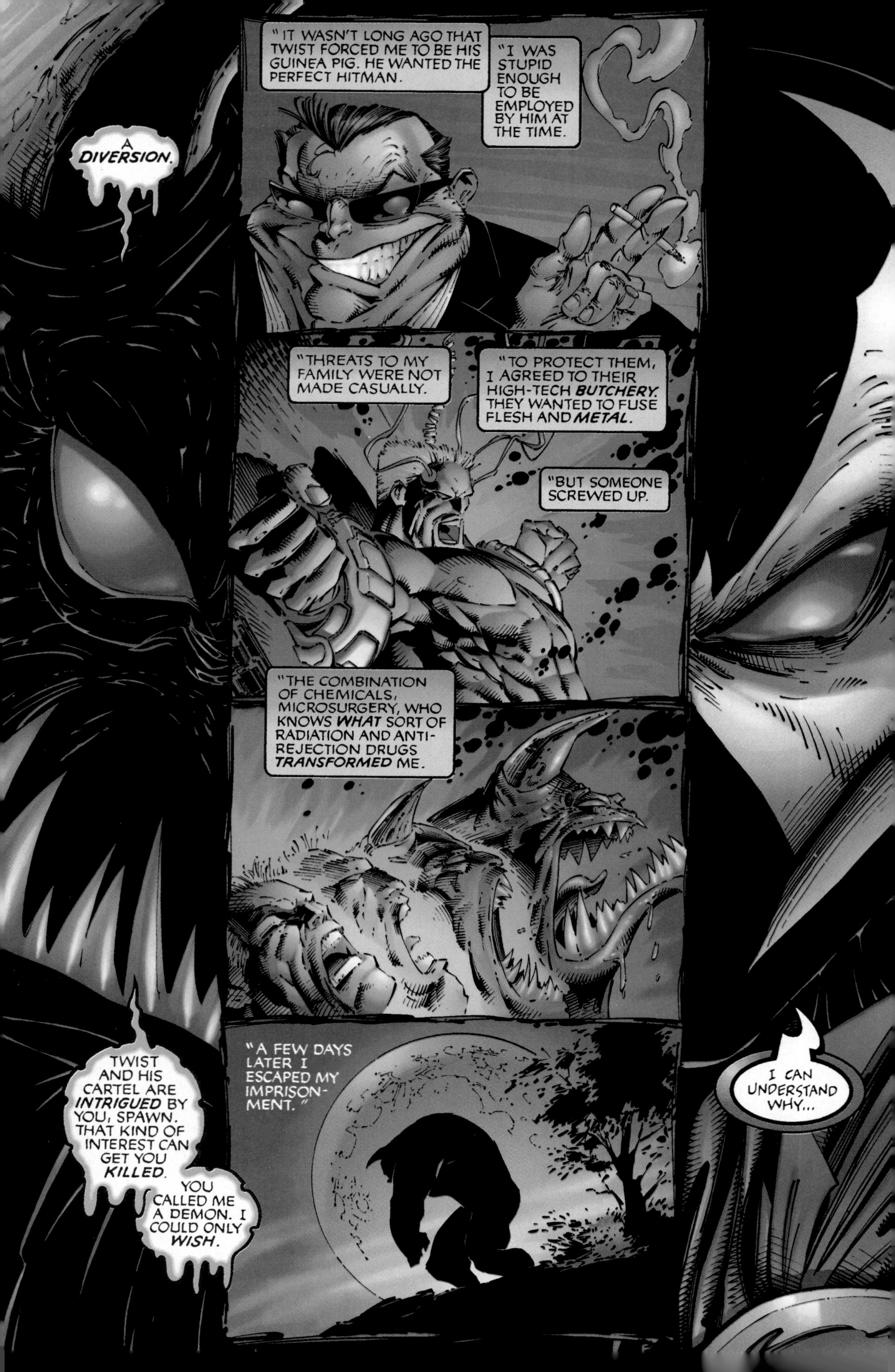
A DIVERSION.
"IT WASN'T LONG AGO THAT TWIST FORCED ME TO BE HIS GUINEA PIG. HE WANTED THE PERFECT HITMAN.
"I WAS STUPID ENOUGH TO BE EMPLOYED BY HIM AT THE TIME.
"THREATS TO MY FAMILY WERE NOT MADE CASUALLY.
"TO PROTECT THEM, I AGREED TO THEIR HIGH-TECH BUTCHERY. THEY WANTED TO FUSE FLESH AND METAL.
"BUT SOMEONE SCREWED UP.
"THE COMBINATION OF CHEMICALS, MICROSURGERY, WHO KNOWS WHAT SORT OF RADIATION AND ANTI-REJECTION DRUGS TRANSFORMED ME.
"A FEW DAYS LATER I ESCAPED MY IMPRISONMENT."
TWIST AND HIS CARTEL ARE INTRIGUED BY YOU, SPAWN. THAT KIND OF INTEREST CAN GET YOU KILLED.
YOU CALLED ME A DEMON. I COULD ONLY WISH.
I CAN UNDERSTAND WHY...

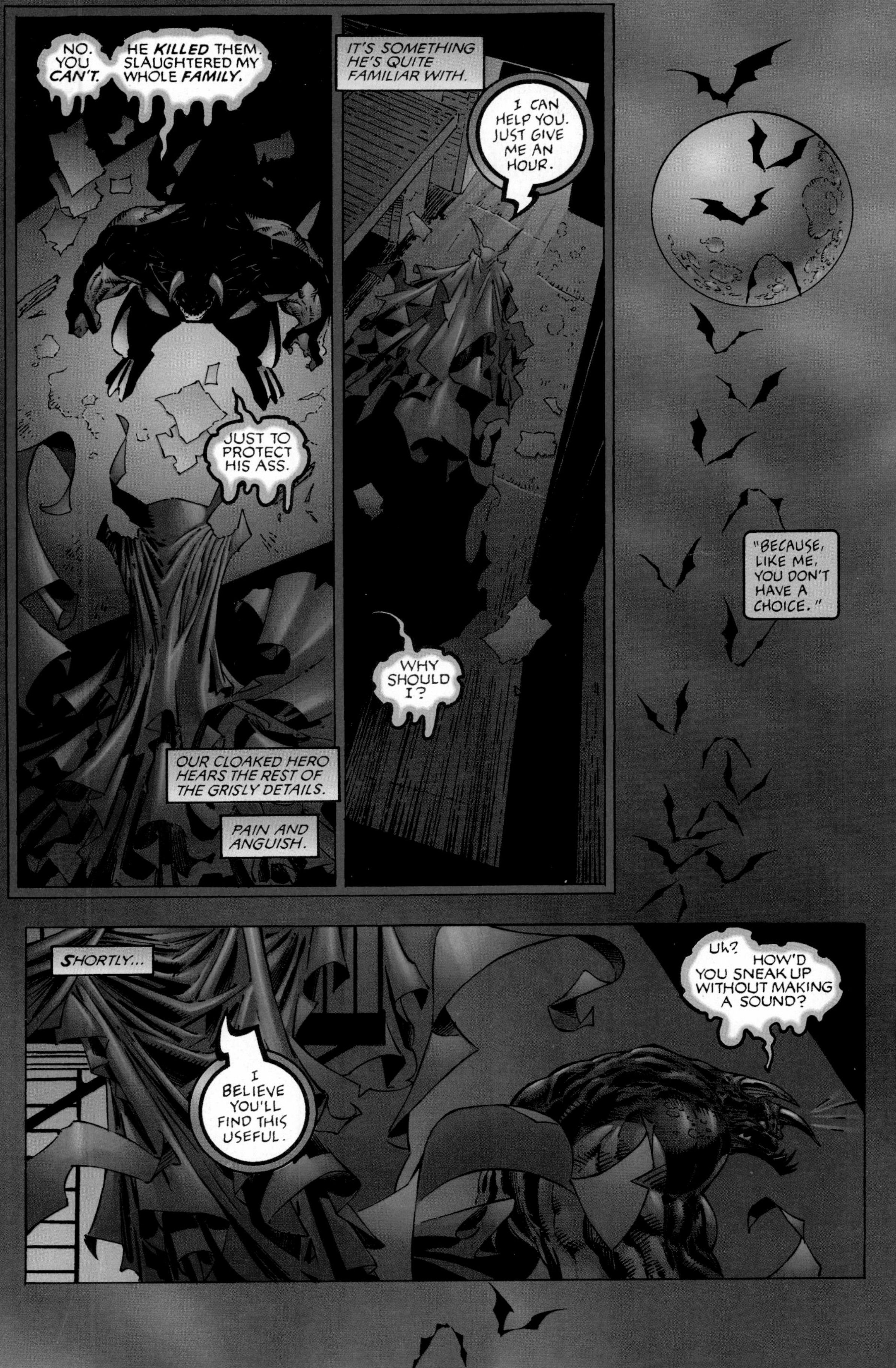
NO. YOU CAN'T.
HE KILLED THEM. SLAUGHTERED MY WHOLE FAMILY.
JUST TO PROTECT HIS ASS.
OUR CLOAKED HERO HEARS THE REST OF THE GRISLY DETAILS.
PAIN AND ANGUISH.
IT'S SOMETHING HE'S QUITE FAMILIAR WITH.
I CAN HELP YOU. JUST GIVE ME AN HOUR.
WHY SHOULD I?
"BECAUSE, LIKE ME, YOU DON'T HAVE A CHOICE."
SHORTLY...
I BELIEVE YOU'LL FIND THIS USEFUL.
Uh? HOW'D YOU SNEAK UP WITHOUT MAKING A SOUND?

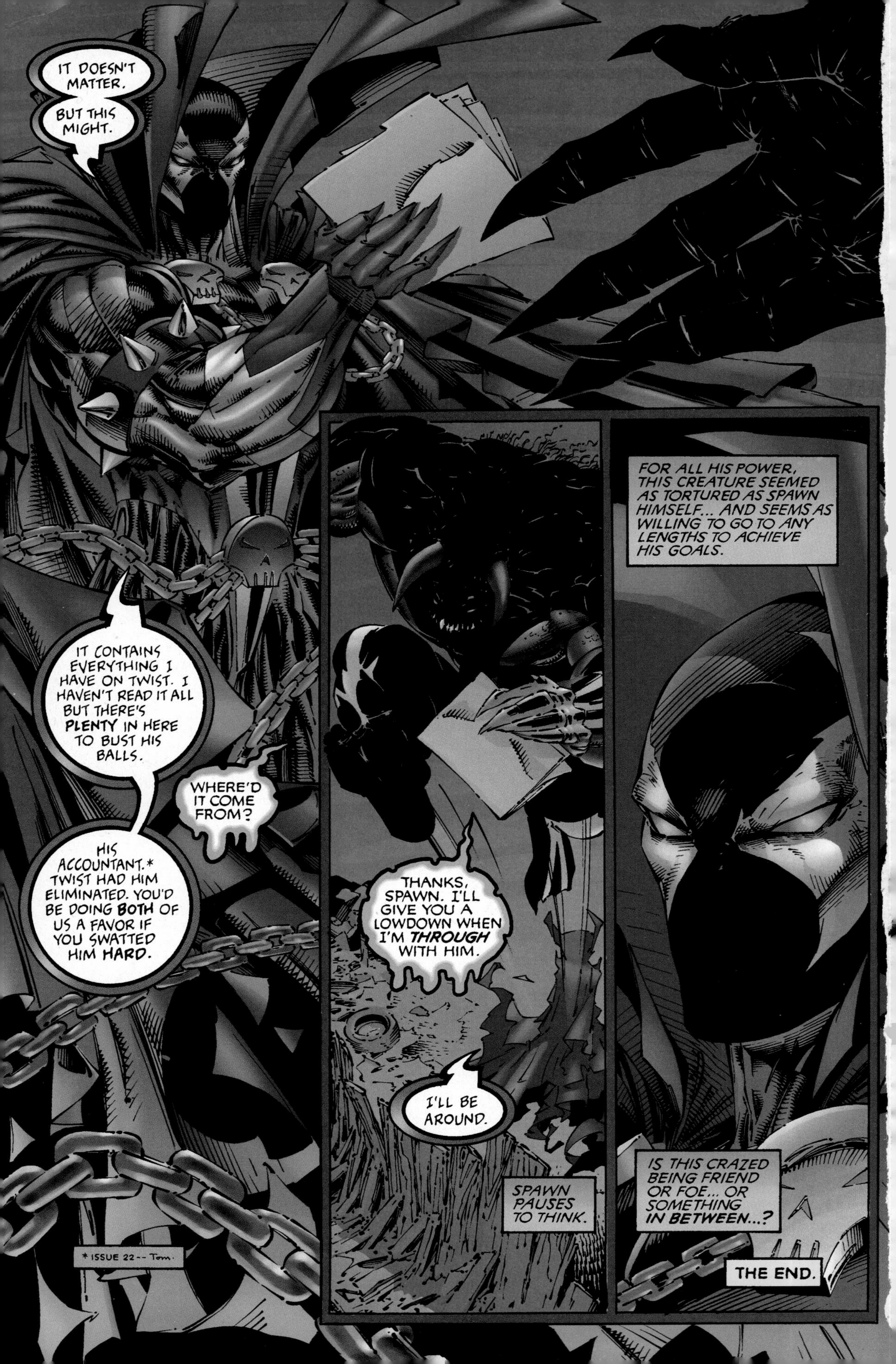
IT DOESN'T MATTER.
BUT THIS MIGHT.
IT CONTAINS EVERYTHING I HAVE ON TWIST. I HAVEN'T READ IT ALL BUT THERE'S PLENTY IN HERE TO BUST HIS BALLS.
WHERE'D IT COME FROM?
HIS ACCOUNTANT.* TWIST HAD HIM ELIMINATED. YOU'D BE DOING BOTH OF US A FAVOR IF YOU SWATTED HIM HARD.
*ISSUE 22-- Tom.
THANKS, SPAWN. I'LL GIVE YOU A LOWDOWN WHEN I'M THROUGH WITH HIM.
I'LL BE AROUND.
SPAWN PAUSES TO THINK.
FOR ALL HIS POWER, THIS CREATURE SEEMED AS TORTURED AS SPAWN HIMSELF... AND SEEMS AS WILLING TO GO TO ANY LENGTHS TO ACHIEVE HIS GOALS.
IS THIS CRAZED BEING FRIEND OR FOE... OR SOMETHING IN BETWEEN...?
THE END.